Discovering
CASTLES IN ENGLAND
AND WALES

John Kinross

Shire Publications Ltd.

ACKNOWLEDGEMENTS

Photographs are acknowledged as follows: Iris Hardwick, plate 1; J. MacCormack, plates 2, 3, 4; D. Uttley, plate 5; J. W. Whitelaw, plates 6, 8, 14, 15, 35, 37; R. D. Bristow, plate 7; J. N. T. Vince, plate 9; Aerofilms Ltd., plates 10, 12, 16, 17, 20, 23, 34, 42; Department of the Environment, plates 11, 49; Jane Miller, plate 13; J. Kinross, plates 18, 24, 25, 26, 44, 45, 46, 47, 48, 50; G. N. Wright, plates 19, 28; Hallam Ashley, plates 21, 22; C. Lamb, plates 27, 33, 36, 51, 52; G. H. Haines, plates 29, 39, 40; N. W. Keiffer, plate 30; A. E. Bristow, plates 31, 32; National Trust, plate 38; and the *Yorkshire Post* and *Yorkshire Evening Post,* plate 41. The ground plans of the four castles on pages 6 and 7 are Crown Copyright and are reproduced by kind permission of the Department of the Environment. The author and publishers acknowledge with thanks the assistance and co-operation of B. J. Stanier, formerly of the Ministry of Public Building and Works, and D. L. Pattison B.A. in the editing of this book. Thanks are also due to those owners of castles who kindly assisted in the preparation of the text. The cover design is by Malcolm Greensmith.

CONTENTS

4

INTRODUCTION

The Romans brought military order to this country with their legions, their great wall and their roads. They built the first stone forts, often on a river crossing or place of similar importance. The Saxon shore forts were castles of a kind. Richborough and Burgh stand today with their massive walls and Dover has always been a military stronghold; their camps were made with earth or wooden walls, as at Launceston, Cornwall.

The Normans were the first people to build what we call castles, that is, a fortified house or fortress used for defence purposes and built for a nobleman or a king. The earliest motte and bailey castles were simple wooden structures on top of a mound or motte together with some form of palisade with a ditch round the motte, not always filled with water, and sometimes round the bailey as well. They must have been uncomfortable places to inhabit and the ring forts like Old Sarum offered considerably more protection from bad weather.

Pevensey was built on the site of a Roman fort and the Normans merely used the fort as an outer bailey for animals, adding a square keep. In the thirteenth century the extra inner bailey curtain with its half-moon bastions and moat was added so that the castle became twice as strong. The fact that it was fortified in 1940 with machine-gun posts proves that the builders did their work well. At Portchester the same thing occurs but a square keep was constructed and the moat is not so impressive.

Rectangular keeps had insufficient living space and this may have prompted castle builders to design shell-keeps. Windsor and Restormel are prime examples. The dwellings were arranged on the inside of the wall with a guard walk round the top of the curtain. Conisbrough keep has a chapel built into its walls and is immensely strong. The bailey towers here are solid and it was a natural step to make them hollow as with the Pevensey inner bailey or at White Castle, Monmouthshire.

The Edwardian castles are utterly different from any others. The unruly Welsh were conquered in 1282 but Edward I wanted to prevent further outbreaks of trouble. The few loyal settlements needed protection and Conway and Caernarvon are perfect examples of fortified towns, with the castle walls playing a vital part in the defensive system. Harlech was an

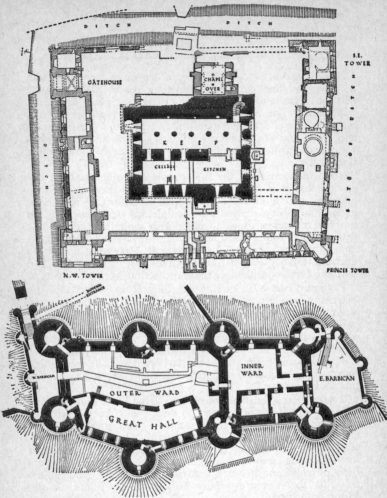

Top: *Middleham Castle, Yorkshire. The twelfth-century keep is one of the largest in England and incorporates the great hall.*

Bottom: *Conway Castle, Caernarvonshire, stands at the mouth of the Afon: its walls played a vital part in the defence of the town which was loyal to Edward I at the time of the Welsh uprising.*

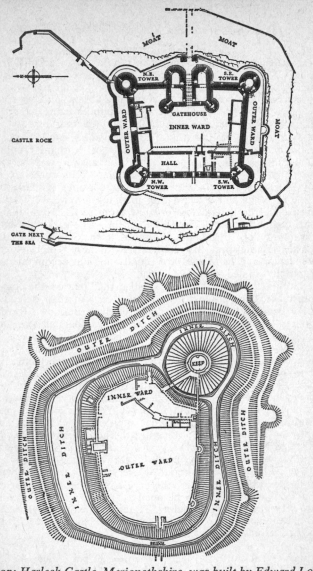

Top: Harlech Castle, Merionethshire, was built by Edward I on a rock overlooking the sea with its gatehouse on the town side.

Bottom: Berkhamsted Castle, Hertfordshire. Little remains of this castle today but the unique double-moat is of great interest.

7

exception because it is built on a rock and is accessible from one side only and that is protected by the gatehouse. The inner curtain was raised so that defenders could fire over the heads of the front line. Keeps are absent and all-round defence is of primary importance. Supplies came by sea so harbours were built at Beaumaris and Caernarvon.

With the increase of military inventiveness, cannon became more powerful and the mighty walls of Norham crumbled under Mons Meg's cannon balls. The answer was to build bastions and widen the moats. Henry VIII's forts are the obvious step. The inner bailey now becomes a passage in time of peace and a death trap in time of war. Every square inch could be defended. Very few large castles were built of this type, however, because by then the castle had gone out of fashion. Queen Elizabeth's Star Fort in the Scillies and Hurst Castle, Hampshire, are impressive gunnery emplacements. Pendennis and St Mawes are equally fine but accommodation is strictly limited.

During the Civil War the castles that put up the longest resistance, due perhaps to the stout hearts of their defenders, were Pembroke and a few small, relatively unknown fortified houses—Lathom, which no longer exists, Boarstall and Donnington which consist of tall gatehouses today, where the earthworks kept the enemy at bay. In Northumberland humble farmers built castles to protect their livestock and themselves. The pele tower was enlarged and haphazard castles like Sizergh appeared. In Scotland the French influence was more prevalent. Hermitage owes no allegiance in style to anything built a few miles away in England. Yet it is a home inside four walls, which is the essence of a castle. Perhaps this is why the most appealing ruins are the homely ones, the semi-fortified homes like Stokesay and Markenfield. These are the essence of English architecture, the outcome of years of defensive thought, the dream of every would-be castle owner.

Castles which are under the care of the Department of the Environment are said to be open at 'normal times' and these are set out in the table below. Times of opening of all castles are, however, subject to alteration and should be checked before setting out to visit them.

	Weekdays	Sundays
March, April and October	9.30 am—5.30 pm	2.00—5.30 pm
May to September	9.30 am—7.00 pm	2.00—7.00 pm
November to February	9.30 am—4.00 pm	2.00—4.00 pm

Closed Christmas Eve, Christmas Day and Boxing Day

BEDFORDSHIRE

AMPTHILL

The fifteenth-century castle of Sir John Cornwall, who fought at Agincourt, was demolished in the late seventeenth century to make way for a house.

BEDFORD

Hugh de Beauchamp's castle at Bedford was built between 1087 and 1132. It was acquired by Falk de Brent who rebelled against Henry III and in 1224 the famous 60 days siege took place. Mangonels, petrariae and two belfries were used by the king who finally invested the keep by undermining it. Camden mentions the lower tower being 'cloven to that degree to show visibly some broad chinks'. It was pulled down, and the final stones of the barbican were removed in 1850.

CHALGRAVE

Near Toddington, Chalgrave has a motte and bailey dating from the twelfth century.

CLOPHILL

The barons de Albini had a castle here which can still be traced on a hill overlooking the village.

EATON SOCON

A Saxon earthwork known as Castle Hill stands on the Ouse which was used to supply the moat. It belonged for a time to the Vaux family who were involved in the Gunpowder Plot.

ODELL

On the Ouse near Bedford, Odell or Woodhill Castle belonged to the barons de Wahul. A new house was built from its stones in the reign of Henry VIII.

RISINGHOE

A fortress stood on the Ouse here. It was built between 1100 and 1200 by William, son of Wigain.

SOMERIES

Leaving Luton by B653, the road to the Vauxhall car factory, the entrance gates to Luton Hoo are straight ahead at a double bend. Less than a mile on is a small road to the left that goes under the railway. At the top of the hill is a farm and a rough track to the left. The brick-built castle gatehouse is in farmland at the end of the track. The remains of the moat are in the field to the north-west.

Someries was founded by Sir John Rotherham, steward to the household of Henry III, on a site once used by Falk de Brent, who was the owner of Bedford Castle and one of King John's most loyal supporters. In 1406 Henry IV granted Luton manor to the Duke of Bedford and later it was acquired by Sir John Wenlock. Sir John was a friend of the great Earl of Warwick during the Wars of the Roses and at one time owned Berkhamsted Castle. He was a notorious turncoat; he fought for the Lancastrians at St Albans in 1455, where he was seriously wounded; then espousing the Yorkist cause he distinguished himself fighting for them at Towton, but finally rejoined Warwick and led one third of the Lancastrian army at Tewkesbury in 1471. History does not record what really happened to him, but most accounts state that during the battle of Tewkesbury he did not advance to help Somerset and that the latter, hard pressed, accused him of treachery and struck him down with his battle-axe before Wenlock could clear himself.

According to Leland, Wenlock's heir, who married a relation of the Archbishop of York, inherited 'three hundred makes of land . . . and a fair place within the parish of Luton called Somerys, which was sumptuously begun by Lord Wenlock (in 1448) but not finished.' Until about 1700 Somerys or Someries was an important building, more of a fortified manor than a house, but the Napier family who acquired it preferred Luton Hoo and they dismantled the high tower.

In the chapel, the first building we come to, there is a squint which once looked into a large south hall and the brickwork round the east window still retains a vestige of originality.

Open at all times. Admission free.

YIELDEN

This Norman castle built by the Baron de Traylly has slight earthworks remaining.

BERKSHIRE

ALDWORTH

The de la Beche family had a castle here on a hill near Streatley. It is now a farm.

BEAUMYS CASTLE

Nicholas de la Beche obtained a licence to crenellate Beaumys in 1338. His castle stood in Swallowfield, but was not strong enough to prevent John Dalton from attacking it soon after its completion and abducting Lady Margaret de la Beche, whom he later married.

BRIGHTWELL

King Stephen had a castle here, traditionally on the site of the manor farm, which was once surrounded by a moat. It is believed to have been built c. 1145 by the Earl of Chester.

DONNINGTON

Just outside Newbury, off the Oxford road, the two drum towers of Donnington Castle's gatehouse stand on the top of the castle mound, having survived a furious bombardment during the Civil War. The manor of Donnington belonged to the Coupelands in the thirteenth century and they sold it to the Abberbury family. It was Richard de Abberbury, one of the Black Prince's knights, who built the castle, obtaining a licence in 1386, just after the licence Dalyngrigge obtained for Bodiam in 1385. In 1393 Abberbury obtained a licence to build the almshouses for thirteen poor men, which, rebuilt by Elizabeth in 1602, still remain in the village.

In 1415 Thomas Chaucer, son of the poet Geoffrey, obtained the castle and it passed in 1434 to his daughter, Alice, who married William de la Pole, Earl of Suffolk. In 1450 Suffolk attempted to flee to the continent but was captured and murdered at sea by English shipmen. His grandson John, Earl of Lincoln, was killed at Stoke in 1487 supporting Lambert Simnel against Henry VII. The earl's brother was attainted and the castle passed to the Crown. In 1514 it was granted to Sir Charles Brandon by Henry VIII, who visited the castle in 1539 and 1541, and later Edward VI held a privy council meeting here in 1551. It was given to Edward's half-sister Princess Elizabeth, who visited it as Queen of England in 1568. Repairs were carried out for her visit. In 1600 she

11

granted it to Sir Charles Howard, Earl of Nottingham, for his services during the Armada.

Lady Russell, Keeper of Donnington, lived here during the Earl's absence and was once refused entry to the castle when Sir Thomas Dolman of Shaw House took it over for his friends. During the Civil War Donnington was owned by John Packer, a Parliamentarian, but, as it was near to Oxford, Charles I seized it and put in a garrison of 200 men and four cannon under Sir John Boys. A four star breastwork was constructed round the castle, with a gap for the road, which in those days ran past the gatehouse. In 1644 Boys resisted two attempts to take the castle and it was the centre of the second battle of Newbury. Waller attempted to make the castle surrender by poisoning the well but Boys sent forty musketeers to clean it and dig it deeper. In 1646 Colonel Dalbier was given the task of reducing the castle, and with a massive mortar he proceeded to batter down the walls. In spite of a royalist sortie by Captain Donne that killed eighty men and captured sixty, Boys knew he must soon surrender. A message from the king at Oxford suggested he obtain the best conditions he could and on 1st April the castle surrendered, each man taking his arms and ammunition and marching to Wallingford.

The Packers continued to live here until the construction of the new house next door. Later the property passed to the Hartleys and in 1946 it was taken over by the Ministry of Works.

Department of the Environment. Open normal times. Admission charge.

FARINGDON

Robert, Earl of Gloucester, built a castle to command the crossing of the Thames at Radcot c. 1144. It was besieged by Stephen, captured after four days and demolished.

HAMSTEAD MARSHALL

Three mounds in the park of the former mansion of Lord Craven mark the site of one of the castles of the first Earl of Pembroke.

NEWBURY

The castle at Newbury was probably Norman in origin. It was besieged and captured in 1152 by King Stephen. In Elizabethan times it became a hospital belonging to the

12

Knights of St John. Later it became a workhouse and in 1723 was demolished when the Kennet Navigation Company built a canal wharf on the site.

READING

No trace remains of Reading's ancient castle, believed to date from Roman times. It was occupied by Stephen but was destroyed by Henry II in about 1153.

WALLINGFORD

William the Conqueror crossed the Thames at Wallingford after a long roundabout march from Hastings and received the submission of Archbishop Stigand and other notable Saxons at the home of the local lord, Wigod. Robert D'Oyly was granted the land and built the Norman castle on the site of a Roman fort. The Abbot of Abingdon was imprisoned here in 1071. It became the centre of Queen Matilda's revolt against Stephen in 1139 and was garrisoned by Simon de Montfort during the Baron's War, which ended with de Montfort's death at Evesham in 1265. During Henry IV's reign the constable was Thomas Chaucer, son of the poet. In 1540 it was described as having 'three ditches, large and well watered'. During the Civil War it was garrisoned by the Royalists under Colonel Blagge, who finally surrendered in July 1646 after enduring a 65-day siege. Today the motte and ditch are all that can be seen in the grounds of Castle House.

WINDSOR

England's largest castle was originally constructed by William the Conqueror on a chalk cliff overlooking the Thames. The site was three miles from the original Saxon settlement at Old Windsor where Edward the Confessor had his hunting lodge. The stone castle was erected by Henry II on the site of William's large motte. There are three baileys – lower, middle and upper – and the total area is thirteen acres. The stone came from Bagshot Heath and by the end of Henry's reign it was a formidable fortress.

Prince John garrisoned it during Richard I's absence but was forced to yield it to Queen Eleanor. The Magna Carta was sealed by John at nearby Runnymede in 1215, in a nine-day ceremony which began a Civil War which was to end with the invasion of the French Dauphin in support of the barons, and John's death in 1216. Windsor was besieged but not taken. Henry III built the west wall and its towers flanking the main street. The first chapel was built where the Albert Memorial Chapel stands. This was made the centre of the new Order of the Garter by Edward III, who established a college with poor knights to organise the Order. The Norman gate and more domestic buildings were built at this time. St George's Chapel was started in 1475 by Edward IV and completed by Henry VII. The body of Henry VI was moved from Chertsey to the chapel in 1485.

Elizabeth I added the gallery, which now forms part of the library, and the North Terrace, which was built so that the queen could reach the Home Park without going through the State Apartments. The latter were rebuilt by Hugh May for Charles II and craftsmen like Verrio and Grinling Gibbons worked on the interior decoration. The famous Long Walk was laid out at this time. The next king to alter the castle was George III, who lowered one of the walls and erected a new window in the chapel, of which Walpole said, 'The Lord appears to be trying to get to heaven in a hurry'. George IV brought in Sir Jeffrey Wyatville, who doubled the height of the Round Tower, changed the skyline with new towers, a new sunken garden and altered the State Apartments. Queen Victoria turned the old chapel into a memorial chapel for Prince Albert and recently a small chapel has been built to the memory of George VI.

Castle precincts open daily 10 to dusk. Admission free. State Apartments and Queen's Dolls' House: open weekdays 11–3 (November–March), 11–4 (April–May), 11–5 (June–September); Sundays 1.30–5 (May–September), 1–4 (October). St George's Chapel: open Mondays to Thursdays, Saturdays 11–4.15, Fridays 1–4.15, Sundays 2.30–4.15 (closed January). Albert Memorial Chapel: open weekdays 10–1, 2–4.45 (April–September), 10–1, 2–4 (November–March). Admission free. Keep: open April–September when royalty not in residence. Admission free. See official guidebook for further details.

BUCKINGHAMSHIRE

BOARSTALL

The fourteenth-century mansion of Sir John de Hanlo was crenellated in 1313 and all that remains today is the gatehouse and part of the moat. Much of the brickwork is seventeenth century. It withstood a Parliamentary siege of eight weeks in

1645 and surrendered on honourable terms. It is now owned by the National Trust but is not open to the public.

BOLEBEC
At Market Hill, Whitchurch, stand the earthworks of Hugh de Bolebec's castle, built in 1147. It was pulled down after the Civil War having been ruinous for many years.

BUCKINGHAM
Walter Giffard built a Norman castle on the site now occupied by the church. In 1821 a limestone wall was unearthed in a cellar on Church Hill; it must have been part of the castle foundations.

CASTLETHORPE
The earthworks of Castlethorpe are more extensive than Whitchurch and mark the site of William Maudit's castle. It was destroyed by Falk de Brent, one of King John's supporters, and William's son moved to Hanslope where he built a fortified mansion, long since destroyed.

HANSLOPE
In the north near the Northamptonshire border, there is a ringwork near the church marking the site of a castle destroyed in 1215.

HIGH WYCOMBE
To the north of the church there was a castle which was in existence between 1257 and 1300 but nothing remains of it today. Desborough Castle on the Marlow road is an earthwork.

NEWPORT PAGNELL
John de Someries built a castle here but, as he had others at Luton and Bordesly, Newport soon fell into disuse. The site is now a cemetery.

PRINCES RISBOROUGH
The ancient seat of the Black Prince stood to the west of the church on land known as the Mount.

WESTON TURVILLE
The remains of the Norman motte and bailey castle in the gardens of Weston Turville Manor mark the site of Geoffrey

de Turville's castle, first mentioned in 1147. John de Moleyns obtained a licence to crenellate his house here in 1333. It was pulled down and rebuilt in the seventeenth century as the Manor House.

WOLVERTON

Manno of Brittany's Norman castle stood by the Old Wolverton church. It later passed to the de Longuiville family.

CAMBRIDGESHIRE

BURNE

A small castle here belonged to the Picotts, then to the Peverils. It was burnt down during the reign of Henry III by Ribald de Lisle.

BURWELL

Within the manor of Ramsey, the castle of the Earls of Worcester was destroyed during King Stephen's reign.

CAMBRIDGE

Built in 1068 on the north bank of the river, Cambridge Castle was finally destroyed by Cromwell during the Civil War.

CAMPS CASTLE

On the Gogmagog Hills stood a castle belonging to the de Veres of Castle Hedingham. It fell down in 1738 and only parts of the moat are visible today.

ELY

The castle here was built between 1070 and 1071 and additional fortifications were added by Nigel, Bishop of Ely in 1138–1139. No trace of it remains today.

WISBECH

The Norman castle built here about 1070 was destroyed by a storm in 1236. Bishop Morton of Ely rebuilt it in 1480 and later it became a royal prison where gunpowder plotter Catesby was confined for a time in 1605. The foundations are now a garden.

CHESHIRE

ALDFORD

Three miles south of Chester, the Aldford family had a harp-shaped castle on Blobb Hill defending a ford across the Dee. It was partially excavated in 1959.

BEESTON

Situated on the A49, Beeston is about half way between Crewe and Chester. The castle stands on top of a 500-foot sandstone crag, approachable only from the south. In 1220 Ranulf de Blundeville, sixth Earl of Chester, built his castle here where he could command the country around and levy his land tax. When the Dauphin attacked Lincoln in 1217, during the Civil War begun by King John, de Blundeville led the royal troops against him. Many barons deserted the French cause and at the 'Fair' of Lincoln they were defeated. After de Blundeville's death and that of his heir the castle was annexed by Henry III. In 1264 Beeston was occupied by Simon de Montfort for a year, and in 1399 Richard II, on his way to Flint, left his treasure here, where it was shortly collected by Henry Bolingbroke as Henry IV.

It was during the Civil War that Beeston really figures in history. Occupied by the Roundheads it was attacked by a small party of Royalists, under Captain Landford, who climbed the north wall and got into the upper ward. Captain Steel, the governor, surrendered and shortly after was shot by his own men in Nantwich. The Royalists were besieged in 1644 but held out until November 1645 when they marched out under their commander Captain Valet. The slighting that took place in 1646 was very thorough.

The inner and outer wards together covered about 450,000 sq. ft. and the outer ward had eight towers in the curtain. The inner ward had a strong gatehouse and three more towers. This is the only part of the castle that remains in any reasonable state. The Tollemache family were the last private owners and in 1959 the Ministry of Works began carrying out extensive repairs.

Department of the Environment. Open normal times. Admission charge.

17

CHESTER
This was once an important walled town with a castle, but only the walls and Agricola's Tower remain. It was a Roman site, strengthened by both Saxons and Normans who built the motte and bailey, and the large buttressed tower was built in the twelfth century. Henry III annexed Chester as a royal castle and from the time of the Black Prince the eldest son of the sovereign has been Earl of Chester. Eleanor, Duchess of Gloucester, was a prisoner in the castle in 1477. In the nineteenth century the gateway, military quarters and assize courts were built. The Regimental Museum is in Agricola's Tower today and inside are relics of Omdurman and the Ashanti Wars and part of a zeppelin.
Museum open daily, except Monday, 10–12.30, 2–6 *April–October;* 10–12.30, 2–4 *November–March.*

DODDINGTON
A few miles from the M6, south of Crewe, a tower near a ruined castle in Doddington Park marks the site of Sir John Delves's fortified mansion, licensed in 1364. He had fought with distinction at Poitiers in 1356, and the stone knights represent Dutton, Hawkstone, Fowlehurst and Delves who, at one point in the battle, defended Sir James Audley against 300 French cavalry.

DODLESTON
Near the Flintshire border is the moated site of the Boydels' castle. Inside the enclosure Sir William Brereton had a house which was his headquarters during the Civil War siege of Chester.

DUNHAM MASSEY
Hamo de Masei had a castle here and an outlying fort at Ullersford. The castle passed through various hands; at one time it was the home of Sir George Booth, 1566–1652. All that is left is the moat, now an ornamental lake, in the grounds of the hall at Altrincham.

FRODSHAM
South of Runcorn, Frodsham ruins stand on Overton Hill. The castle was destroyed by fire in 1654 on the same night as Sir John Savage, its owner, died. In the eighteenth century a Mr Ashley built a new house which incorporates some of the castle dungeons in its cellars.

18

HALTON

Near Frodsham on a high hill, Halton was once an important castle. Built in Henry II's reign, it had nine large towers in the curtain wall, two of which defended a strong gate. The de Lacys lived in it for many years and John of Gaunt used it as a hunting lodge. During the Civil War it was garrisoned by Lord Rivers, captured by Lord Brereton and demolished. The remaining walls, 20 to 30 feet high, are now part of Runcorn New Town.

MACCLESFIELD

The Earls of Chester had a castle here on Castle Field near the Congleton road.

MALPAS

Near the church is part of a 40-yard diameter motte of a border stronghold, built by the first Earl of Chester to keep out the Welsh.

PULFORD

A Saxon stronghold once stood on the Wrexham-Chester road, near the river Alyn. It was built by the Pulfords and during the Glyndwr rising in Wales, Sir Thomas Grosvenor, the then owner, set out from Pulford with an army of Cheshire men to defend the Welsh Marches.

SHIPBROOK

On the Weaver near Northwich is Castle Hill, where Richard Vernon built a castle; it was still standing at the end of the seventeeth century.

SHOCKLACH

Shocklach, on the Dee, was an important link in the line of castles from Aldford to Malpas. It was occupied by Lord Dudley, in Elizabethan times by the Corbetts of Stoke, and later by the Breretons.

SHOTWICK

Between Chester and the sea, Shotwick was a pentagonal castle with a gatehouse and six bastions, one of which was six storeys high. Troops were once dispatched to Ireland from this place and in the mid thirteenth century it was one of Cheshire's principal strongholds.

STOCKPORT
The Earls of Chester once had a castle near the church, probably built on a Roman site. In 1173 it was held by Geoffrey de Costentin against Henry II.

CORNWALL

BOSCASTLE
Near Tintagel the de Bottreaux family built a castle during the reign of Henry II. It stood on a grassy hill called Jordans.

CARDINHAM
Near Bodmin, the Dinhams built a castle by the church and its ruins were visible in Victorian times.

CASTLE DORE
A ringed earthwork stands near Fowey which was fortified by the Parliamentarians in the Civil War. It was possibly the site of a medieval castle.

FOWEY
By the harbour mouth were two forts connected by a chain. The French invaded the port in 1457 and Place House was fortified by Thomas Treffry, whose wife beat off the French from her doorstep with the help of one servant, and in Henry VIII's reign St Catherine's Fort was built. It mounted four cannon and was restored in 1855 (*see also* Polruan).

HELSTON
The Earl of Cornwall had a castle here; it is mentioned by Leland and stood on the site of the bowling green.

INCE
Near Antony House (National Trust), Ince was a seventeenth-century castle, fortified during the Civil War for the king and later turned into a farmhouse. It was restored in 1920 and is a private house.
Grounds open in summer under the National Gardens Scheme.

LAUNCESTON
Robert de Mortain built the first castle on the high hill above the town. It was probably of wood and was not replaced by stone until Richard of Cornwall obtained the property and built the shell-keep with a round tower inside and a

strongly protected passage to the curtain from the gatehouse. This design is unusual in English castles. The space between the central tower and the curtain could be roofed over to permit extra fighting space if there was a siege. The central tower has a fireplace. Later an extra building was added as a gaol.

The east gate contains the constable's quarters and here, under the gatehouse, is a room where George Fox, the Quaker, was imprisoned in 1656 for wearing his hat in court. During the Civil War, although ruined, the castle changed hands five times. The outer ward was still enclosed at that time but has long since been encroached upon by the town. *Department of the Environment. Open normal times. Admission charge.*

LISKEARD

Robert de Mortain had a castle here. In 1540 it was in disrepair. It had a large park with 200 deer but nothing remains of either park or castle today.

PENDENNIS

Pendennis and St Mawes castles were built by Henry VIII in 1548 to protect Carrick Roads at Falmouth. Pendennis stands 300 feet above the sea and consists of a circular tower 56 feet in diameter, with walls 11 feet thick pierced in three tiers with embrasures for guns. In Elizabeth's reign a large angular rampart wall was added, covering nearly two acres. The entrance is across a drawbridge from Castle Drive and through a gateway over which the arms of Henry VIII are prominently displayed.

During the Civil War, Colonel Arundel of Trerice was the governor. He had anticipated a siege and had strengthened the defences with a pentagonal redoubt and other earthworks, constructed so that enemy cannon could not approach within range. Provisions for nine months were stored inside and the garrison consisted of 800 men. When Fairfax arrived in March 1646 Arundel refused to surrender and held out until 17th August by which time his supplies had run out and 200 of his men had fallen sick. Only Raglan in Wales held out longer—two days longer in fact.

There is a fine collection of arms and armour inside the castle and in the Elizabethan part is a Youth Hotel. *Department of the Environment. Open normal times. Admission charge.*

PENGERSIC

A three-storey embattled tower joined to a smaller tower dates from Henry VIII's reign. It once belonged to the Duke of Leeds.

POLRUAN

This square harbour tower with two storeys and fireplaces was built at the same time as St Catherine's Fort, to defend the harbour (*see* Fowey).

RESTORMEL

The most picturesque castle in England, Restormel was built by Baldwin Fitz Turstin, owner of Bordardle manor. In 1100 it passed to the Lord of Cardinham, whose grandson Robert was a king's justice. In 1270 it became the property of Richard, Earl of Cornwall, and since 1299 has belonged to the Duchy of Cornwall. Originally an earthwork, the gate was built up in 1100 and Robert was responsible for the circular curtain wall. This forms a keep on its own and the buildings erected inside were of a later date, the chapel projecting on the east and an arch being cut through the curtain for access. The east window was blocked during the Civil War when the chapel became a gun emplacement and look-out post. During the battle of Lostwithiel, on 21st August 1644, the Royalist Sir Richard Grenville captured Restormel. The Earl of Essex had withdrawn most of the Parliamentary garrison before the attack and the commander, Colonel Weare, was in doubt as to his orders. He surrendered to Grenville.
Department of the Environment. Open normal times. Car park. Admission charge.

ST MAWES

Begun in 1540 and generally considered the finest of Henry VIII's coastal forts, St Mawes lies across the estuary from Pendennis and Falmouth. It took three years to build and consists of a large central tower, surmounted by a small watch-tower, and three semicircular bastions arranged in a clover-leaf. A drawbridge, protected by musket loops and an outer blockhouse, leads to the first floor.

The garrison varied from 16 to 100 men and the only time it saw action was during the Civil War when Lieutenant Bonython surrendered to Fairfax in March 1646 after reasoning that the castle could not be defended against guns mounted on the higher, landward side. The Vivian family have always been the traditional governors. The castle now stands in gardens but during the last war it was an important part of the coastal defences of Falmouth.

Department of the Environment. Open normal times. Admission charge.

ST MICHAEL'S MOUNT

Opposite Marazion, the island of St Michael's Mount rises high out of the water some 600 yards from dry land. It is supposed to be part of the lost kingdom of Lyonesse, and as early as 1044 was associated with Mont St Michel in France when a Benedictine monastery was formed there, a cell of the French monastery.

The first person to realise the military importance of the island was Henry de Pomeroy from Berry Pomeroy who landed here in Richard I's reign with a force disguised as monks. They seized the island in the name of Prince John and remained there until Richard's return, when the Archbishop of Canterbury successfully led his troops against them.

The same ruse was used in the fifteenth century when John de Vere, Earl of Oxford, after escaping from the battlefield of Barnet in 1471, made his way to Wales and sailed round the coast to capture the Mount. He fortified it and eventually surrendered on honourable terms to Edward IV. Sent to France as a prisoner, Oxford escaped and joined the Duke of Richmond's army. His military experience was invaluable and he led the vanguard at Bosworth, becoming Henry's most able general and subsequently Lord Chamberlain.

During the Civil War the Mount was garrisoned by the Royalists under Sir Francis Basset, who spent most of his own money on the provisions. The Mount was used as a gaol for important prisoners, including the Duke of Hamilton and the Royalist Sir Richard Grenville, who was arrested by his own side for insubordination to Sir Ralph Hopton—an event that led to the King's defeat in Cornwall. When Parliamentary troops moved in they found fifteen guns and 400 stands of arms.

From the Restoration and prior to its acquisition by the National Trust the Mount belonged to the St Aubyn family. The Lady Chapel has been converted into Gothic-style drawing-rooms. The refectory is known as the Chevy Chase room because of its plaster frieze executed during the Civil

War. A north wing was erected in 1927. There are no visible remains of the twelfth-century building.

National Trust. Open Wednesdays and Fridays all year, and Mondays June–September (additional rooms including armoury). Guided tours 10–4.30 June–September, 10.30, 12, 2 and 3.30 October–Easter; 10.30, 12, 2.30 and 4 Easter to May. Ferry in summer, or walk at low tide. Admission charge.

TINTAGEL

The site of King Arthur's legendary castle on the edge of the cliff, the ruins today are of the great hall, probably built in 1145 by Reginald, Earl of Cornwall. Henry III's brother Richard added an outer ward connected by a drawbridge to the island ward. It also had a fortified landing-stage.

Open to the public. Access by foot or Land Rover. Admission charge.

TREGONY

The Pomeroys had a castle here overlooking the river Fal. Nothing remains today.

TREMATON

One of the most interesting castles in Cornwall, Trematon is a few miles from Saltash. The castle, mentioned in Domesday Book, stands high over the Lynher river. Built on a Saxon site by Robert de Mortain, it later passed to the Crown, and in the reign of Richard I belonged to Reginald de Valletort, who was responsible for much of the construction. His grandson passed it to Sir Henry Pomeroy whose son made it over to Edward III. It then became part of the Duchy of Cornwall.

The building consists of a shell-keep similar to Restormel but standing on its own mound with its own ditch. The curtain wall then extends west and south in a great loop, enclosing almost an acre. The gatehouse on the south-east is a fine example of its kind with two portcullises and with arrow loops on either side and a guard chamber above. There is a west postern.

In 1594 Sir Richard Grenville and his wife were surrounded in Trematon by the rebels of Kilter's rising, who seized the place and stripped their prisoners and the contents of the castle. After this it appears to have been little used, although in 1650 petty courts were held here every three weeks.

In 1808 a house was built in the bailey for the Surveyor-General of the Duchy and the curtain wall was partly destroyed so that he could see the sea. Today the castle is in private hands and is not open to the public.

ISLES OF SCILLY

CROMWELL'S CASTLE
Built in 1651, Cromwell's Castle is a round tower and forebuilding on the west coast of Tresco. It is remarkably well preserved and is worth visiting. It had a garrison of 20 men and was supplied from St Mary's by sea. The entrance was by a wooden ladder.

KING CHARLES'S CASTLE
Built before Cromwell's Castle on the main Tresco cliff, it was converted into a fort during the Civil War and possibly the stones were taken away to build Cromwell's Castle.

STAR CASTLE
On St Mary's Island, Star Castle was built by Robert Adams, a surveyor, in 1593. It is an eight-pointed building surrounded by a rampart wall. It had gun embrasures and inside was a basement and two storeys. It had a garrison of 25 in 1637 with a further 25 Cornishmen for six months. Charles I came here, when prince, with the Duke of Buckingham. It has a gateway defended by a portcullis and an eighteenth-century bell tower. After its capture by Parliament in 1646 Star Castle was used as a prison for the Duke of Hamilton and other Royalists. In 1660 Sir Harry Vane was imprisoned here by Charles II, who knew the building well. In 1669 there was a garrison of 200 men and later it was used as the governor's residence. Today Star Castle is an hotel.

CUMBERLAND

ARMATHWAITE
A pele tower stands beside the river Eden which was built by the Skeltons. John Skelton was Henry VIII's poet laureate but the tower is older than this. It was altered in Georgian times and in the nineteenth century belonged to the Earl of Lonsdale.

ASKERTON

Near Kirkcambeck and Naworth, Askerton is a fortified house built by Lord Dacre on the river Cambock. In the shape of a quadrangle, it mostly dates from the fifteenth century and was used as the base for the Land Sergeant of Liddesdale who, under Elizabeth, was Thomas Carleton, an opportunist who sided with the Scots if it suited him.
Askerton is a private house, not open to the public.

BEWCASTLE

A remote spot on a Roman site, Bewcastle is a few miles off the Brampton-Newcastleton road. The castle is a square structure with a gatehouse and one stair remaining. It had some sort of moat but must have been easy prey to the Scots. The first owner was Giles Bueth; it then passed to the Vaux and Musgrave families; it belonged to the Grahams in the seventeenth century. In 1639 there was a garrison of 100 men here watching the border but Parliamentary supporters destroyed it in 1641.
Open to the public, provided permission is obtained from the farmer. Entrance is by a gate behind the farm.

CARLISLE

Both the Romans and the Saxons considered Carlisle an important border stronghold, for the rock is a natural defensive position. The first castle, however, was built by William II in 1092. The Scottish king, David I, was responsible for building the city walls and improving the castle but it is not clear whether he used wood or stone. Building continued throughout the middle ages. For a time it was the home of the ill-fated Andrew Harcla, Earl of Carlisle, executed in 1322 for making a pact of friendship with Robert the Bruce. By 1526 the castle was much decayed and structural repairs were undertaken in 1541 by the Master of Works, Stefan von Hashenperg, known as 'The Almain', and the garrison was strengthened with 800 German mercenaries. Queen Elizabeth kept Mary, Queen of Scots, at Carlisle for two months in 1568, and built a range to add to her father's half-moon battery.

During the Civil War, Sir Thomas Glenham held the castle for the king after Marston Moor. It was besieged by the Scots under Leslie and finally surrendered after Naseby, the garrison being so starved they were reduced to eating 'rats, linseed meal and dogs'. Leslie's Scots repaired the castle with stones from the cathedral.

The most exciting episode in the long history of Carlisle was the entry of the Jacobite army in 1745. The garrison, mostly militia men, held out for seven days and then surrendered to the Duke of Perth. The Jacobite army captured a hundred barrels of gunpowder and, having taken the valuables which had been stored there for safety, sent the news of victory to Prince Charles Edward at Brampton. A small garrison was left there and on the retreat this was increased to about 400 men under John Hamilton of Aberdeen. After a few shots at the Duke of Cumberland's army, Hamilton surrendered and the garrison was marched to London where Hamilton and another officer were hanged, drawn and quartered. After Culloden many Scots were imprisoned there and their cells are shown to visitors to the keep.

Rebuilding occurred between 1824 and 1835 when the great parade ground was built and the new barracks replaced the great hall and the Elizabethan barracks.

Department of the Environment. Open normal times. Car parking. Admission charge.

CATTERLEN HALL

Near Newton Reigny, which is three miles from Penrith, Catterlen is a pele tower with a sixteenth-century hall, altered in the seventeenth century. It belonged to the Vaux family before being bought during the Civil War by Christopher Richmond of High Head Castle.

COCKERMOUTH

Once an important castle, Cockermouth was built by William de Fortibus in the thirteenth century and was rebuilt in 1360 by Anthony de Lucy, a powerful friend of both Edward II and Edward III. It passed to the Percys and after 1585, when the eighth earl died in the Tower under suspicious circumstances, it fell into decay. The next owner, Charles, Duke of Somerset, repaired it and it remained virtually intact until the Civil War when it was besieged by the Royalists and later dismantled. The outer gatehouse has a spiral staircase and the inner gatehouse was once a prison. There is an eighteenth-century building in the grounds and parts of the castle were restored during the last century.

Open Monday–Friday 9.30–6, Saturdays 9.30–12, 2–6, Sundays 2–4. Limited car park. Admission charge.

CORBY

Like many northern castles, Corby, near Carlisle, started as a pele tower, and like Catterlen belonged to the Vaux and Richmond families before passing to Andrew Harcla, Earl of Carlisle. When the latter was executed for treason in 1322 it passed to the Salkelds who added to the tower. In 1812 the Howards, with the aid of Peter Nicholson, altered it to its present form.

DACRE

One of the most perfect pele towers a few miles from Ullswater on the river Eamont, Dacre is still a family home. It was built in the thirteenth century by Ranulph Dacre, whose family built Naworth. Thomas, Lord Dacre, made some alterations to it in 1674, adding the large windows and placing his arms over the entrance. There is a strange horseshoe-shaped moat on the lake side and twin parallel walls once ran down to the moat, so there could have been two baileys with a double wall protecting the inner one. The earthworks between the moat and the castle may indicate an earlier building where, according to tradition, Constantine of Scotland and Eugenius of Cumberland placed their kingdoms under Athelstan of England in 927.

DALSTON

This nineteenth-century house was constructed on a pele tower built by the Dalstons in 1500. Sir William Dalston was a leading Royalist in the Civil War and, during the siege of Carlisle, General Leslie captured Dalston tower and used it as his headquarters.

DISTINGTON

Hayes Castle, where the Morseby family once lived, consists today of a single wall.

DRAWDYKES

Near Houghton, Drawdykes pele stands on the Roman wall. In 1676 it was given a three-storey front by John Aglionby.

DRUMBURGH

Near Bowness-on-Solway in the fifteenth century, Lord Dacre built a defensive tower out of the Roman wall on the site of an earlier tower. In 1860 it was altered, again by John Aglionby.

EGREMONT

The ford over the river Eden at the south end of the town is commanded by the hill on which William de Meschines built his castle, one of the oldest in the county, in 1130. The vast gatehouse and herringbone curtain wall date from this period and there used to be a round keep. The great hall was on the north side and only a portion of two windows and an outer staircase remain. It belonged to the Moultons and later to the Percys but seems to have been in ruins for a long time.

GILSLAND

The castle of Triermain at Gilsland is now only a fragment of one of the four towers that once enclosed a courtyard and moat. It is described in Sir Walter Scott's *Guy Mannering*.

GREYSTOKE

Very little of the existing castle of Greystoke is medieval. It belonged in turn to the Greystokes, Dacres and Arundels, was burnt down during the Civil War and rebuilt in the nineteenth century by the Howards.

HARBYBROW

A pele tower on the Eden now forms part of a farm at Mealsgate, near Aspatria.

HAYTON

At Allonby, Hayton Castle is a fortified fifteenth-century house, the home of the Musgraves. Nearby is a motte and bailey castle.

HIGH HEAD

Nine miles south-west of Carlisle, High Head Castle was demolished and rebuilt in 1744. It was burnt down in 1956 and only the facade of the mansion remains. The original castle was built in Edward III's reign by William Engleys who held it from the crown on annual payment of a rose. It figures in a Buck's print as a formidable fortress.

HIGHHEAD

Burnt down in 1956, Highhead at Ivegill, eight miles south of Carlisle, was once a pele tower belonging to Andrew Harcla. It was turned into a mansion by Henry Brougham in the eighteenth century at a cost of £10,000.

29

HUTTON JOHN

Near Dacre Castle, Hutton John was a fourteenth-century pele tower built by William Hutton. In 1564 one Margaret Hutton married Andrew Hudleston, a Catholic. Father Hudleston from Hutton John attended Charles II on his death bed, and the house is still owned by the family.

IRTON

This Victorian house incorporating a pele tower is near Seascale. Sir Thomas Irton was knighted at Flodden and an earlier Irton fought in the Crusades and saw the capture of Jerusalem by Godfrey of Bouillou in 1099.

KIRKANDREWS TOWER

This sixteenth-century pele tower belonging to the Grahams is now a farm.

KIRKOSWALD

One tower remains of this castle, with portions of the moat. Built by Hugh de Merville c. 1201, it was the favourite home of Lord Dacre and his wife Elizabeth. One of the ceilings from Kirkoswald was transferred to Naworth by Lord Howard and the stones were re-used in the seventeenth century. In 1610 Sandford described Kirkoswald as 'the fairest fabrik that ever eyes looked upon'.

LIDDEL

At Kirkandrews on the Scottish border, Liddel belonged to Ranulf de Soulis in 1174. It became Crown property, then passed to the Earl of Cumberland. It is now merely an earthwork on the Esk.

LINSTOCK

At Houghton, once the residence of the bishops of Carlisle, Linstock is a square pele rebuilt by James Nicholson in the eighteenth century. It had a moat.

LORTON

A pele tower south of Cockermouth, Lorton was enlarged in the seventeenth and nineteenth centuries.

MILLOM

At the south-west tip of Cumberland, Millom Castle consists mainly of a fifteenth-century pele tower built into a thirteenth-century castle. It belonged to the Hudlestons (*see* Hutton John, Cumberland).

MUNCASTER

The Pennington family built this pele tower at Ravenglass, with outworks on the Esk estuary. During the Wars of the Roses Sir John Pennington, a Lancastrian, is said to have sheltered Henry VI, who was found wandering on the moors. The king gave Sir John an enamelled bowl saying that the luck of Muncaster would be preserved if the bowl was kept intact. As the Penningtons still own the castle the luck has been safeguarded. In 1826 the north-west tower was added by Salvin and Muncaster became a stately home. The gardens are renowned for the azaleas and rhododendrons and the castle contains many fine paintings and furniture.

Castle open to the public Easter–30th September, Wednesdays, Thursdays, Saturdays, Sundays and Bank Holidays 2–5 pm. Admission charge. Grounds and bird garden open. Admission charge.

NAWORTH

Naworth is the home of the Earl of Carlisle. It can be easily seen on the road to Lanercost Priory from Brampton which goes across the park. Like many other northern castles it started life as a pele tower, built in 1335 by Ranulph de Dacre, Sheriff of Cumberland. The most famous owner was Lord Thomas Dacre, who commanded the reserves of the Earl of Surrey at Flodden in 1513. He married a ward of the king, Elizabeth of Greystoke, whom he carried off one night from neighbouring Brougham Castle.

The Dacres were involved in the rising of the northern earls against Henry VIII in 1536. Robert Aske and Lord Dacre were executed and it was not until 1603 that Lord William Dacre was restored to his property and made Warden of the Marches. He married Elizabeth, his half-sister, and was known as 'Belted Will'. The castle was restored in Tudor style and some of the panelling from nearby Kirkoswald was included in its rooms. The disastrous fire in 1844 ruined much of the castle, which was restored the following year by Salvin. The fire revealed secret chambers and a staircase. Fortunately, a strong door prevented it from destroying Belted Will's tower. The Great Hall is one of the largest and finest in England, measuring 78 feet by 24 feet, and although the roof is Victorian, Salvin restored it as near as possible to the original.

Not open to the public.

PENRITH

Substantial remains of a large rectangular but rather un-exciting castle can be seen by the railway station. It was crenellated in 1397 by William Strickland, later Bishop of Carlisle. The castle was captured by General Lambert in 1648 and used as his headquarters during the Second Civil War. Never intended to be a building of active defence Penrith was built more as a shelter for the townsfolk until help could be obtained from Brougham or Carlisle.

ROSE CASTLE

The home of the bishops of Carlisle since the thirteenth century, Rose Castle is seven miles south-west of the city. It is mostly the work of Thomas Rickman in 1828, but was originally a pele tower. It had an elaborate moat and outer-walled defence system so that when garrisoned during the Civil War it held out with only thirty Royalists against a regiment of Roundheads who turned it into a prison for the garrison when they captured it. It has been burnt twice and extensively repaired by Bishop Percy, who removed Pettenger's Tower from the south-west corner, so called because an unfortunate of that name hanged himself inside.

SCALEBY

Built by Richard de Tilliol during Henry I's reign, Scaleby is about six miles from Carlisle. It was originally a tower house which was made into a castle in 1307 by Robert de Tilliol. Later owners added to it and built the moat, which still holds water. It was damaged during the Civil War and Sir Edward Musgrave, a Royalist, was forced to surrender it in 1648. It had already suffered from a siege in 1645 and was in no condition to face another. He sold it to Richard Gilpin who restored it and in 1737 further repairs were carried out. Today only the old pele is ruinous and Scaleby is the home of Lord Henley.

Not open to the public.

SHANK CASTLE

Near Stapleton and not far from Bewcastle is this ruined pele tower.

SOWERBY

Owned by Robert de Vaux c. 1175, Sowerby is a few miles west of Skelton. There are no visible remains.

1. *St Michael's Mount, Cornwall, was thought to be part of the lost kingdom of Lyonesse.*

2. St Mawes, Cornwall, was considered the finest of Henry VIII's coastal forts. Pendennis is just visible in the background.

3. The present remains at Tintagel, Cornwall, date from 1145 and are on the site of King Arthur's legendary castle.

4. *Restormel Castle, Cornwall, has belonged to the Duchy of Cornwall since 1299.*

5. *During the eighteenth century Powderham Castle was transformed into one of the most spectacular homes in Devon.*

6. *Donnington Castle, Berkshire, survived furious attacks during the Civil War before the Royalists eventually surrendered it.*

7. *The magnificently sited Corfe Castle, Dorset, has been a defence-point since Saxon times and is one of England's noblest ruins.*

8. *The unspoilt village of Castle Hedingham in Essex is dominated by a Norman keep as large as that of Rochester in Kent.*

9. *Colchester Castle, Essex, was built in the reign of William I and has the largest keep in England.*

10. *Berkeley Castle, Gloucestershire, was popular with both sides in the Civil War and so remains even now in excellent condition.*

11. Hurst Castle, Hampshire, was effectively adapted by the artillery during the First World War.

12. Goodrich Castle, Herefordshire, stands on a spur commanding the country over the river Wye.

STONEGARTHSIDE

Three miles from Nicholforest near the Northumberland and Roxburghshire borders, Stonegarthside is a tower later converted into a large farmhouse. It has a massive staircase and a courtyard that was once roofed over, but the owner removed the lead and sold it for its silver content. The Forsters owned Stonegarthside and built the nearby pele tower.

WOLSTY

Remains of a moat are all that can be seen of the castle of the abbots of Holme, crenellated in 1349. It passed to the Chambers family who moved to Hanworth, Middlesex.

DERBYSHIRE

BOLSOVER

Just off the M1 near Chesterfield, Bolsover stands high on a rocky hill in a coal-mining area. Originally built by William Peverel in Norman times, the castle was forfeited to the Crown when his son fell from favour for poisoning the Earl of Chester. King John sent the Earl of Derby to capture Bolsover from his barons and for six years the custodian was Gerard de Furnival. The castle then passed through numerous hands until in 1613 it was sold by the Talbots to Sir Charles Cavendish, son of the Countess of Shrewsbury. Lady Shrewsbury, the famous 'Bess of Hardwick', had already designed a new castle with her builder-architect John Smythson. The building that stands today is the Smythson castle, designed in the Jacobean Romantic style with angle towers, a central cupola and vaulted rooms. Later a long gallery was added and Sir Charles' son William, Marquis of Newcastle, built a riding school which, with the gallery, is in ruins.

Charles I stayed here in 1633 before the building was completed. His entertainment, together with a masque by Ben Jonson, cost £15,000. During the Civil War the Marquis was commander-in-chief of the Royalist forces in the north and midlands. Bolsover was garrisoned but in 1644 it was taken by Major General Crawford and the Marquis fled abroad. It was slighted but partly rebuilt by young Charles Cavendish for his brother at great expense after the war.

Department of the Environment. Open normal times. Admission charge.

33

CODNOR
Near Alfreton and the Nottinghamshire border, Codnor ruins stand high over the Erewash valley. The castle belonged to the Greys and later to the Lords Zouche. It consisted of two courts joined by a turreted gatehouse. Most of what remains today dates from the fourteenth century.

DUFFIELD
The Ferrars family built a massive castle here with a keep (excavated in 1886) measuring 95ft. x 93ft. and walls fifteen feet thick. It guarded the royal deer forest known as the Frith. During the reign of Henry III Robert de Ferrars, Earl of Derby, rebelled against the Crown and was defeated by Prince Edward at Chesterfield. The castle was burnt and Robert, captured hiding in the church, was banished. The property passed to the Duchy of Lancaster.

GRESLEY
Near Ashby-de-la-Zouch nothing remains of the Gresley family castle except a mound known as Castle Knob.

HORSLEY
On the A61 north of Derby, Horsley or Horeston Castle was built by Roger de Buron in the twelfth century. It was destroyed by quarrying. Excavations in 1888 showed that the multi-angular keep stood much higher on the rock than the rest of the castle.

MACKWORTH
The front wall of the fifteenth-century gatehouse still stands a few miles north-west of Derby. John Mackworth was Dean of Lincoln and lived mostly in London where his coat of arms can be seen at Barnard's Inn, Holborn. Sir Thomas Mackworth sold the castle to Sir John Curzon in 1655 but it was in all probability destroyed before this during the Civil War.

MELBOURNE
On B587 south of Derby, Melbourne Castle was built in 1311 by Robert de Holland and later passed to his brother Henry. It was acquired by marriage by John of Gaunt and remained part of the Duchy of Lancaster until 1604 when bestowed on the Earl of Nottingham. Later it passed to the Earl of Huntingdon and the Marquis of Hastings. For eighteen years John, Duke of Bourbon, was a prisoner here after his

capture at Agincourt. Dismantled during the Wars of the Roses there remains only a wall near Castle Farm of what was once a magnificent structure consisting of a square gate-house, twelve large towers, and living quarters surmounted by odd-shaped chimneys.

PEVERIL

On the A625 near Chapel-en-le-Frith, Peveril Castle, some-times known as Peak Castle, stands in a virtually impregnable position on a rock outcrop. William Peverel was granted the land by William the Conqueror who had lead mines nearby. Peverel had already built Bolsover Castle and was the lord of over 100 manors in Nottinghamshire and Northamptonshire as well as Derbyshire. His son William inherited all this and lost it when his estates were forfeited in 1155 for his part in the murder of the Earl of Chester. Peveril passed to Henry II who appointed a caretaker at the annual salary of £4 10s. The castle was much improved, especially the living quarters, and a square tower keep was erected in 1176.

Later, Peveril was owned by Simon de Montfort, by Prince Edward, and in 1310 was granted to John de Warenne, Earl of Surrey. Edward III granted it to John of Gaunt and it became a possession of the Duchy of Lancaster. Much of the building material in the south curtain wall is re-used Roman stone from Brough. This work dates from the thirteenth century when a hall and a chapel were built within the curtain. The hall appears to have become too uncomfortable, for a new hall was built at the bottom of the courtyard. When the tower was built the entrance was altered to the north-east corner instead of the south-west corner, where there might have been a bridge at one time.

Department of the Environment. Open normal times. Admission charge.

DEVON

AFFETON BARTON

The fortified manor of the Stucleys was altered in Victorian times, but the gatehouse and one tower remain.

BAMPTON

The manor house of the Paganels was fortified in 1336 by Richard Cogan, an Irish landowner. Nothing remains on the site today.

BARNSTAPLE

A mound remains near the municipal offices, where there was once a circular keep similar to Launceston. Most of the castle was destroyed in 1842.

BEARSCOVE

In Bayard's Cove at Dartmouth is a Henry VIII fort. *Open at all times. Admission free.*

BEER

The Ferrers family had a castle here and licence to crenellate was obtained in 1337. It was beside the Tavy river.

BERRY POMEROY

A few miles from Compton and only found with a good map, Berry Pomeroy ruins are in the middle of a dense wood. The Pomeroys came over with the Conqueror in 1066 and lived in their castle until 1549 when a riot over the reform of church services led to Sir Thomas Pomeroy leading 2,000 men on Exeter. His army was defeated by Lord Russell's mercenaries and he fled. His property was confiscated by the Crown and sold to the Seymours.

Sir Edward Seymour erected the fine Elizabethan house inside the walls but never finished it. It was struck by lightning in 1685, set on fire and ruined. In spite of this, William of Orange's army camped here on their way from Torbay to London in November 1688. The old ruined Norman building had been demolished after the Civil War but the gatehouse remains and most of the massive curtain wall.

Berry Pomeroy has a legend. The young Lord Berry and his cousin Genevieve were attacked by robbers while walking outside the castle. The robbers took her to a cave and she woke up to find them dead, killed by her cousin's standard-bearer, Raby Copeland. The latter was very badly wounded and she bound the wound with her scarf. He recovered and admitted his love for the girl. Lord Berry, who had hoped to marry Genevieve himself, gave his consent and the couple were married. Another version of the legend, however, says that he killed them both in a room in the gatehouse, and that their ghosts can be seen on certain nights, trying to touch each other.

Open every day, 10–6. Admission charge. Free car park at the castle.

COLCOMBE

Near Colyton the Pole family had a fortified house which is now incorporated in a farmhouse.

COMPTON

Off the main A381 between Newton Abbot and Totnes, Compton lies in a valley. The fortified manor, built by Geoffrey Gilbert in 1329, is a splendid sight from the minor road and must be one of the few medieval manors left in its original form. The Great Hall was rebuilt in 1954 like the original fourteenth-century hall, with screens, passage and minstrels' gallery. In 1450 a withdrawing room was built at the west end and the Gilberts, who have lived here since 1320 and were granted the right to use a portable altar, built a small chapel next to this room about the same period.

In 1520 the buttery and pantry were rebuilt and a huge larder and kitchen were added. The 24 foot high courtyard wall was built at this time as well as the towers, which have loopholes to cover all the walls of the house. There are two portcullis entrances, one of which is defended by a spear hole for thrusting at attackers. The roofed towers have machicolations over each face. The French attacked Teignmouth in the fifteenth century and this may account for the fortification work.

The most famous of the Gilberts was Sir Humphrey. He was Sir Walter Raleigh's half-brother and by taking possession of Newfoundland he founded the British Empire. He was lost at sea on the return journey in September 1583. A tablet in the chapel commemorates him. The building has recently been very carefully restored by Commander Walter Raleigh Gilbert.

National Trust. Open to the public April–October, Mondays, Wednesdays, Thursdays 10.30–12.30, 2–5. Admission charge.

DARTMOUTH

This harbour fortress was originally built in 1481 by Edward IV; the Kingswear section was later added by Henry VII and once anchored a chain which stretched across to the other side in order to block the harbour. In the Civil War the town was fortified by the Royalists and there were forts called Gallant's Bower, Paradise and Mount Flaggon on one side of the river, and Kingswear fort on the other side. Tunstall church was fortified and there were batteries at Hardress and Mount Boon. In spite of this Colonel Pride and others attacked the defences in January 1646 and the governor Sir Hugh Pollare surrendered the following day.

Department of the Environment. Open normal times. Admission charge.

EXETER

The Romans built a fort here which the British called Caer Wisc and King Alfred had a fortress of great importance on the Exe. A large Norman castle was begun in 1068 and altered by Stephen in 1138. It was called Rougemont in Shakespeare's day, because it was built of red sandstone, but in 1773 most of the castle was pulled down to build the County Court. There remain today only the walls and one gate.

FORT CHARLES

This fort on the Kingsbridge river is surrounded by water at high tide. It dates from Tudor times and was resolutely defended for the king by Colonel Fortescue and 63 men in 1646, finally surrendering on 7th May. The colonel escaped abroad and the castle key is still in the possession of his descendants.

GIDLEIGH

Near Chagford, Gidleigh was built in Norman times by the Prowse family. In later years it belonged to the Coades and Ridleys. Today it is a ruined dungeon and a few stones are all that can be seen.

HEMYOCK

On the Somerset border near Wellington, stand the remains of the Norman castle of the Hidons. They married into the Dynham family in the fifteenth century and Sir John Dynham was High Treasurer to Henry VII. The castle was dismantled in 1660 having been used as a prison by Parliament, and a farm now stands on the site.

LYDFORD

On an artificial mound within a bailey stands a square tower, believed to have been built by Richard, Earl of Cornwall and brother of Henry III. It has three rooms on one floor and above these are two others, one with a fireplace.

Department of the Environment. Open at all times. Car park opposite. Admission free.

MARISCO CASTLE

On Lundy Island, Marisco Castle is named after a piratical family who lived there until the twelfth century. The moat and outer walls are still visible, as is the rectangular keep.
Steamers from Ilfracombe, October–May. Landing fee.

OKEHAMPTON

The castle ruin is behind the telephone exchange on an isolated spur. Only the rectangular keep stands on an artificial motte. It belonged to the Norman Baldwin Fitz-Gilbert. One of his descendants was sheriff of Devon under Henry I, and from his line the Courtenays, Earls of Devon, obtained possession.

The Earl of Devon was a Lancastrian during the Wars of the Roses and twice the castle was forfeited but in 1504 Edward Courtenay defended Exeter for Henry VII against Perkin Warbeck. In 1538 Henry Courtenay, Marquis of Exeter, was involved in a plot with Cardinal Pole and Thomas Cromwell convicted him of treason. Courtenay was executed and his castle reduced to the ruin that stands today.

The main living accommodation, kitchens, gatehouse and chapel are at the bottom of the slope; the keep is isolated and appears to have been built at two separate times. From a defensive point of view, Okehampton is unsatisfactory and a determined enemy could probably have attacked the keep without fear of molestation from the rest of the castle.
Department of the Environment. Open normal times. Admission charge. Small car park.

PLYMOUTH

Leland speaks of a 'strong castle' here with 'at each corner a great round tower'. It was demolished in Charles II's reign and the citadel was built on the site.

PLYMPTON ST MAURICE

Near Plymouth and also known as Plympton Earl, the castle mound, now a local view point, is all that remains of Richard de Redvers's castle. Built during Henry I's reign, it was destroyed in 1136, rebuilt in 1204 and confiscated by the Crown. It was still more or less intact in 1642 when it was used as the Royalist headquarters in the unsuccessful attack on Plymouth.

POWDERHAM

On the A379 a few miles south of Exeter, Powderham has been the home of the Courtenays for 600 years. It was built, according to Leland, by Isabel de Fortibus, widow of the first Earl of Devon. The site was probably first occupied by a tower guarding the estuary against the Danes and in Norman times it belonged to the Count d'Eu. In 1325 the Courtenays came into possession of it when Hugh Courtenay married the granddaughter of Edward I, Margaret de Bohun. It passed to their sixth son, Philip, who was responsible for building the present structure.

There was virtually no disturbance at Powderham until 1538 when Henry Courtenay, a cousin of Henry VIII, was imprisoned and executed the following year on a trumped-up charge of treason. His son Edward was also imprisoned, but was released after fourteen years by Queen Mary and restored to his property. Later he was suspected of participation in Wyatt's rebellion and fled to Italy. During the Civil War the castle, garrisoned by Sir Hugh Meredith for the Royalists, beat off an attack in 1645 by Fairfax's troops, but surrendered the following year on honourable terms. The castle escaped destruction, perhaps because Sir William Waller's daughter married a Courtenay. The eighteenth century saw Powderham turned into one of the most spectacular houses in Devon with a grand staircase decorated with elaborate plaster-work and two libraries. James Wyatt added a music room in 1770. *The Earl and Countess of Devon. Open 27 May–13 July, every day except Saturdays and Mondays, 2–6; 15 July–7 September daily except Saturdays. Deer park. Admission charge.*

TIVERTON

Next to the church remains the gatehouse of one of the largest castles in Devon. It had three round and one square tower and a wide double moat. It fell into decay in Tudor times after its owner, the Marquis of Exeter, was executed for treason by Henry VIII. During the Civil War it was garrisoned by 300 Royalists but General Massey captured it after a lucky shot broke the drawbridge chain and exposed the inner courtyard. The remains of a fourteenth-century hall and chapel are also visible.

TORRINGTON

A castle belonging to the baron of Torrington once stood here.

TOTNES

A shell-keep similar to Launceston, Totnes was never of great military importance. Built by the Nonants in the eleventh century, it passed to the Zouche family. In later days it was used as a prison. There used to be a square tower in the keep and a second bailey was constructed for cattle on the outside of the moat to the north. The structure is in excellent condition.

Department of the Environment. Open normal times. Admission charge. No car park.

DORSET

BROWNSEA

On an island in Poole Harbour Henry VIII had a defensive blockhouse, which was used by Sir Christopher Hatton to extract money from passing ships. It was mostly burnt down in 1895.

National Trust. Open April–September. Admission charge. Boats from Rockley, Sandbanks and Shell Bay.

CHIDEOCK

Only the moat remains of Sir John Arundell's fourteenth-century castle. It changed hands three times during the Civil War and was slighted by Colonel Ceely in 1645 at a cost of £1 19s.

CORFE

One of the noblest and best known ruins in England, Corfe stands high up in a gap in the Purbeck Hills. The first building was probably erected by King Edgar, whose son Edward was murdered here in A.D. 978. His stepmother is said to have had him stabbed.

The Duke of Britanny and several French captives were imprisoned here by King John and twenty-two starved to death in a dungeon. Henry III turned it into a royal palace and Edward II spent a night here on his last journey to Berkeley. The ill-starred Duke of Clarence owned it during the reign of Edward IV, and the Protector Somerset until his execution for treason in 1552. In Elizabethan times the Hattons owned it and in 1635 it was sold to Sir John Bankes. He was with Charles I when the Parliamentary forces from Poole attacked Corfe, which was defended by his wife

41

and their small garrison. Two attacks were beaten off but in 1646 a Colonel Pitman turned traitor and admitted the enemy, forcing Lady Bankes to surrender. The slighting was very thorough and one of the gatehouse towers was split in two. The wall between the gatehouse and keep remains.
Open 10–dusk, April–September.

DORCHESTER
Nothing remains of Dorchester Castle, although the arms of the town show a keep and four towers. It was north of Sheep Lane on the Frome, was badly damaged during the Civil War and was finally demolished in 1794.

LULWORTH
The seventeenth-century castle stands on the site of the Newburghs' Norman castle.

MAIDEN CASTLE
The largest earthwork in Britain, this is not strictly a castle but an Iron Age fortification. It was captured by the Romans in A.D. 43 and in 70 it ceased to be occupied. In 1937 excavations revealed a number of skeletons, one with a Roman arrow-head in the spine.

MARSHWOOD
There are signs of a motte and bailey castle here which was first mentioned in 1215.

PORTLAND
Henry VIII built a blockhouse here to command Weymouth. It was manned at the time of the Armada. It was captured by Royalists during the Civil War and held until April 1646.

POWERSTOCK
A motte and bailey castle near Bridport had stone buildings visible until the eighteenth century.

RUFUS CASTLE
On the east coast of Portland Bill are the remains of William Rufus's castle, with its loopholes guarding Church Ope Cove. It is also known as Bow and Arrow Castle.

SANDSFOOT
Henry VIII built a fort on the beach near Weymouth. It was destroyed by the sea and now has round it some gardens with a fountain.

SHAFTESBURY

A motte on Castle Hill is all that remains of what was probably a castle of Stephen's reign.

SHERBORNE (OLD CASTLE)

Roger de Caen's building at Sherborne is well situated on a commanding hill with steep ground to the north and west and a wide moat on the other two sides. Roger, Bishop of Salisbury, was Regent to Henry I during the latter's frequent journeys abroad. He also built Devizes, Old Sarum and Malmesbury castles. In 1139 Roger was imprisoned by Stephen for his friendship with Matilda. His castle fell into decay and subsequently had several owners, including Lord Somerset, until Elizabeth I presented it to Sir Walter Raleigh. He, however, decided that it was too decayed and built the new castle nearby.

There were three gateways to Sherborne; the north, with its long vaulted passage, is not yet completely restored; the north-east is completely ruined; the south-west is the best preserved. The main buildings are in the centre with the great hall on the ground floor and the chapel on the first floor. There is a large Norman pillar supporting a bay window which faces south, an alteration dating from the sixteenth century. In James I's reign the Earl of Somerset was sent to the Tower for his part in the murder of Sir Thomas Overbury and the castle passed to Baron Digby, former Ambassador to Madrid. His descendants, the Wingfield-Digbys, own the land today.

During the Civil War the castle was garrisoned for the King and was besieged twice. In 1642 the Parliamentarians were driven off and in 1645 there was a fifteen-day siege in which the Portsmouth siege train had to be brought up to batter down the walls before Sir Lewis Dives surrendered.
Department of the Environment. Open normal times. Admission charge.

STURMINSTER NEWTON

A motte and bailey castle built c. 1208 stood here south of the river, but very little remains.

WAREHAM

The Normans built a shell-keep at Wareham which was used as a prison for Robert of Normandy in 1106. It was held by

43

Royalists during the Civil War until betrayed in 1645 and dismantled. The west bank became known as the Bloody Bank because it was the scene of executions after Sedgemoor.

WOODSFORD

A fortified house was built in 1337 by Guy de Bryan on the Frome near Wareham. It was once four-sided, with towers on each corner, but only part of one tower remains. It is still inhabited after being restored during the last century by Lord Ilchester.

DURHAM

AUCKLAND

The castle at Bishop Auckland is still the home of the Bishop of Durham. It was built by Bishop Bec and rebuilt by Wyatt and has a great hall, now the chapel, and a fine wood-panelled private chapel off the throne room. It once had a stone curtain wall. In the grounds stands an eighteenth-century deer shelter, somewhat similar to that at Sudbury in Staffordshire.

Open to the public, with the grounds, usually on the third Sunday in July. Admission charge.

BARNARD CASTLE

Barnard was built on the Tees in 1130 by Bernard Balliol. (The site had been given to Guy Balliol of Bailleul by William Rufus.) The next owner, Hugh Balliol, was a favourite of King John. During the Barons War in 1216 the castle was besieged but one of Hugh's men killed the Lord of Alnwick, who was fighting for the Scots, with a shot from his cross-bow, and the attackers retreated. After passing to the Nevilles the castle came to Charles, Earl of Westmorland, who was one of the supporters of Mary Queen of Scots during the Rising of the North in 1569. He was forced to flee the country after trying unsuccessfully to drive out Sir George Bowes, who in his absence captured Barnard for Queen Elizabeth. The Crown confiscated the property, leasing it to various people including the Vanes. This family held Barnard for the Royalists during the Civil War, when it was badly damaged by Parliamentary cannon and captured.

There are four baileys, the large outer and town baileys

and the smaller middle and inner ones. The main keep, Balliol's Tower, was so strongly built that at one time it was used as a shot tower, thereby damaging its vaulting and floor. The chapel was in the outer bailey and part of a pier is still visible in a cowshed.

Department of the Environment. Open Sundays 1st April– 30th September 9.30–7. Admission charge.

BRADLEY HALL

Near Wolsingham, a fortified manor was crenellated by Bishop Langley in 1431 and surrounded by a moat. The south range is a ruin.

BRANCEPETH

A few miles south-west of Durham is Brancepeth Castle, built by the Bulmers before 1100 and inherited by the Nevilles in 1174. Today it is mostly eighteenth and nineteenth-century work that stands but parts remain of Ralph Neville's fourteenth-century castle. Ralph, grandfather of Warwick the King-maker, was Marshal of England for 26 years, 1399-1425.

In 1569 the sixth Earl of Westmorland fought in the Rising of the North and the property was confiscated by the Crown. It was owned for a time by the Earl of Somerset and in 1701 was bought by Sir Henry Belasyse.

In 1796 William Russell, a Sunderland banker, bought it and, with his son Matthew, the richest commoner in England, spent more than £120,000 restoring it. The work was carried out by an Edinburgh architect called Patterson who had a fondness for Norman work but not very much imagination. Today Brancepeth is a research laboratory for a firm of glass-makers and is not open to the public.

DURHAM

Standing inside an incised meander of the river Wear, Durham Castle makes a handsome partner to the great cathedral. It was a Norman stronghold and the original castle was built by William I c. 1072. It was strengthened and enlarged by Bishop Pudsey in 1174. The present entrance has massive sixteenth-century doors which lead into a court-yard. Bishop Bec's Great Hall is on the left. It has a large collection of paintings and armour and has seen many famous guests, including Sir Walter Scott and the Duke of Welling-ton. The kitchen was once a guardroom. Above is Bishop

Pudsey's Norman doorway; to reach it one goes up the Black Staircase, installed in 1663 by Bishop Cosin. The Senate Room has a sixteenth-century tapestry and underneath is a small chapel, dating from 1070, the oldest room in the castle. A new chapel was built in 1542 nearby with fittings from Auckland Castle. The massive keep was converted into rooms for students in 1840 and the castle is now University College.

Open to the public July–September and the first three weeks of April, 10–12 and 2–4.30 weekdays only. The rest of the year on Mondays, Wednesdays and Saturdays 2–4. Admission charge.

HOLLINSIDE
A ruined, fortified manor stands by the Derwent.

HYLTON
A few miles north-west of Sunderland on the Wear, Hylton is a fourteenth-century tower, measuring 66 feet by 36 feet, with raised turrets, one of which has a clock. The Hylton family were fortunate to escape the Pilgrimage of Grace in 1536 and, although Royalists, did not lose their property during the Civil War.

Hylton has a shield over the gateway known as the Washington shield, with stars and stripes similar to the USA flag. It is a favourite photographic subject for visiting Americans.

There is a legend about the castle. One of the owners accidentally killed a stable boy and threw his body into a pond. The boy's spirit haunted the castle and at night cutlery and plates were hurled about. If servants left the dining hall in disorder, however, the next morning all was neat and tidy. The spirit finally departed when a fine green coat was left for it on the hearth. The last Hylton died in 1730 and about this time a boy's bones were found in the pond.

Department of the Environment. Open normal times. Admission charge.

LAMBTON
An eighteenth-century castle, built on the site of an older castle, Lambton is now an educational institution.

LUMLEY
South of Chester-le-Street, Ralph, first Baron Lumley, crenellated his house in 1392. He did not live long enough to

enjoy it as he joined the plot against the new king Henry IV in 1400 and was killed at Cirencester fighting for Richard II. This revolt sealed Richard's fate and he died within weeks. Sir John Lumley fought at Agincourt and was killed at Anjou in 1421. Another Lumley was executed for his part in the Pilgrimage of Grace in 1536, and Richard, Viscount Lumley, fought for Charles I at Bristol. Richard Lumley, Earl of Scarborough, fought at Sedgemoor. He commissioned Sir John Vanbrugh to alter Lumley and Vanbrugh rebuilt the south and west front windows, added a staircase and, under the ballroom, a library divided into three by pillars.

Lumley belongs to Durham University and is not open to the public.

RABY

At Staindrop on the main A688 road between Bishop Auckland and Barnard Castle, Raby is one of the finest fourteenth-century castles in the country. Sir John Neville, who as a boy had seen his father victorious at Neville's Cross, obtained a licence to crenellate his home in 1378. He was High Admiral of England and his son Ralph played safe by supporting both Richard II and the usurper Henry Bolingbroke. First Earl of Westmorland, Ralph fought at Agincourt. His first wife was Margaret, daughter of Hugh, Earl of Stafford; his second was Joan Beaufort, John of Gaunt's daughter. He had 21 children by his two wives and the youngest of them, Cicely, was known as the 'Rose of Raby'. She married Richard Plantagenet, Duke of York, and was the mother of Edward IV and Richard III. The sixth Earl, Charles, was the last Neville to bear the title of Westmorland; he escaped abroad following the Rising in the North in 1569 and later died in Holland. Raby was forfeited to the Crown.

In 1626 it was purchased by Sir Henry Vane. The Vanes were Parliamentarians during the Civil War and, although the Royalists from Bolton captured it in 1645, Sir Henry Vane retook it before it suffered any damage. In 1698 Christopher Vane was created the first Lord Barnard and in 1714, attempting to injure his son's inheritance because the latter had married unexpectedly, he stripped the lead off Raby's roof and attempted to pull down the walls. Luckily the law intervened and Raby was saved. Raby Castle still belongs to the Vane family and the present owner is Harry John Neville, the 11th Baron Barnard.

The castle lies on a slight hill. There used to be a wide

moat round it. The entrance is by the north gatehouse in the curtain wall and a fourteenth-century inner gatehouse leads into the courtyard. Clifford's Tower is the largest in the castle with walls 10 feet thick, but Bulmer's Tower at the other end is the oldest, built in the twelfth century though increased in height in the fourteenth. It is five-sided. The south facade was altered by the architect Burn in 1840 but it was done in such a way that the effect of the castle from a distance is dramatic.

Open to the public. Easter; Spring Bank Holiday; Sundays to end of May; and November–February; Wednesdays, Saturdays and Sundays in June, July and September; every day except Friday in August. Admission charge.

RAVENSWORTH

Four miles from Gateshead, this castle, recently demolished, was completely rebuilt in 1808 but once belonged to the Lumleys. Later it passed to the Liddells, who commissioned Nash to redesign it and it was finally finished in 1846 with the later drawing being completed by Lord Ravensworth's son, the Hon. H. T. Liddell. In its heyday it was the finest romantic revival building in the north of England.

STOCKTON

There was a bishop's castle here which was rebuilt in the fourteenth century and restored in 1578 by Bishop Barnes. It was destroyed in the Civil War and only the names Castle Street and Moat Street remain.

STREATLAM

Two miles north-east of Barnard Castle, Streatlam was once a Balliol castle but was rebuilt in 1718-1720 by Blakiston Bowes and is now a ruin. It was the scene in 1767 of the elopement of Lady Strathmore, a young widow, with Andrew Stoney, a worthless scoundrel. Stoney spent her money and shut her up in Streatlam. She escaped but Stoney recaptured her and rode off to Darlington with her across his horse's neck. They were, however, overtaken by local people; Lady Strathmore was rescued and Stoney was sent to prison.

WITTON

This imposing castle on the Wear dates mostly from the nineteenth century but the north tower is fifteenth-century and was built by Ralph Eure, although the castle belonged to the

48

bishops of Durham. It passed to the Darcys and in 1743 was acquired by William Cuthbert for £15,000. It once had one square and three circular towers with curtain walls and bartizans and must have been very strong. Today it is a caravan park and the grounds are open to the public although the castle is private.

ESSEX

CASTLE HEDINGHAM

One of the surprises of Essex is Castle Hedingham, a charming unspoilt village dominated by a Norman keep as large as that at Rochester in Kent. To reach it take the A604 from Colchester or from Cambridge and the village is four miles north of Halstead.

The castle was built in about 1130, of Barnack stone brought from Northamptonshire, and has a basement and three storeys, rising to 110 feet at the battlements and a further 20 feet to the top of the two remaining towers. The walls are 12 feet thick at their base and, as at Colchester, the first storey windows are loopholes, those higher up being larger to let in the light. The entrance is on the west side at first storey level and was defended by a gatehouse, now destroyed, and a portcullis. The hall, with its gallery on the second floor, has an arch across it to support the floor above; the floor below had a similar arch, now destroyed. The third floor, reached from a staircase in the north-west corner that runs from top to bottom of the structure, has access to a parapet walk and to the two turrets that remain of the original four. Outside the keep is a sixteenth-century bridge over the moat and the remains of the encircling wall which enclosed three acres. In its day it must have been one of the strongest castles in England.

The owners, the De Vere family, were frequently at war. Robert, second Earl of Oxford, fought against King John and, after the latter's death, the castle, which was in Crown hands in 1214, was two years later occupied by French soldiers who came over with the Earl of Winchester. Robert de Vere's son fought for Simon de Montfort at Lewes and another de Vere, the seventh Earl of Oxford, fought at Crecy. The ninth earl was a favourite of Richard II and married Edward III's granddaughter. He was created a marquis, the first in England.

The most famous earl of Oxford was the Lancastrian soldier who fought with Warwick at the battle of Barnet. Unfortunately he lost the enemy in the fog and attacked his own side by mistake. He was imprisoned for many years by the Yorkists in France but escaped to land with Henry Tudor at Milford Haven in 1485 and to command his vanguard at the decisive battle of Bosworth Field. The miserly king, although no doubt grateful, was entertained by the earl at Castle Hedingham, who was afterwards fined 15,000 marks (over £10,000) for keeping so large an army of uniformed retainers.

In 1604 the seventeenth earl dismantled part of the castle to spite his relative Lord Burleigh, who inherited it. The two had quarrelled over the trial of the Duke of Norfolk. (Norfolk, a friend of the Earl of Oxford, was accused of supporting Mary, Queen of Scots.) In 1713 the castle passed to the Trentham family and later to the Ashurst family from Lancashire. Today it is owned by Miss Majendie, a relation of the Ashursts, and Dr Margery Blackie.

Open Easter Monday, May–September, Tuesdays, Thursdays and Saturdays. 2–6 pm. Admission charge.

COLCHESTER

Colchester Castle was built in the reign of William I on the site of a Roman temple. The rectangular keep, the largest in England, was originally built one storey high surrounded by ramparts. The outer bailey extended to the walls north of the town. At a later date three other storeys were added and the entrance was from the north wall at second storey level entered by a flight of wooden steps. Both the battlements and the north ramparts could defend it, so it is surprising that the present large south doorway was ever built. Presumably the other one was too small and did not lead into the great hall. Also the townfolk could withdraw into the protection of the keep in times of trouble, taking their possessions with them, and by entering from the south they would have the protection of the gatehouse and portcullis, which must have been built for this purpose. The present cupola is an eighteenth-century addition, for at that time the ruined keep stood in the garden of Holytrees, now a museum containing later antiquities and costumes.

The massive ruin was roofed over and fitted with galleries in 1932. On the first floor are four enormous fireplaces with bricks built in herring-bone pattern and a chapel positioned in the south-east corner similar to that in the White Tower of the Tower of London. The similarity between the two castles suggests that they were designed by the same man.

The history of the castle is the history of Colchester. It belonged to Eudo, steward to William I and Henry I, and on his death it reverted to the Crown. Hamo St Clare was constable in the twelfth century and later this office passed to William de Lanvalei. King John distrusted the third generation de Lanvelei and replaced him with a Fleming, Stephen Harengoot, who fortified the castle with two 24-inch and six 12-inch ballista from London. After Magna Carta the castle was once more restored to Lanvalei, who was one of the rebellious barons. In 1215 7,000 men landed in Suffolk from France and a force under the Earl of Winchester, including many French soldiers, occupied the castle. It was attacked by Savaric de Mauleon and King John. The French fought furiously, using the ballista, but were defeated and once more Harengoot was installed as constable.

Shortly after this the keep was used as a prison, but during the Civil War the Royalists held Colchester for three months against Fairfax and the New Model Army. After a twelve week siege the town finally surrendered in August, 1648. Sir Charles Lucas and Sir George Lisle, two of the leaders of the revolt, were imprisoned traditionally in the long vault near the wellhouse until, as an example to others, they were taken outside to face the Parliamentary firing squad. Sir Charles Lucas, whom Clarendon describes as 'a gallant man but of a nature not to be lived with, more intolerable than the siege', was a cavalry leader and a veteran of Marston Moor. He was shot first and Lisle ran over to pay his respects before he too faced the firing squad. 'He had the softest nature imaginable, loved all and beloved of all' said Clarendon of the hero who had removed his coat at the second battle of Newbury, so that his own men, as well as the enemy, could see him in the twilight. When the firing squad captain said 'I'll warrant you Sir, we'll hit you', Lisle remarked 'Friends, I have been nearer to you when you have missed me'. Today a stone outside the castle keep marks the spot where they died.

Another man who died for a cause in Colchester was young James Parnell, a Quaker who was imprisoned in a cell so small and high up, that the ladder to it did not reach it and he injured himself in a fall. Later he was left in the open courtyard on a winter night, which treatment made him so ill that he died. He was nineteen years old.

The structure was partly pulled down in 1683 by a local ironmonger who happily found the task too great, and soon gave it up. Colchester Castle is now the Colchester and Essex Museum. It contains an extensive archaeological collection, including some of the best Roman remains in Britain.
Open weekdays 10–5, Sundays (summer only) 2.30–5. Vaults and cells tour on weekdays only.

HADLEIGH

In south Essex, not far from Leigh-on-Sea and just off the A13 from London to Southend-on-Sea, stand the remains of Hadleigh Castle on a hill overlooking the Thames estuary. It was built by Hubert de Burgh, Chief Justiciar of King John and Henry III, of Kentish stone ferried across the river and up a creek that has since silted up. Henry VIII's 'Flanders Mare' Anne of Cleves who 'spoke only German and spent her time chiefly in needlework' lived here after her divorce.

The castle, made famous by John Constable's painting, differs from the usual medieval design in having no keep. The two remaining towers at the north-east (now partially collapsed) and south-east have walls 5 feet thick and the latter has two hexagonal rooms, chimney flues and slit windows. The entrance was on the north, protected by a barbican adjacent to a large tower which may have acted as the keep, protected by a drawbridge and portcullis. The main offices were to the south-west where there were timber buildings against the wall and a circular tower with a dungeon. Hadleigh is one of the finest remaining late medieval ruins left in Essex.
Department of the Environment. Open normal times. Admission charge.

PLESHEY

> *What shall he at Pleshey see*
> *But empty lodgings and unfurnish'd walls,*
> *Unpeopled offices, untrodden stones?*

Thus Shakespeare described Pleshey Castle near Chelmsford, but today the walls have vanished and the lodgings nearby are full. Originally a motte and bailey castle of the twelfth century, Pleshey still has a motte 50 feet high, a moat crossed by a fifteenth-century bridge and a huge outer bailey that covers most of the village. Geoffrey de Mandeville, owner of Saffron Walden Castle, was the first known owner. He surrendered it to King Stephen in 1142. It was ordered to be destroyed in 1157 but was refortified 1167–1180. It passed to the Bohuns, Earls of Hereford. Eleanor de Bohun was the wife of the Duke of Gloucester, uncle of Richard II. The Duke tried to rule the young King and opposed the marriage of his own brother's son to his wife's younger sister Mary de Bohun. Richard set out with a party of soldiers for Pleshey and enticed the Duke away. On their way back to London the party was ambushed and the Duke was carried off to Calais on Richard's orders. The unfortunate man was later strangled and brought back to Pleshey to be buried next to his wife. His family got their revenge three years later when the Duke of Exeter, who had been responsible for the ambush, was beheaded by a mob outside the castle walls.

In 1629 Robert Clarke, the then owner, pulled down most of the castle to build a house called the Lodge. This was later sold to Sir William Joliffe, whose monument can be seen in the church. There is a stone from the castle in the church-yard which has on it the name 'Richard II' inscribed in Latin. *Ruins open at all times. Admission free.*

RAYLEIGH

This motte and bailey castle passed into Crown hands in 1163. It was repaired in 1173 and again in 1183. In the Prittlewell Priory Museum at Southend is part of its pre-conquest oak gangway.

SAFFRON WALDEN

Little remains of this castle. In Church Street are the flint walls of the keep dating from the eleventh or twelfth centuries. There used to be another building west of the keep, reached by a staircase. At the time of Domesday the manor belonged to Geoffrey de Mandeville who probably built the castle. His grandson, also Geoffrey, fought for Queen Matilda against King Stephen and had to forfeit Saffron Walden, together with Pleshey Castle and his position as Constable of the Tower of London. He was later killed by an arrow while attacking Burwell Castle near Cambridge.

Later the castle passed to his niece Beatrix de Saye, wife of the Chief Justice of England and a friend of King John. When they died the property passed to their daughter Maud, wife of the Earl of Hereford, Lord High Constable of Eng-land. In 1347 Maud's son Humphrey obtained a licence to crenellate what must have been mainly a domestic building.

On his death it reverted to the Crown and became part of the Duchy of Lancaster. Henry VIII presented it to the Lords Audley and from this family it descended to the Howards, Earls of Suffolk.

STANSTED MOUNTFITCHET

Near the railway station are the remains of a small Norman castle, a circular inner bailey and another bailey to the east. It was built by the Mountfitchets and destroyed in the reign of King John after Richard de Mountfitchet, who fought for the barons, was defeated.

GLOUCESTERSHIRE

BERKELEY

The building of the present castle was begun by Roger de Berkeley in 1117 and completed by his son, also Roger, in about 1153. The castle was granted to Robert FitzHarding, following the younger Roger's opposition of Henry II, who was created Baron Berkeley. The Berkeleys opposed King John and later joined Simon de Montfort's rebellion. In spite of this they continued to hold their property, due mainly to Thomas Berkeley who fought valiantly for Edward I in the latter's northern campaign. During the deposition of Edward II by Queen Isabella and Roger Mortimer, Thomas Berkeley was turned out of his castle, which was used as a prison for the king under two guardians, Lord Maltravers and Thomas Gurney. One of the cruellest deeds in English history took place on 21st September 1327 when 'the shrieks of death through Berkeley's roofs did ring, shrieks of an agonising King'.

Thomas Berkeley was exonerated from any complicity in the murder and young Edward III soon had his revenge on Mortimer (*see* Nottingham Castle). Thomas's grandson was one of Henry Bolingbroke's supporters in the deposition of Richard II and when he died in 1417 the ownership of the castle and estate was disputed between his son-in-law and his nephew James Berkeley. The latter was awarded the estate but during the Wars of the Roses the daughter's grandson Lord Lisle and James's son William waged a private war that had no connection with the major war that was going on elsewhere in England. In 1470 at the battle of

Nibley Green, Lisle was defeated and killed. William had no heirs and rather than recognise any of his cousins he granted the castle to Henry VII in exchange for the title of Earl Marshal in 1486. For sixty-one years the castle was held by the Crown until the great grandson of William's brother Maurice inherited it on the death of Edward VI.

During the Civil War Berkeley Castle was occupied by both sides and finally the Royalist Sir Charles Lucas surrendered to Colonel Rainsborough in 1645 after a three day siege. The usual slighting was not attempted as Berkeley was popular with both sides. Only the outer wall was demolished and the keep breached, as it remains still. In 1679 George Berkeley was made an earl but owing to a complication in inheritance in 1810 the 'Berkeley Peerage Case' left the castle in different hands for a hundred years until the earls once again possessed it in 1916.

The Norman shell-keep has been flattened on the top to give more space. This leads out to the inner ward, where there is the chapel, the great hall built during the reign of Edward III and the residential quarters—all somewhat similar to an Oxford or Cambridge college. Edward II's prison was in one of the three semi-circular keep towers although he is believed to have been murdered in a room above the fore-building, described by Horace Walpole as 'a dismal chamber in a square tower'. The gatehouse is small and the moat narrow, so that it is remarkable that this castle has survived to the present age in such excellent condition.

Major R. J. G. Berkeley, MFH. Open April–September every day (except Monday) 2–5.30. Bank Holiday Mondays 11–5.30. Sundays only in October, 2–4.30. Admission charge. No dogs.

BEVERSTONE

On the A435 between Tetbury and Dursley, Beverstone belonged to Berkeley manor at the time of Domesday. During the reign of Henry I it passed to Robert Fitzharding and his son Maurice fortified the manor without permission from Henry III. The castle commanded the main road to Cirencester and was built in a square with corner towers and a moat. It was altered in Elizabethan times, the banqueting hall being converted into a farmhouse. Garrisoned for the king during the Civil War it was captured at the second attempt by General Massey in 1644. The ruins of the west front remain with a dungeon and a fine fourteenth-century chapel.

BRIMPSFIELD

A few mounds mark Brimpsfield Castle on the edge of Ermine Street between Cirencester and Gloucester. It was the home of the Giffards one of whom rebelled against Edward II. The latter sent soldiers to demolish the building but the work does not seem to have been carried out for the next inhabitant was Hugh Despencer. After the murder of Edward at Berkeley the property passed to John Maltravers, who was involved in the murder. Edward III granted it to his son Lionel, Duke of Clarence, and thereafter it remained Crown property until its destruction, probably in the seventeenth century.

CIRENCESTER

A castle once stood next to the church. It was demolished by King Stephen.

DURSLEY

Roger de Berkeley's castle was built here in 1153. It had a deep moat but has since vanished, the material being used to build Dodington House.

DYMOCK

On the Herefordshire border, Dymock is a small village on B4125 with a motte and bailey earthwork built in the twelfth century. It was granted to William de Braose by the Earl of Hereford 1148–1154.

ENGLISH BICKNOR

There was a motte and bailey castle here, first mentioned in 1190. It was near Symonds Yat.

GLOUCESTER

Where the County Gaol stands was once a Norman castle with two baileys, a square keep, a deep moat and 'a private chapel for the King, another for the Queen and their separate apartments paved with tiles'. The gatehouse still stood by the river in 1721 but by the nineteenth century this had vanished.

HAILES

At Winchcombe near Cheltenham are the ruins of Hailes Abbey. Near Hailes Green Farm Ralph of Gloucester had a castle, the stones of which were probably removed in 1246 to build the abbey.

LYDNEY

A small castle, excavated in 1930, stood on Little Camp Hill to the south of Lydney. It had a rectangular keep and a curtain wall with two towers.

MISERDEN

A motte and bailey castle in the grounds of Miserden Park, north of Stroud, was once the home of Robert Musard, a Norman baron. It was destroyed during the Wars of the Roses. The Park gardens are occasionally open to the public.

ST BRIAVELS

On the Monmouth bank of the Severn at the head of a wooded valley on the Wye stands the small twelfth-century castle of Milo FitzWalter. It consists of a massive gatehouse and kitchen, the keep having fallen down in the eighteenth century. Most of the present structure dates from 1276 but during the reign of King John the castle was used as a hunting residence. Apparently Milo's son, Mahel, who was 'cruel and covetous', entertained Walter de Clifford here and a small fire in the castle brought down a stone on Mahel's head which killed him. This may account for the old chapel, which was made into a court room, being converted back into a chapel at a much later date.

SUDELEY

The fortified manor of Sudeley near Winchcombe, off the A46, is famous as the last resting place of Queen Catherine Parr, the sixth wife of Henry VIII and who survived him. The building that stands today was designed by Sir John Soane and later by Sir Giles Gilbert Scott.

Catherine Parr married Thomas Seymour after the death of Henry VIII, and he was presented with Sudeley. In 1549 he was put to death by Somerset and Catherine's brother William took possession of the property until his execution for his participation in Wyatt's Revolt in 1554. The next owner, Sir John Brydges, Earl of Chandos, was a supporter of Queen Mary and his son later became Constable of the Tower, a duty which he exercised with great tact: Queen Mary ordered Princess Elizabeth to be executed but young Brydges delayed the warrant and saved her life.

George Brydges, sixth Earl of Chandos, was an ardent Royalist and raised his own regiment to fight for Charles I. Unfortunately during his absence on New Year's Day, 1642, Colonel Massey arrived from Gloucester and set fire to some outbuildings, capturing the castle under cover of the smoke and his guns. Lord Chandos returned in 1643 and recaptured it but not for long and for many years it was a ruin. In 1837 John and William Dent of Worcester restored part of it with care and Catherine's tomb, which had been broken open in 1782, was with its chapel made into 'a most exquisite gem of ecclesiastical architecture'.

Open daily (except Mondays) 24 March–14 October. Sundays 12–5.30. 24 March–26 May 2–5.30; 29 May–23 September 12–5.30; 25 September–14 October 2–5.30; other days 11–5.30. Admission charge.

TEWKESBURY

The remains of a motte and bailey castle are clearly visible on the A38 opposite Gupshill Manor Inn. Here the army of Henry VI's queen Margaret spent the night before its defeat at the battle of Tewkesbury on 4th May, 1471.

THORNBURY

Edward Duke of Buckingham's fine house, built in 1511, has an elevation of 205ft. with the towers rising to over 60ft. It was built more for comfort than defence and never completed because the duke, who was the last High Constable of England, was tried on a trumped-up charge of treason against Henry VIII and executed in 1521. In 1824 the Stafford Howards restored and improved the property, which is a few miles north of the Severn road bridge.

UPPER SLAUGHTER

A motte and bailey castle once stood near the church in this Cotswold village.

GREATER LONDON

BAYNARD'S CASTLE

Ralph Baynard, one of William the Conqueror's supporters, built this castle on the bank of the Thames by St Paul's Cathedral. It was famous as the home of the barons Fitz-Walter and in the fifteenth century became the palace of Humphrey, Duke of Gloucester, and later of Edward IV and Richard III. It was burnt down in the Great Fire of 1666 and never rebuilt.

ENFIELD

In 1347 Humphrey de Bohun obtained a licence to fortify his manor, which is believed to have stood at Oldbury near the church.

MONTFICHET

Near Addle Hill in the city, Gilbert de Montfichet built a castle which was demolished in 1276 to make way for a Dominican friary.

RAVENGER'S CASTLE

Granted to Geoffrey de Mandeville in 1141, it may have been one of the castles erected after William's entry to London in 1066. There is no known site for this castle but it may have been near the Tower.

TOWER OF LONDON

The building of the White Tower or keep was probably begun by William I in 1078, on the site of the original ditch and palisade set inside the old city wall. Strangely, the sides of the White Tower are not regular and three corners are not right angles. At ground level the walls are 15 feet thick. It marked the eastern flank of the structure and the ruined Wardrobe Tower forms the half-way point in the east wall which ran from the Bowyer Tower to the Lanthorn Tower. In the thirteenth century the castle was enlarged to its present size of 18 acres and today it has examples of all ages of architecture.

The Tower was a royal palace until the reign of James I. The palace buildings were situated between the White Tower and the Inner Wall, east of the Bloody Tower. Many famous prisoners have been kept in the White Tower and in the Queen's House, among them Robert Dudley, Earl of Essex, Sir Walter Raleigh, Judge Jeffreys, the Duke of Monmouth, Lord Nithsdale, Sir Roger Casement and Rudolf Hess. In the White Tower is the Chapel of St John, which was restored by Wren. On the south side of the tower two children's skeletons were discovered during the reign of Charles II. They were supposed to have been those of the two princes, sons of Edward IV, who vanished during the reign of Richard III and whose murder remains a mystery.

For the visitor, the two main attractions of the Tower are the Crown Jewels and the Armouries. The jewels date mostly from the seventeenth century as the original ones were broken up by the Parliamentarians during the Civil War. The only older pieces are the Anointing Spoon, of the twelfth century, and the eagle-shaped Ampulla, which dates from Henry IV's reign. Both St Edward's Crown, made for Charles II's coronation, and the Imperial State Crown, made in 1838, are on display. The Armouries contain weapons and armour from Henry VIII to the present day. Small arms are kept on the ground floor and swords and daggers on the first floor. On the top floor are personal weapons of the kings of England. The Mortar Room has an interesting collection, including a gun from the *Royal George,* sunk by accident in Portsmouth Harbour in 1782. In the Cannon Room are cannon from the *Mary Rose,* sunk in action against the French in 1545.

The Royal Fusiliers have a special museum containing three VCs won by the regiment and models of the battles of Albuera, Alma, Mons, and Monte Cassino. In the Royal Chapel of St Peter ad Vincula are buried the remains of the prisoners executed at the Tower, the last three being Scottish lords beheaded in 1747 for their part in the Jacobite Rising. On Tower Green scaffolds were erected for the execution of two of Henry VIII's wives—Anne Boleyn and Catherine Howard, as well as Lord Hastings, Lady Jane Grey, Margaret Countess of Salisbury, Jane Viscountess Rochford, and Elizabeth I's Essex.

In 1673, the Martin Tower was the scene of the desperate attempt to steal the Crown Jewels by a Hampshire soldier, Colonel Blood. Hiding the crown in his cloak and the orb in his pocket, the Colonel and his accomplices attempted to file the sceptre in half to conceal it. The keeper's son found them and after a fight they were captured. Blood was pardoned by Charles II who gave him a pension and some Irish estates—one of the mysteries of the Tower never satisfactorily explained.

Among various ceremonies associated with the Tower is the Ceremony of the Keys, which takes place at 10 pm every night. The Chief Yeoman Warder and four men close the gates and then there is the guard's customary challenge, to which the Chief Warder replies ending with the salute 'God preserve Queen Elizabeth', and the keys are taken to the Queen's House for the night. Royal salutes are fired from the Tower by a detachment of the Honourable Artillery Company and there is an impressive ceremony on the installation of a new Governor. The famous ravens are kept

in a cage by the Lanthorn Tower and given 15 pence worth of horseflesh each week by the Yeoman Quartermaster.
Department of the Environment. Open daily weekdays March–October 9.30–5. November–February, Sundays March–October 2–5. Admission charge. Wharf front open weekdays 7–dusk, Sundays 10–dusk. Admission free. Permits must be obtained from the Constable's office for photography in the Chapels Royal, Armouries, Beauchamp and Bloody Towers. The Tower is closed over Christmas and on Good Friday.

HAMPSHIRE

ASHLEY
William Briwere had a licence to fortify his manor at Ashley or at Stockbridge c. 1200. The remains of a motte and bailey castle can be seen near the church.

BASING HOUSE
A fortified house constructed on the site of a thirteenth-century ringwork and bailey, Basing is famous for its defence during the Civil War by the Royalist Marquess of Winchester. The Paulets added a fifteenth-century crenellated house of which only the gatehouse, a few walls and the remains of the keep stand today. During the famous three-year siege, which ended in a bloody fight on 14th October 1645, some 2,000 Parliamentarians lost their lives. The castle was completely demolished and the marquess and Inigo Jones were taken prisoner with a few of the survivors. Two small museums and the gatehouse remain together with a secret tunnel.
Temporarily closed.

BISHOPS WALTHAM
About 1135 Bishop Henry of Blois built here a moated residence which was converted into a palace by William of Wykeham. Fortified by the Royalists during the Civil War, it was captured in 1645 and demolished, the bishop escaping in a dung cart.
Department of the Environment. Open normal times (closed Mondays). Admission charge.

CALSHOT
A small blockhouse erected at the time of Henry VIII, Calshot was constructed to defend the entrance to Southampton harbour. It has a round tower and platform with a

surrounding gun terrace and embrasures. It once stood on an island.

CHRISTCHURCH

The castle mound and remains of the keep stand near the abbey on high ground once surrounded by a rectangular moat connected to the Avon. It was built by Richard de Redvers, Earl of Devon, and his son during the reign of Henry I and was captured by Walter de Pinkney in 1147. In the grounds belonging to the local bowling club stands the constable's house dating from c. 1160. It has the remains of a water gate and a remarkable chimney and flue which make it appear entirely separate from the rugged remains of the keep.

Department of the Environment. Keep open at all times. Admission free. Guidebook obtainable from E. A. Burge's confectionery shop.

HIGHCLIFFE

Near Bournemouth, Highcliffe is a nineteenth-century castle famous for being the home of the Kaiser for three weeks in 1907. It is also unique as it was constructed from three demolished French buildings, one of which was the Chateau Les Andelys, destroyed in 1820. Lord Stuart bought the famous oriel window which had witnessed the death of Anthony de Boulon, father of Henry IV of France, in 1568 after the siege of Rouen. Highcliffe is therefore a modern castle constructed from an old one.

HURST

Near Milford-on-Sea, Hurst is situated at the end of a two-mile stretch of shingle facing the Isle of Wight, where James Wursley built a tower in about 1536 which together with Hurst, commanded the Solent from 1544, the date of its completion, until the Second World War, when Hurst was principally an anti-aircraft battery fortress.

Similar castles were built in Henry VIII's reign at Southsea, Netley and Calshot but Hurst is the most extensive. It originally consisted of a central twelve-sided tower with a curtain wall, and three large semi-circular bastions containing unusual eyebrow gunports. Until the seventeenth century the castle was not well maintained and only in 1635 was it equipped with iron guns in place of the brass ones. During the Civil War it was held for Parliament and Charles I was brought here from Carisbrooke shortly before his execution.

He arrived on 29th November 1648 by boat and left on 18th December escorted by Colonel Harrison. His room at the castle on the second floor was only 8 feet by 4½ feet, a mere cell.

During the years following the Restoration thirty guns were installed and in the eighteenth century it was used as a prison. In 1861 the entire castle was enlarged and built round so that only from the inside today is it possible to realise the size of the original building. There is a narrow-gauge rail network built for transporting shells for the naval guns, and Hurst must surely be the only English castle with a railway running over its drawbridge. There is an ingenious lift from the basement magazine for lifting shells to the ground floor. During the First World War heavy coastal artillery was installed, and the tracks and mooring stanchions are still in place. The entrance in the north-west bastion is protected by a caponiere built in the nineteenth century for covering the moat with musket fire should an attempt be made to capture the castle from the land side.

Department of the Environment. Open normal times. Admission charge. To get there from the mainland, take Ernie's Ferry from Keyhaven or walk at low tide (about 35 minutes).

MERDON

On the hill above Hursley, behind a dilapidated fence, is one of the most interesting castle sites in Hampshire. Bishop Blois constructed his castle in about 1138 with a double moat and an ivy-covered keep. It was destroyed in 1155. In the centre of the one ward is a well which was excavated some time this century in a search for Cromwell's treasure, for his son 'Tumble-down Dick' lived at Hursley until his death in 1712. According to legend the well connected with a pothole at Otterbourne, six miles away. Two ducks were put down it once and they swam to Otterbourne but came out with no feathers.

The castle stands on private land and is not open to the public.

NETLEY

Henry VIII built a fort here near the abbey. It became a private house in 1627, the last date in which the garrison of ten were paid. The building was considerably altered and enlarged in the nineteenth century but the original outer walls, now in the dining room, are still about 12 feet thick.

ODIHAM

King John's castle, in which a gallant force of thirteen men held out for two weeks in 1216 against the French, is on the canal at North Warnborough. Part of the keep remains and is noted as the only octagonal keep in the country.

Open at all times. Admission free.

PORTCHESTER

This is probably the best surviving Roman fort in England. It was square and covered nine acres but after the Romans abandoned Portchester, it was not inhabited again until an Augustinian priory was established in 1133 in the south-east corner of the square. At about that time Henry I built the stone keep in the opposite corner. The two top storeys of the tower were added later, together with the inner ward.

Portchester has always played an important part in history because the fleet could shelter beneath its walls. It was held by Simon de Montfort for a time, and from here Henry V set sail on his Agincourt campaign. Henry VI's queen, Margaret of Anjou, arrived at Portchester from France and Elizabeth I often used it.

During the Napoleonic Wars it became a prison and at one time there were 4,000 men here. One story is that one day a senior officer left his horse at the gate while he was seeing the governor and returned a few hours later to find that the French, who were always short of food, had in that time, stolen and eaten it.

The inner ward was protected by its own drawbridge with a 15 foot long passage somewhat similar to that at Prudhoe. The water gate of two storeys was built by the Romans but has been repaired on several occasions.

Department of the Environment. Open normal times. Limited parking. Admission charge.

PORTSMOUTH

In 1848 the downfall of the French monarchy and the advent of Napoleon III caused general alarm in England. Lord Palmerston set about building a series of forts to protect the fleet at Portsmouth, which had by then become a naval port more important than Chatham. An outer line of forts protecting Gosport was planned but only Fort Fareham, now used as a store, was built. An inner line extended from Fort Gomer near Alverstoke to Fort Elson, with, in between Fort Grange (now an R.N. building), Fort

64

13. *Hever Castle, Kent, was the family home of Anne Boleyn, and here she was courted by Henry VIII.*

14. *At Rochester, Kent, was built the first great square keep c. 1126. The first castle was built c. 1080.*

15. *Deal Castle, Kent, was one of a series of circular forts built along the south coast by Henry VIII.*

16. *The magnificent castle at Leeds, Kent, has held many prisoners, including Richard II.*

17. *Lancaster Castle, on the site of a Roman fort built by Hadrian, was briefly occupied by the Jacobites in 1715.*

18. *The famous Ashby-de-la-Zouch Castle was Sir Walter Scott's scene for the jousting tournament in 'Ivanhoe'.*

19. *The building accounts for Kirby-Muxloe, Leicestershire, survive from 1474 and show an expenditure of £1,088 17s. 6¾d. over four years.*

20. *At Tattershall Castle, Lincolnshire, is some of the most remarkable fifteenth-century brickwork surviving in England.*

21. *The stairway entrance to the keep at Castle Rising, Norfolk. Edward III had his mother imprisoned here.*

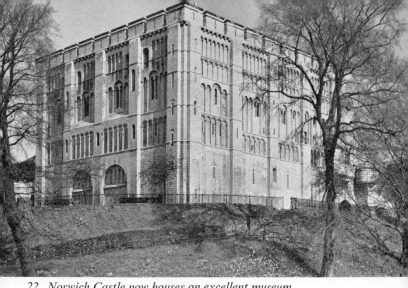

22. *Norwich Castle now houses an excellent museum.*

23. *The original Barnwell Castle, Northamptonshire, now stands in the grounds of the seventeenth-century Barnwell Manor.*

24. *Rockingham Castle, Northamptonshire. The massive twin towers of the gatehouse date from 1275.*

25. *The present keep of Warkworth Castle, Northumberland, was restored by the Duke of Northumberland in the nineteenth century.*

Rowner (R.N.) and Fort Brockhurst. The latter is being restored by the Department of the Environment. The forts are very solidly constructed with caponieres (covered passages) and underground barracks with fireplaces. The ramparts are equipped for both guns and rifles and built of granite as well as brick. To prevent an encircling movement and an attack from the north, Palmerston placed six forts on Portsdown Hill. These are Fort Wallington at Fareham, Fort Nelson, Fort Southwick, Fort Widley, Fort Purbrook and Farlington Redoubt. Only Southwick and Purbrook are used by the armed services, and Widley belongs to Portsmouth Corporation. These forts are much larger and well worth exploring. The gun emplacements are well protected by chalk banks and are well concealed. To the east, Portsmouth was defended by the Cumberland Fort, erected in 1789 and still intact. In 1860, when England and France were supporting Italy in her struggle with Austria, Palmerston built four forts in the middle of the Solent which are well-known landmarks for yachtsmen today.

SOUTHAMPTON

Part of the bailey wall still remains on Western Esplanade. Once a wooden structure, it was the centre of the walled town that was stormed by the French in 1338. Sir John Arundel repaired it and in 1377 it held out against a further French attack. A block of flats has been built on the site of Lord Stafford's banqueting hall. The castle had a water gate and vault which still remain, and the bailey covered three acres. The eastern gate has recently been uncovered and restored. The town walls are, with Berwick-upon-Tweed, the best surviving in the country.

SOUTHSEA

One of the most interesting Hampshire castles, Southsea was built in 1543–44 by Henry VIII; a square keep within a diamond. It was restored and strengthened in 1814 by Major General Fisher of the Royal Engineers, who also enlarged it to accommodate his 200 men, and some 32 lb cannon, but none of the original ones are on display. The Tudor gun ports are also visible and at one time the roof of the keep supported four traversing guns fed by ammunition hoists in the roofs of the first-floor galleries.

The first year after completion the castle saw action when the French invaded the Isle of Wight in 1545. The enemy

DC—5   65

retired after three days, having failed to do any serious damage. In 1626 there was a serious fire so that the governors had no proper accommodation until repairs were carried out in 1635. In 1642 the governor, Captain Challoner, holding the castle for the king in support of Colonel Goring in Portsmouth, was surprised at night by the enemy under Colonel Norton of Southwick. He surrendered without a shot.

In the eighteenth century there was a further disaster when hot embers from a fire fell into the powder room and the resulting explosion killed seventeen people. In 1850 the advent of Napoleon III occasioned the improvement of the defences of Portsmouth, and Southsea was given two outer ramparts.

The building was garrisoned in both world wars, was bought by Portsmouth Corporation in 1960 and was opened to the public in 1967. Inside there are maps, armour and a very interesting collection of model ships.

Open daily, November–February 10–5; *May–August* 10–9; *other times* 10–6. *Admission charge.*

TITCHFIELD

The foundation stone of the abbey was laid in 1219 and its church consecrated in 1238. At the Dissolution of the Monasteries (1537–38) the abbey was surrendered to the Crown and was given to Thomas Wriothesley, Earl of Southampton, by Henry VIII. He converted the abbey into a fortified mansion, 'Palace House' (later Place House), incorporating the nave of the original church. In 1741 the house was sold to the Deline family who used much of the stone to build elsewhere. The building has been in a state of disrepair since 1810.

Department of the Environment. Open normal times. Admission charge.

WINCHESTER

The ancient capital of England had, to the north-west of the cathedral, a castle which was burnt down in 1141. A new one was built which was the scene of Queen Matilda's rescue by the Earl of Gloucester and sixty men during her war with King Stephen. Today the Great Hall is the courthouse and is open to the public. It contains 'King Arthur's Round Table', which may well have been constructed in the sixteenth century.

Open weekdays, summer 10–5, *winter* 10–4; *Sundays* 2–4.30, *April–September.*

WOLVESEY

The ruins of Bishop Blois's castle stand east of Winchester cathedral. It was Norman and was destroyed during the Civil War. Much archaeological work has been done here recently. *Open at all times. Admission free.*

WOODWARD

Near Beaulieu Abbey was a sea fort built during Henry VIII's reign.

ISLE OF WIGHT

CARISBROOKE

The Romans had a camp at Carisbrooke and in A.D. 530 the invading Jutes under Cerdic and Cynric defeated the islanders at Withgarasburh, or Carisbrooke. William the Conqueror gave the island to William Fitz Osbern who built the Norman keep; his son Roger completed the castle. He was imprisoned by William for rebellion and the Crown owned the land until it was granted to Richard de Redvers in 1100. His son Earl Baldwin retreated here after his defeat at Exeter in 1136 when he was fighting for the Empress Maud, Henry I's daughter, against Stephen. The castle, described as 'ornately built of stone' with a high motte and two square baileys, surrendered when the water supply gave out. The Great Hall, or part of it, was built by Baldwin's younger son and the castle was enlarged by the last of the de Redvers family to hold Carisbrooke, Isabel Countess of Albermarle. When she died she left her property to Edward I and it remained with the Crown until Edward III granted it to his daughter Isabel in 1355.

Richard II granted it, together with the lordship of the island, to William de Montacute, Earl of Salisbury, and he constructed the three-storey block next to the Great Hall. The defences must have been in good condition for in 1377 the French burnt Yarmouth and Newtown but failed to take Carisbrooke whose constable, Sir Hugh Constable, forced them to retire on the death of the French commander and the payment of a thousand marks to the troops. During the Wars of the Roses Carisbrooke belonged to the Duke of Gloucester, the Duke of Somerset and Lord Scales, all of whom were convicted of high treason. During Elizabeth I's reign elaborate surveying and strengthening were carried out against the threat of possible Spanish invasion. A falcon gun of this period can still be seen in the museum.

The most famous person to stay at Carisbrooke was Charles I. He was brought here in November 1647 by his friends hopeful that some kind of settlement could be made with Parliament and that Charles would win over to his cause the governor, Colonel Hammond, a Puritan related to John Hampden. When Charles signed a treaty with the Scots to restore him to the throne he soon found he was not a guest but a prisoner, and he made three attempts to escape. He could not get through the window because of an iron bar and later when Henry Firebrace, his gaoler, gave him a file, one of the officers of the watch, a Major Rolfe, betrayed him to Hammond. On another occasion he found a crowd waiting for him under the window so he did not move. Finally after a year on the island, the king was moved to Hurst Castle in Hampshire, from where he left for Whitehall and his execution in January 1649. Charles's two young children, Princess Elizabeth and Prince Henry, lived here after his death. Elizabeth died in September 1650 of an illness and young Henry was allowed to join his brother Charles in Holland in 1652, a rare example of Cromwell's kindness. Princess Beatrice, youngest daughter of Queen Victoria, was Carisbrooke's last royal resident.

The gatehouse bears the arms of Anthony Woodville and others on its fifteenth-century doors. The chapel is dedicated to St Nicholas and is the island war memorial. The museum contains pictures and relics of the island's history. The well house with its donkey wheel is a great attraction for the younger visitors.

Department of the Environment. Open normal times. Admission charge.

COWES

West Cowes Castle was built by Henry VIII and its terrace is now that of the Royal Yacht Club.

NORRIS

At East Cowes, Norris Castle was built in 1799 for Lord Seymour. East Cowes Castle, built by John Nash, has been destroyed, but like Norris it was never built for defence.

NORTON

Fort Victoria was built in the nineteenth century on the site of an earlier fort built by Wursley in 1536. It provided an effective gun position for defending the Spithead when used in conjunction with Hurst opposite.

YARMOUTH

Behind the George Hotel, Yarmouth Castle was built in 1547 by Henry VIII, and was one of the chain of forts erected to defend the south coast against French attack after the alliance of France and the Holy Roman Empire in 1538. This is different from Cowes and Hurst because it is square, and it differs from earlier castles in being built with cannon in mind. It has the first arrow-head bastion in England and an earth bank in the north hall for supporting heavy guns at second-floor level. The living quarters were mostly built in 1632.

Department of the Environment. Open normal times. Admission charge.

HEREFORDSHIRE

ALMELEY

A few miles from Kington, Almeley had a castle next to the church. Sir John Oldcastle lived here. A supporter of Wycliffe, he was burnt in chains in London. The first Protestant martyr, he was outlawed after the Lollard meeting in St Giles's Fields in 1414.

ASHPERTON

Near Ledbury, the moat still remains of the castle of the Grandison family. It was built in 1292 and consisted of a fortified manor with the church included in the outer bailey.

BRAMPTON BRYAN

On the Radnor-Shropshire border, this is the fourteenth-century home of the Harleys. The old gatehouse is dwarfed by the new hall, built mostly in the eighteenth century. During the Civil War Brampton was held for Parliament by Lady Harley who surrendered only after it had been reduced to ruins. A month later she died of 'a verie bad cold'.

BREDWARDINE

Not far from Moccas to the west of Hereford, Bredwardine's castle of the Baskervilles and Vaughans stood on the banks of the Wye. Until recently cellars and underground passages existed beneath the mound. There are two knights' monuments in the church. One is an effigy of Sir Robert Vaughan, who died defending Henry V at Agincourt.

BRONSIL

At Eastnor, below Midsummer Hill, stand the remains of the Beauchamps' castle. It had quadrangular walls with corner towers and intermediate towers. There was a west gatehouse of which part of one tower remains, together with the moat.

CASTLE FROME

Between Bromyard and Ledbury, a motte and bailey castle was built about 1162 near the church.

CLIFFORD

On A438 by the Welsh border the ruins of Clifford Castle stand on a small hill beside the Wye. There is a thirteenth-century shell-keep with five projections and a ruined chapel, turned into a cottage.

Built by William FitzOsbern, builder of Wigmore, it passed to Ralph de Todenei whose descendants were Cliffords. Henry II's mistress, Fair Rosamund, eldest daughter of the first Clifford, was born here.

In 1547 Clifford manor and castle were given to Lord Clinton, the English admiral who supported Lord Somerset in his victory over the Scots at the battle of Pinkie.

Mr Parkinson. Open to the public by permission. Admission free.

CROFT

Approached by a long oak avenue, Croft Castle is mostly a fourteenth- and fifteenth-century building with four large round towers. It was Gothicised in the mid eighteenth century when it passed from the Croft family to Richard Knight, son of a Shropshire mine owner.

The Crofts were warriors. Sir Richard Croft, whose tomb can be seen in the church, was a veteran of Tewkesbury, Stoke and Mortimer's Cross—the last named battle was fought a few miles to the south-west of the castle. He was the friend and governor of young Edward IV and was knighted on the field of Stoke by Henry VII. One of his descendants was comptroller of Queen Elizabeth's household and one of a later generation was killed at Stokesay fighting for Charles I. The Crofts were forced to sell the castle in 1746 but bought it back in 1923. The National Trust acquired it in 1957.

National Trust. Open Easter to 30th September—Wednesdays, Thursdays, Saturdays and Sundays; October—Saturdays and Sundays 2.15–6, also Bank Holidays. Admission charge.

CUSOP

On the Welsh border stood a pele castle once belonging to the Clavenogh family.

DORSTONE

Near Moccas, Dorstone had a castle that covered two and a half acres. It was built by John Le Breton, one of the murderers of Thomas à Becket.

EARDISLEY

Eardisley had a motte and bailey castle mentioned in Domesday. It was the property of the de Bohuns, the Cliffords and later the Baskervilles. Although destroyed in the Civil War, the gatehouse was occupied until about 1680.

EASTNOR

Built for the Earl Somers in 1812, Eastnor is a Norman Revival castle built as a private home and never intended for defence. Inside are some fine pictures and armour.

Open Sundays, June–September 2.15–6, also Bank Holiday Mondays 2.15–6. Admission charge.

ECCLESWALL

At Linton-by-Ross are the earthwork remains of the Talbots' castle. Until the last century a tower stood near the farmhouse and near it was found the silver seal of Philip de Henbury.

EWYAS HAROLD

One of the most important Welsh border castles, this was rebuilt by William FitzOsbern, a Norman who supplied ships for William's invasion in 1066. It has a motte over 40ft. high on which there was once a shell-keep.

GOODRICH

Near the Gloucestershire border, Goodrich is the most imposing ruin in Herefordshire. Built of red sandstone in the late thirteenth century it stands on a spur overlooking the

Wye. Entered by a barbican which is at an angle to the main gateway, it must have been a formidable castle to storm as the two drawbridges swing on central pivots dipping down into pits between the barbican and the main gatehouse. The Norman keep is small and is overshadowed by the south-west tower. There is a great hall 65 feet long and a chapel with a room above overlooking the gatehouse.

The Earl of Pembroke, a supporter of King John and governor to Henry III, was the first known owner of Goodrich. His sons left no male issue and after their deaths his eldest daughter succeeded to the estate with her husband Warren de Mont Cenis. Their son William supported Simon de Montfort and forfeited his estates after being captured by Henry III at Kenilworth. Henry granted the property to William de Valence and later it passed to the Talbots. John Talbot's son was killed defending his king at Northampton in 1460, but the Talbots continued to live here until the seventeenth century when it was inherited by Elizabeth Grey, Countess of Kent. During the Civil War it was garrisoned for Charles I and held out under Sir Henry Lingell until 1646 when it was captured by increased Parliamentary opposition and slighted by artillery.

Department of the Environment. Open normal times. Admission charge.

HEREFORD

'One of the fayrest, largest and strongest castles in all England', Leland wrote of Hereford, which once covered over five acres. Today the bailey is Castle Green and only some ramparts remain by the eighteenth-century promenade.

Built by the Norman Ralph in 1048, it was destroyed by the Welsh in 1055 and rebuilt by FitzOsbern, Earl of Hereford. Roger Milo, son of the Constable of England, was granted it by Queen Matilda and his son Roger became governor. During the de Montfort rebellion young Prince Edward was held prisoner here and succeeded in escaping from his captivity by setting out on a hunting expedition with his captors. When they were tired, he spurred his horse on and reached the safety of Wigmore Castle.

During the Civil War Hereford surrendered to Sir William Waller but it soon passed into Royalist hands again. After Naseby Charles I and his cavalry came here from Ashby and the Scots under Leslie besieged the town which held out until the Royalists were strong enough to force Leslie to retire. Later in the year Colonel Birch attacked in deep snow and captured the castle and town taking 'one hundred and twenty lords, knights and officers in commission, eleven pieces of ordnance and a great store of ammunition'.

HUNTINGDON

A few miles from Kington, Huntingdon Castle was the seat of the Bohuns and consists of the remains of the inner bailey wall and a north tower. Humphry Bohun set out from here to fight for Simon de Montfort at Evesham and the Duke of Buckingham was captured here trying to escape from Richard III to join Henry Tudor.

KILPECK

Once an enclosed village, the castle still boasts two fragments of a large keep. It belonged to William de Waleran and later to William Herbert, Earl of Pembroke, who was executed after the battle of Edgecote in 1469.

KINGTON

Near the church there was a castle mentioned in 1187.

KINNERSLEY

Between Eardisley and Weobley, Kinnersley had a medieval castle belonging to the de la Beres, but the present castle is Elizabethan and was built by Roger Vaughen. It was rebuilt and altered in the eighteenth and nineteenth centuries.

LONGTOWN

One of the best preserved of the many Herefordshire castles, Longtown keep stands on a high mound, once the site of a Roman fort, off the A465 near Abergavenny. The keep, mostly thirteenth and fourteenth century, has two storeys and three projecting buttresses, in one of which is a spiral staircase. The entrance was on the first floor with steps outside, now destroyed. There were two baileys, and the keep was on the apex of the inner bailey.

It belonged to the de Lacy family and passed by marriage to John de Verdon, one of Edward I's crusaders. When he died it passed to his grand-daughter Elizabeth and her husband Bartholomew de Burghersh who was knighted for his service in the French wars of Edward III. Their son Thomas supported Richard II and lost both his land and his life for his loyalty. Longtown then passed to the Nevilles in whose hands it remained for many centuries.

LYONSHALL

Not far from Madley, off A348, stand the moated remains of the thirteenth-century keep of the Devereux family castle.

MOCCAS

A motte and bailey castle stood here, but nothing remains of a fortified manor built on the same site by Hugh de Frene.

MORTIMER'S CASTLE

At Much Marcle the remains of a motte and bailey castle, seat of the Mortimers, stand near the church. The motte is over 20 feet high and 150 feet in diameter.

MOUSE

A motte and bailey castle, about a mile north of Cusop, can still be seen but is in a bad state of preservation.

PEMBRIDGE

A few miles to the north of Monmouth at Welsh Newton is the thirteenth-century moated castle of Ralph de Pembridge. During the reign of Edward III Richard Pembridge, Lord Warden of the Cinque Ports, lived here. He fought at Poitiers and Crecy and was buried in Hereford Cathedral. Occupied by both sides during the Civil War, it was slighted, but repaired in 1675 by George Kemble.
Open May–September, Thursdays 10–7. Admission charge.

PENYARD

At Weston-under-Penyard near Ross is the ruin of a farmhouse, which was once the fortified manor of the Talbots.

RICHARD'S CASTLE

Built by Richard Fitz-Scrub before the Norman Conquest, Richard's Castle stands on the Herefordshire bank of the Teme overlooking Ludlow. It is a massive earthwork with a wall across the top and a semicircular wall round the perimeter. Most of the stone has long since vanished but there is still one piece 12 feet high and signs of the wall that enclosed the church. During the Civil War Sir Thomas Lansford was defeated here by Colonel Birch, one of Cromwell's officers, in one of the last engagements of 1645.

ST DEVEREUX
In the grounds of Didley Court Farm near Kilpeck stood a motte and bailey castle.

SNODHILL
At Peterchurch near Dorstone are a few remains of the Chandos family castle – a Norman keep and a fourteenth-century gatehouse and bailey.

STAPLETON
On the Radnor border stand the ruins of a seventeenth-century farmhouse, once a castle belonging to the Cornwall family.

WEOBLEY
To the west of Hereford Street are the earthwork remains of the de Lacy castle. Once it had four circular towers and a keep with walls 12 feet thick.

WIGMORE
On A4110 not far from Mortimer's Cross are the ruins of the Mortimers' border castle. Ralph de Mortimer was a relation of William the Conqueror and took the Wigmore property from Edric, Earl of Shrewsbury. The main castle was built by William FitzOsbern, Earl of Hereford, who was the owner at the time of Domesday, but the Mortimers seem to have gained possession shortly after this date. Roger Mortimer was a supporter of Henry III in his war against Simon de Montfort and was one of the commanders of the Royal army at Evesham. After the battle de Montfort's head and hands were cut off and sent to Wigmore as a grisly present for Lady Maud Mortimer. Roger's son built Chirk Castle and founded the second Mortimer line, known as the Mortimers of Chirk.

In 1322 Roger, the eighth Baron of Wigmore and first Earl of March, became the lover of Edward II's queen. He was imprisoned in the Tower and rescued by Queen Isabella. He joined her in France and when the young Prince Edward crossed the channel to meet his mother, the unpopular Edward II was unable to retain the throne and was subsequently brutally murdered at Berkeley Castle. Mortimer was now the virtual ruler of England and transferred his seat to Ludlow Castle. His friendship with the queen led to his eventual downfall and execution at Tyburn in 1330. His son married a Plantagenet, and their grandson become rightful heir to the throne; on his death in Ireland in 1398, this claim passed to Anne Mortimer, grand-mother of Edward, Earl of March, later Edward IV.

Until the seventeenth century Wigmore belonged to the Crown. In 1601 it was acquired by Thomas Harley of Brampton Bryan and here Sir Robert Harley, Queen Anne's states-man, was born. Lady Harley had not the men to garrison it during the Civil War so it was slighted at an early date. Today the remains are mostly fourteenth century and include one tower, a ruined wall and a south gatehouse.

WILTON

At Bridstow is the thirteenth-century ruin of Hugo de Longchamp's castle which defended a bridge over the Wye. Later it belonged to the Greys and Lord Grey sold it in 1555 to pay for his ransom when captured by the French. It was bought by the Brydges family who kept it until 1732 when it became the property of the trustees of Guy's Hospital. The parapet wall, part of the bailey and the north-west polygonal tower remain, but the Elizabethan house was burnt down in the Civil War.

HERTFORDSHIRE

ANSTEY

The remains of a motte and bailey castle can still be seen.

BENINGTON

A small keep, near 'The Lordship', a much altered Georgian house, is all that remains of Alexander Balliol's castle. It was destroyed in 1212 when owned by Robert FitzWalter.

BERKHAMSTED

Near the railway station, Berkhamsted is one of the most important castles in the country, although little remains today except the motte and bailey and a unique double moat. Plans are being made to fill the moat completely.

The route taken by Duke William after the Battle of Hastings crossed the Thames at Wallingford and he approached London from the west. At Berkhamsted he was greeted by Edgar Aetheling, Earl Morcar and Edwin, who came out from London to submit to his authority. William gave the Saxon castle at Berkhamsted to his brother Robert, Count of Mortain, who built a strong keep here on top of a motte. It had its own well and staircase. The two-acre bailey was ultimately enclosed in the twelfth and thirteenth centuries by a massive wall interspersed with half circular defensive towers. The entrance was by the south – not the present entrance but across a causeway – and there was a small dernegate over two drawbridges to the north-east. The most unusual features of Berkhamsted are the earth platforms or small malvoisins outside the north moat. These are believed to be mangonel platforms built by the French army that attacked and captured the castle in 1216. They may have been part of the defences but if so, why were they outside and not inside the moat?

The Earl of Cornwall lived here after the Count of Mortain's death as did Thomas à Becket when he was Lord Chancellor. King John obtained the castle from the property of Richard I's wife Berengaria and spent about £250 on repairs. His queen was here when the barons and the Dauphin's French army attacked and captured the castle. John's second son Richard, Earl of Cornwall, inherited it and built a three storey tower and numerous apartments for his family. King Edward I granted it to his queen, Margaret of France, and in 1309 Edward II gave it to Piers Gaveston, his favourite, who married the king's niece.

During the building of Windsor Castle, Berkhamsted was an important royal palace. The Black Prince spent his last days here in 1376 and the captive King John of France was brought here from Somerton. The final inhabitant of note was Cicely, Duchess of York, who made it her home until she died in 1496. Queen Elizabeth leased it to Sir Edward Carey for the rent of a red rose each year in memory of Cicely, the 'Rose of Raby', who was born a Lancastrian but married a Yorkist. Carey built nearby Berkhamsted Place out of stones from the castle, which remained part of the Duchy of Cornwall until 1930 when it passed to the Commissioners of Works.

Department of the Environment. Open normal hours. Admission charge.

HERTFORD

Hertford Castle was built by William the Conqueror soon after 1066 to guard the ford where the Great North Road crossed the river Lea about 20 miles north of London. The internal buildings of the castle were demolished early in the seventeenth century: all that remains is the gatehouse, built in

77

1463, which is now the Council offices, the Norman motte, the postern gate and most of the curtain walls, over 20 feet high.

During the Baron's War against King John, Hertford was besieged by the Dauphin Louis who captured it from the King's forces. In 1304 the Castle and Honour of Hertford were granted to Queen Margaret and was used as a royal palace until the accession of James I in 1603. During this period it was used by the kings and queens of England. It was also used as a royal prison for David II of Scotland (after his defeat at Neville's Cross in 1346), for John of France (after the battle of Poitiers in 1356), and for Margaret of Anjou, the queen of Henry VI (after the Yorkist victory at St Albans in 1455). In 1360 the castle was granted to John of Gaunt and was part of the Duchy of Lancaster until 1628.

Queen Elizabeth I spent some of her childhood at Hertford and held the Law Courts here when there was plague in London. It is known that during her reign the Court of the Star Chamber held its sessions at Hertford Castle. During the reign of Charles I it passed to William, Earl of Salisbury, but it was leased to various occupants, particularly the East India College in the reign of George III. Today the gatehouse with its four towers stands in a pleasant park. The windows and the south-west wing were added in the late eighteenth century: and the west wing was built in 1936, all this work being in the Gothic style to match the original gatehouse. Recently the whole building was restored, exposing the fifteenth-century ceilings: over the doorway can still be seen the coat of arms of Edward IV.

Grounds open every day until 6. Admission free. Gatehouse open Saturdays by prior arrangement.

SOUTH MYMMS

Geoffrey de Mandeville had a castle here, built in 1141–1142.

WAYTEMORE, BISHOPS STORTFORD

The Norman castle of the bishops of London stood in Bridge Street. The mound still has a few flint stones and the bailey is now a park. It had a wall around the motte lip. The castle was destroyed by King John but the dungeon was in use in Queen Mary's reign and was known as 'The Bishop's Hole'.

HUNTINGDONSHIRE AND PETERBOROUGH

CONNINGTON
Near Stilton and just off the Great North Road are faint traces of the Earl of Huntingdon's castle. He was the son of Malcolm Canmore and became King David I of Scotland, great-grandfather of Robert the Bruce.

ELTON HALL
This is a fifteenth-century fortified manor with many later additions.
Not open to the public.

GREAT STAUGHTON
There was a motte and bailey castle at Old Manor Farm and traces are still visible.

HUNTINGDON
A Saxon or Roman fort here was converted into a castle in 1068. It was destroyed by Henry II.

KIMBOLTON
This was the ancient seat of the Mandevilles and Montagus. The present 'castle' was refaced and largely remodelled by Vanbrugh and the fourth Earl and fifth Duke of Manchester between 1707 and 1720.
Open: Bank Holidays, Thursdays and Sundays, July 30–September 3. Admission charge.

LONGTHORPE
In the Soke of Peterborough, Longthorpe Tower was added to the manor in 1300. It has unusual fourteenth-century wall paintings of Biblical scenes.
Department of the Environment. Open normal hours. Admission charge.

NORTHBOROUGH
Seven miles from Peterborough is the fortified manor of the de la Mare family erected about 1350 and much altered in the seventeenth century. Cromwell is alleged to be buried in the churchyard alongside his wife who died in the village in 1665.

RAMSEY
A twelfth-century motte and bailey castle stood on Booth Hill.

SAPLEY

Near Hartford is a 9 foot motte with a moat and earthwork which was probably a castle site.

WOOD WALTON

There is the site of a large motte and bailey castle on Castle Hill.

WOODCROFT

In the Soke of Peterborough, Woodcroft House was built in the late thirteenth century and altered during Tudor and later periods. Only one of the towers that remain is original. Here lived Charles I's chaplain Dr Hudson, who was the model for Sir Walter Scott's Dr Rochecliffe in *Woodstock*. He was an ardent Royalist and, after escaping from the Tower, fortified the castle for the king in 1648. He was promised quarter on his surrender but was cut down while clinging to a gargoyle and fished out of the moat by a soldier who later exhibited the unfortunate man's tongue as a trophy. He is buried at Uffingham.

KENT

ALLINGTON

Just before Maidstone, after turning off the motorway from London, a lane leads down through a new housing estate to one of the most beautiful castles in southern England. It is now a Carmelite Friary.

The first castle was built in King Stephen's reign although there had been a Roman and a Saxon encampment here. In 1282 Stephen of Penchester obtained a licence to crenellate 'with a wall of stone and lime and hold thus strengthened their house at Alinton.' A copy of the sealed document hangs on the chapel wall today. Penchester built the great hall and Solomon's Tower opposite.

The Wyatts are the best-known inhabitants of Allington. Sir Henry Wyatt, a friend of Henry VII and Henry VIII, bought the castle in 1492, adding the Tudor building and the long gallery. His son Thomas was a poet and friend of Anne Boleyn. He introduced the Italian sonnet into English literature but died in his thirties in 1542. His son Thomas led the rebellion against Queen Mary's intended Spanish marriage. Lord Cobham, Wyatt's father-in-law at Cooling Castle, was forced to join Wyatt when the rebels stormed his castle. The rebellion ended with a march on London. Wyatt and his men were separated and many deserted; Wyatt was executed together with the other leaders of the revolt.

Allington now passed to the Crown and the great hall, chapel and north-east tower were burnt down. For a time John Astley, Master of the Jewels to Elizabeth I, lived here but his descendants moved into Maidstone and the castle was rented to a Catholic family named Best. In the eighteenth and nineteenth centuries the Astleys sold it to the Marshams and in 1905 it was bought by Lord Conway who spent 25 years restoring it to its present condition. A total of £70,000 was spent and today only one wall remains a ruin. In 1951 Allington Castle was acquired by the Carmelite Order and is now a centre for conferences and for ecumenical and youth work.

Order of Carmelites. Open every day 2–4. Admission charge.

BAYFORD

Near Sittingbourne, not far from a Danish encampment, stood the fortified manor-house of Robert de Nottingham. It later passed to the Cheney and Lovelace families, but nothing remains.

BRENCHLEY

On a hill nine miles south-west of Maidstone, there is a double defensive ringwork which, although badly damaged today, marks the site of Knowle Castle.

CANTERBURY

At the end of Wincheap lies the Norman keep of Canterbury on the corner of two busy roads and surrounded by an iron railing. The castle was built by William I and was in existence by 1086. During the middle ages the Roman Worth Gate gave access to the Castle ground, but it was blocked up in 1548 and demolished in 1791 when Castle Street was made. The castle eventually fell into disuse in 1600. The famous Dane John motte nearby possibly predates the existing castle; the name derives from the medieval 'donjon'. The town walls, which were mostly built in the fourteenth century, are well preserved and the West Gate (1380), built to replace an earlier gate that may have been of Roman origin, is worth visiting for its collection of arms and prison ironmongery. In 1971, following Ministry of Works repairs, the original Norman forebuilding was excavated.

Castle open on application only at Royal Museum, High Street, Canterbury. Grounds open dawn to dusk.

CHATHAM

In Stuart times Chatham became an important naval base and after the disgrace of the Dutch attack on the Medway in 1667 a series of forts was built to protect the harbour. In 1758 a row of forts called the Chatham Lines stretched from Gillingham to the south end of Chatham Reach. In 1778 Fort Amherst was built and so later were Fort Delce, Fort Pitt and Fort Clarence. The last three were not completed until after Waterloo but in 1865 a royal commission recommended more forts to protect the harbours and by 1867 no less than 76 had been constructed, 'well made, with flanks, palisades and doublefoss with room for four or five hundred men'. A French emigré, Dumouriez, took a leading part in planning the defences against the first Napoleon and his influence remained in the planning of the later forts.

Tilbury was improved and Gravesend fort was constructed by General Gordon, whose statue stands at Chatham today. Fort Borstal, Fort Horstead, Fort Luton and Fort Darland were built round Chatham and a line from Tilbury to Gravesend constructed with further gun emplacements at Cliffe Creek, Slough Point, Grain, Sheerness, and Shornmead. Later, two further forts at Halstead and Westerham were constructed. Today little can be seen of these fortifications although some of the first have been put to other uses, like Fort Pitt which is a girls' technical school.

CHILHAM

On A252 between Canterbury and Charing, the keep of Chilham Castle stands next to the Jacobean house of the same name. Originally a Roman then a Saxon stronghold, a keep was begun by Bishop Odo of Bayeux which was completed by a Norman knight called Fulbert de Lucy. His daughter married Richard Fitzroy, a bastard son of King John. Their younger daughter married the Earl of Atholl who was executed for treason against Edward I. The Jacobean castle was built by Sir Dudley Digges to designs by Inigo Jones. It is one of the finest examples of architecture of that time. During the Wars of the Roses, Chilham belonged to Lord Rees, who was attainted after Towton. It reverted to the Crown in the early sixteenth century and Henry VIII granted it to Sir Thomas Cheney, Warden of the Cinque Ports. The gardens, at one time modified by Capability Brown, contain the first wisteria to be planted in England. *Viscount Massereene and Ferrard. Gardens open to the*

*public Easter–September, daily except Mondays and Fridays
2–6. Admission charge.*

COLBRIDGE

Near Egerton and not far from Charing, Colbridge Castle
was built by Fulk de Peyforer in 1314. It later belonged to
the Earl of Huntingdon and the Duke of Lancaster. In the
eighteenth century it passed to Sir Edward Wotton and much
of the stone was used for nearby Boughton Malherbe Manor.

COOLING

On the promontory between the Medway and the Thames,
Cooling Castle still boasts a fine gatehouse. The Cobhams
obtained a licence to crenellate in 1380 and lived here for
350 years. During Wyatt's rebellion against the Spanish
marriage of Queen Mary, in 1554, the castle was captured
by the rebels. Wyatt forced Cobham and his two sons to
march with him on London. The unusual design of the
castle – the two wards joined by a drawbridge – must have
made it difficult to capture and Wyatt only succeeded by
battering down the west wall of the outer ward with cannon
and then attacking the inner ward after crossing the drawbridge.

The other famous person connected with the castle is Sir
John Oldcastle, a friend of Wycliffe and leader of the Lollard
rising which was suppressed by Henry V in 1414. Oldcastle
escaped from the Tower, and spent three years in hiding
before being captured and burnt to death for heresy and
treason at St Giles Fields in 1417.

DEAL

The Reformation, the dissolution of the monasteries and
the alliance between France and the Holy Roman Empire
made Henry VIII's England liable to attack from abroad.
To counter this, the south coast was fortified by a series of
circular forts, designed to hold a captain and twenty-four
men. Deal is larger than Walmer and Sandown and has three
tiers. A dry moat surrounds six semicircular bastions and
inside this are six smaller bastions with a top storey from
which further guns could be fired. The central stair provided
a means of escape as it connects by passages with the outer
bastion and there is a sally-port leading into the moat. There
was also an oven for heating cannonballs – a devastating
means of attacking wooden shops. Above the entrance are

machicolations through which grenades could be dropped while the attackers were trying to force the portcullis (now gone) and the outer gate.

The only time the castle saw any fighting was in 1648, during the Second Civil War, when Sandown, Deal and Walmer castles were fortified for the king and part of the fleet supplied them with men, munitions and food. Colonel Rich attacked Walmer with an army of 2,000 but as he had no artillery the Royalists held out for some time before surrendering. Deal held out for a few more weeks and in August a strong naval force attempted to relieve the garrison. The Royalist commander, Major-General Gibson, was captured with 100 men, so the following day the garrison surrendered. Sandown Castle capitulated shortly after.

During the eighteenth century the present battlements were added for aesthetic reasons and a governor's lodge was constructed on the seaward side. This was rebuilt in 1802 for Lord Carrington but in 1941 a bomb demolished it and the castle was later restored to its original form. An archaeological museum occupies the gatehouse.

Department of the Environment. Open normal times. Admission charge.

DOVER

Continuously fortified from the early Iron Age and Roman times until 1958, Dover Castle is one of the strongest in England and, because of its position, is second only to the Tower of London in military importance. The Roman lighthouse, or Pharos, still stands next to the church of St Mary-in-Castra. The Saxon fortress had a gatehouse, enceinte and well.

The Normans built 27 towers in the outer wall and 14 square watchtowers in the inner wall. The cliffs form the seaward wall, so there was no moat, although the entrance bridge straddles a dry ditch. The first constable of Dover, appointed by William I, was John de Fiennes. He was assisted by eight knights, who were granted land elsewhere on the condition that they provided a garrison on a rota basis throughout the year.

King Stephen died in Dover in 1154 and Henry II constructed the inner bailey wall and the vast keep, which houses the Waterloo model and a collection of arms. Hubert de Burgh defended Dover for King John against Louis, Dauphin of France, in 1216. The French attacked the northern gate, which they breached with a mine, and would have entered had not de Burgh blocked it with timber. When the siege was over an additional spur and outer barbican were built and the old gate was permanently closed. In 1265, during the de Montfort rebellion, Dover was in rebel hands but twelve prisoners from Lewes managed to capture two of the towers and helped Prince Edward (later Edward I) to retake the castle.

During the Civil War a Royalist garrison surrendered to a party of twelve Parliamentarians led by a local merchant called Drake. They climbed over the north-east wall and talked the Royalist commander into surrender. Another 120 men were rushed in from Canterbury and by the time the Royalists had rallied Drake had the castle secured.

In 1794 the circular Valence and Mortimer towers were added, and another tower, which still remains though in a much altered state, was built over Colton's Gate, which leads to the Pharos.

During the Napoleonic Wars Lieutenant Burgoyne, Inspector General of Fortifications, installed gun positions on the keep roof, built many bastions, and excavated a series of underground passages defended by an ingenious system of remote-controlled doors which could trap attackers. Provision was made for a total of 231 guns of all sizes to defend the castle. The constables in the nineteenth century were William Pitt, the Duke of Wellington and Lord Palmerston. In the twentieth century George VI was constable when he was Prince of Wales, and he was succeeded by Sir Winston Churchill. The castle was an important military headquarters in the Second World War.

Department of the Environment. Open normal times. Admission charge.

EYNSFORD

In the Darent valley on A225, Eynsford Castle stands opposite the Castle Inn. It was built by William D'Eynsford and is D-shaped with flint walls 30 feet high in places. D'Eynsford quarrelled with Thomas à Becket but after the latter's murder, he was filled with remorse and vowed never to live in his castle again. The keep was recently excavated and it was discovered to have originally been a timber tower built over a well, replaced at a later date by a stone shell-keep.

FAIRSEAT

A motte in a square enclosure, Fairseat was excavated in 1964. Signs of a wooden tower were found.

FOLKESTONE
Overlooking the harbour there was a motte and bailey castle which was mentioned in 1137.

GILLINGHAM
The ruins of the Stuart fort built to defend the Medway still remain. It was not strong enough to afford any protection against the Dutch raid of 1667.

HEVER
Near Edenbridge, Hever is one of the finest inhabited castles in the country. A licence to crenellate was granted to Sir John de Cobham in 1384. In 1462, the castle was bought by Sir Geoffrey Bullen (Boleyn), Lord Mayor of London, who made considerable alterations to it. The building was completed by his grandson, Sir Thomas Boleyn, father of Henry VIII's unfortunate queen, Anne. Henry first met her in the garden at Hever. They were married in 1533 and in 1536 she was arrested, accused of adultery and executed. Henry then married Jane Seymour, who produced the son and heir the king wished for so dearly.

After Sir Thomas Bullen's death, the castle passed to Anne of Cleves, Henry's fourth wife, and when she died it was sold to Sir Edward Waldegrave. From the Waldegraves it passed to Sir William Humfreys, Lord Mayor of London in 1714, and then to Sir Timothy Waldo. The castle today owes its appearance and beautiful gardens to the first Viscount Astor, who bought it in 1903 and built a mock Tudor village for his guests in the grounds. The castle gatehouse, with its machicolations, its wide moat and the surrounding gardens, is one of the finest sights in Kent.

Lord Astor of Hever. Open Easter Sunday, 22nd April–17th October, Wednesdays, Sundays, and bank holidays, and Saturdays in August and September, 1–7. Admission charge.

KINGSGATE
Built by Lord Holland in 1760, Kingsgate is a sham castle perched on the cliff edge between Margate and Broadstairs.

LEEDS
Just outside Maidstone, on the main road to Canterbury, the magnificent castle at Leeds is surrounded by an artificial lake. It was built by the Saxons and after the Norman conquest was enlarged by the Crevecour family. During the

Baron's War of Simon de Montfort, Robert Crevecour changed sides and was dispossessed by Henry III who granted the castle to Roger de Leybourne.

Later Edward I owned Leeds and his son Edward II gave it to one of his barons, Lord Badlesmere, with his queen Isabella nominally in possession. However the constable, Walter Colepeper, refused permission for the queen and her party to enter and six of the queen's men were killed trying to do so. The king laid siege to Leeds and Badlesmere, attempting to relieve it, was forced to withdraw. Colepeper was captured and executed, along with eleven of his men.

Reverting to the Crown, Leeds was used as a prison for the unfortunate Richard II for a short time, and later for the wife of Henry IV. Henry VI was here in 1431 when his aunt Eleanor of Gloucester was tried for 'necromancy, witchcraft, heresy and treason' in front of Archbishop Chichele. She was sentenced to life imprisonment in the castle. During the seventeenth century there were Dutch and French prisoners here under the charge of John Evelyn, who 'flooded the dry moat, made a new drawbridge and brought spring water into the court'. It later belonged to the Culpepers, one of whom was Governor of Virginia from 1680 to 1683.

In the nineteenth century Leeds belonged to the Wykeham-Martin family and the mock Tudor buildings were erected on the central island – the castle stands on three islands connected by bridges. The inner island, known as the Gloriette, is the keep. There is a bath-house erected by Edward I, now used as a boathouse. Inside the castle are some interesting paintings (including a portrait of Sir Peter Lely) the oldest pendulum clock in England, and Anne Boleyn's shoes.

Hon. Lady Baillie. Open once a year under the National Gardens Scheme.

LEYBOURNE

Near West Malling on the A228 to Rochester, the Leybourne family castle was built mostly in the fourteenth century and the remaining portion is now part of a modern house. It once belonged to Sir Joseph Hawley, whose horses won the Derby four times.

LYMPNE

The present castle incorporates the Square Tower, which is very old and believed to be the Roman watch-tower for the Saxon shore fort 300 feet below (known in Roman times as *Portus Lemanis*). The Great Hall, built in 1360, replaced an early Norman one of the late eleventh century and the Great Tower was built between 1360 and 1420. Minor restoration was undertaken in 1905 by Sir Robert Lorrimer who also built the New Wing. Most of the castle lies untouched since the fourteenth century.

H. Margery. Open April–October Wednesdays, Sundays and Bank Holidays 2–6, and daily except Mondays from June–September, 10.30–1, 2.30–6. Admission charge.

QUEENBOROUGH

On the Isle of Sheppey, two miles south-west of Sheerness, a fort was built in 1361 'for the strength of the realm and the refuge of the inhabitants'. It was considerably strengthened during the reign of Henry VIII and repaired by Elizabeth I. It was a circular castle, the outer bailey being defended by a moat and a strong wall. The keep was defended by six circular towers. It had twelve rooms in the basement and forty on the upper floor. The original architect was William of Wykeham and among the constables were John of Gaunt, the Duke of Clarence and, at the time of the Armada, Sir Edward Hoby, custodian of Signor Jeromino, a Spaniard captured by Sir Francis Drake.

The castle was dismantled by Cromwell in 1650 and was sadly missed a few years later when the Dutch landed at Sheerness. Today very little remains.

RECULVER

Between Birchington and Herne Bay, Reculver was a stone fort before Richborough had walls. Originally known as *Regulbium* it is famous today for the remains of its church, founded by Egbert in A.D. 669. The south and east walls remain in parts but the north wall vanished under the sea many years ago. A copy of a charter granting the monastery of Egbert at Reculver to Christ Church, Canterbury, and signed by Dunstan, Abbot of Glastonbury, can be seen today in Canterbury Cathedral library. The twin towers of the church, which was demolished in 1809, were kept as a landmark. According to legend they were erected by an abbess whose sister was shipwrecked off the Reculver cliffs. *Department of the Environment. Church open normal hours. Admission charge.*

RICHBOROUGH

Just outside Sandwich one mile from the Canterbury road, the massive Roman walls of Richborough look down over the railway line and the site of the old Roman port of *Rutupiae*. Here Claudius landed with his invasion army in A.D. 43 and built a supply base. Agricola destroyed the wooden buildings and erected a cruciform structure in A.D. 85, probably to commemorate the final conquest of Britain. The cross rests on a masonry platform which covers an underground passage and the masonry descends to a depth of 30 feet. A house and three surrounding ditches were built in the second half of the third century. The famous walls date from about A.D. 287, when Richborough was one of the castles erected by the Count of the Saxon Shore. Modern historians consider that the chain of forts from Brancaster in Norfolk to Portchester in Hampshire was erected by Carausius to prevent the Roman army under Diocletian from invading Britain.

The walls have a central west gate where Watling Street entered and there is an outer causeway with guard chambers on each side. St Augustine is supposed to have landed at Ebbsfleet, 3 miles from Richborough, in 597 to meet Ethelbert of Kent. The imprint of his foot was kept on a stone and a chapel was built by the Saxons to house the relic. Excavations during the 1920s revealed a number of coins and skeletons, including the grave of a Roman soldier with shield, spear and sword. The principal finds are in the museum on the site and include a remarkable Anglo-Saxon sword with a blade made of strips of iron welded together.

Department of the Environment. Open normal times. Admission charge.

ROCHESTER

On a bend in the river Medway, Rochester was once a Roman camp commanding a bridge on the road from London to Dover. Later it became a Saxon castle, *Hrofe Caestre,* which was a fortified enclosure of seven acres and a motte known as Boley Hill. The manor was bestowed on Odo, Bishop of Bayeux, by William I but the first castle was built in about 1080 by Bishop Gundulf.

Rochester keep was constructed c. 1126 by William de Corbeuil in an enceinte measuring 160 yards by 130 yards. It is over 100 feet high and has a square forebuilding and walls 12 feet thick. This was the first great square keep to be constructed in an English castle and it was soon put to the test. William d'Albini held it against King John for three months in 1215 and only by undermining the south-west tower did the king's forces get into the bailey and dislodge the garrison from the keep.

In 1216 the French Dauphin Louis recaptured Rochester for the barons, but the castle successfully withstood a siege by Simon de Montfort in 1264. In 1381 it was captured by Wat Tyler's rebels who were supported by the local townsfolk. After this it fell into decay although Edward IV spent some time and money trying to repair it. Its constable from 1413 onwards was Lord Cobham, whose family were involved in Wyatt's Rebellion of 1554 (*see* Allington, Kent).

In 1883 it was bought by the Corporation of Rochester and opened to the public.

Department of the Environment. Open normal times. Closed on Good Friday. Limited parking. Admission charge.

SALTWOOD

On the top of the hill above Hythe, Saltwood Castle is tucked away from view on the other side of the road from the church. It is recorded that Aesc, son of Hengist, 'built a castle in this place' in 488, but during the Roman occupation it was important, as it stood just off Stane Street. Saltwood was then a fortified port, Hythe being under water.

The present castle was built by Henry de Essex, Henry II's standard-bearer. Accused of cowardice, Essex became a monk and the castle reverted to the Crown. It was already, however, the joint property of Becket, Archbishop of Canterbury, and the Warden of the Cinque Ports, formerly Henry de Essex himself. There was a quarrel between Becket and Henry II about this property. The king's nominee at Saltwood, Randolph de Broc, was also an enemy of Becket and he sheltered the four knights who landed from Normandy on 28th December 1170 and murdered Becket at Canterbury the following day. Afterwards they returned to Saltwood.

Later owners included Archbishop Courtenay. He built the twin-towered gatehouse which was converted in Victorian times by the Deedes family and is now the inhabited part of the building. Cranmer, the last archbishop to live here, gave it to Henry VIII in 1540. Forty years later a surprise earthquake rendered it uninhabitable, until restored by Deedes and by Lady Conway, who reroofed the Archbishop's Hall. It was recently made into a library. Protected by two baileys and a moat round the inner triangular one, this is one of the finest and least known small castles in the south of England.

Hon. Alan Clark. Open to the public only on certain days during August and September.

SANDGATE
In Castle Road, Sandgate, almost part of Folkestone, is another of Henry VIII's circular castles, built from the stones of two demolished priories. Elizabeth I spent a night here at the time of the Armada. The keep, all that remains, is now a private house.

SANDOWN
The largest of Henry VIII's forts, Sandown, of which only a few stones remain, is just to the east of Deal. Colonel Hutchinson, Ireton's cousin, was imprisoned and died here after the Restoration. His wife ably describes the place in her diary: 'the walls were four yards thick, yet it rained in through the cracks in them'. In 1894 two flanking gun positions and a central one were blown up by the Royal Engineers because they were unsafe.

SANDWICH
The ancient Cinque Port of Sandwich still has both a barbican tower protecting its bridge and Fisher Gate on the river bank. Edward III used the port frequently and a castle is mentioned at that time. In 1383 the English fleet captured a large French ship carrying a prefabricated wall, 20 feet high, 3,000 feet long, with turrets every 12 feet, capable of holding ten men each. This was assembled at Sandwich by its inventor, an Englishman, and for a time acted as part of the defences of the port. In 1451, however, the Great Bulwark was erected in the south-east corner of the town. This was of two storeys and well provided with cannon. On 20th August 1457 Pierre de Breze landed with a French raiding party and captured the Bulwark with great difficulty, but got no further. He retired with considerable spoils and to this day the mayor wears a black robe of mourning in memory of the raid. The Bulwark, never really a castle, was held by the bastard Fauconberg for the Earl of Warwick during the Wars of the Roses but seems to have been demolished shortly after the battle of Barnet in 1471.

SCOTNEY
Originally a fourteenth-century moated castle built by Roger Ashburnham in the reign of Richard II, Scotney, near Lamberhurst, is a romantic round tower set in the garden of a late Georgian mansion. In 1422 it was acquired by Archbishop Chichele who gave it to his niece and her husband Thomas Darell of Ashford. They were Catholics

and secret chambers were built to hide their priests. One of these, Father Blount, with Bray his servant, remained hidden for a week while the Darells were out of the castle and it was occupied by their enemies. Today it is famous for its gardens.

National Trust. Open Wednesdays to Sundays and Bank Holidays 2–6, Easter Saturday–October. Admission charge. No dogs allowed.

SHURLAND

The sixteenth-century manor-house near Minster-in-Sheppey is built on the site of Sir Robert de Shurland's castle. According to the *Ingoldsby Legends* Sir Robert once buried a friar in the grave in which the friar had refused to inter a pauper. Sir Robert is supposed to have ridden his horse two miles out to sea to get pardon from the queen for his sins and on his return an old woman told him that his horse would be the death of him. Thereupon he knifed the unfortunate animal there on the beach, but many years later stumbled over the skull which poisoned his foot and caused his death.

SISSINGHURST

Not far from Cranbrook, Sissinghurst was built by the Speaker of the House of Commons, Sir John Baker, in about 1530. During the Seven Years War it held French prisoners-of-war and today only the Tudor gatehouse and moat remain in the famous garden restored by the late Miss V. Sackville-West.

National Trust. Open April–October daily 10–6. Admission charge. No dogs.

SUTTON VALENCE

Protecting the road from Rochester to Rye, Sutton Valence is a few miles south of Maidstone on A274. The ruined castle stands on a hill by the church. Only a portion of the keep remains.

The castle was built by one of Henry III's many, unpopular half-brothers William de Valence, who married a Pembroke heiress and later became Earl of Pembroke. During de Montfort's rebellion, he supported Henry III at Lewes, and after Evesham was made governor of Goodrich Castle. Three Pembrokes owned Sutton Valence until it passed to the Cliffords. When Mildred Clifford, who had four husbands, died, her first husband Sir Edward Harper inherited it. He sold it to Sir Edward Hales, whose family lived here for many years. In 1956 the site was excavated and pottery dating from 1150 was discovered together with parts of the forebuilding and staircase.

THURNHAM
Near Maidstone, on the Downs are the remains of Godard's castle mentioned in a charter of 1215.

TONBRIDGE
Richard FitzGilbert built a castle on a prehistoric mound at Tonbridge, so called because the manor had been given to Richard de Tonbridge who fought for William I at Hastings. It was surrounded by a moat fed from the river. During 1088 the castle held out against William Rufus, but FitzGilbert was wounded during the siege and the castle surrendered. He died in Normandy in 1091. In the thirteenth century Richard de Clare built the gatehouse which stands today. In 1264 Gilbert de Clare set out from here to lead the centre of Simon de Montfort's army at Lewes but he quarrelled with Simon and joined the king's side at Evesham the following year, later marrying Prince Edward's daughter Joan. In 1314 their only son Gilbert was killed at Bannockburn, so that Tonbridge passed to his sisters. One of these married Hugh de Audley who rebelled against Edward and consequently forfeited his castle. Edward III restored it to Audley and on his death it passed to his daughter Margaret who married Lord Stafford, a great soldier who commanded the van at Crecy in 1346. One of the Staffords was killed fighting for Henry IV at Shrewsbury, in 1403. Later Staffords, Dukes of Buckingham, also met violent deaths, one being killed at Northampton in 1460, another at St Albans in 1461, and Henry, the second duke, being executed in Salisbury by Richard III. His son Edward, restored to the title, became High Constable of England but, falling foul of Cardinal Wolsey, was accused of treason, tried and beheaded in 1520.

Held for Parliament during the Civil War, the castle was not demolished until 1793 when it was bought by Thomas Hooker of Peckham who constructed the present Gothic building, now used as municipal offices, next to the gatehouse. The bailey is a garden and only a small piece of the wall remains.
Open every day 9–5. Admission charge.

TONG

Near Teynham, between Faversham and Sittingbourne, Tong was originally an earthen fortress erected by Hengist and his Jutes. The Celtic leader Vortigern offered Hengist as much land as he could cover with an ox-hide and the latter chopped it into thongs and enclosed many 'hides', this one being known as 'Tong'. The site contained a castle that belonged to the Mortimers and later passed to the Crown. Today only a mound remains, as it is thought that the area was abandoned after the plague.

UPNOR

In 1561 an Elizabethan fort was constructed on the river Medway at Upnor, near Rochester. It was a long three-storey building with a tower at each end and a ravelin in front with gun platforms and stockade. The only time the guns fired against an enemy was in 1667 when De Ruyter invaded the Medway. His leading ships crossed over the chain at Upnor and set fire to two guard-ships, the *Mathias* and the *Charles V*. Two other ships, the *Royal Charles* and the frigate *Unity,* were captured and four more were set on fire almost under the noses of Upnor Castle's inefficient gunners. This, according to Evelyn, was 'as dreadful a spectacle as Englishmen ever saw and a dishonour never to be wiped off'.
Department of the Environment. Open normal times. Admission charge.

WALMER

On the edge of the beach where Caesar landed in 55 B.C., Walmer Castle was built for Henry VIII by Hugh de Albertsmil to guard the coast against invasion. Not as large as Deal or the three other 'castles of the Downs', Walmer consists of four large bastions with a central circular one. The moat was once filled by the sea at high tide and was, like Deal Castle, covered by gun ports lest the enemy should attempt to cross it.

Since the eighteenth century Walmer has been the official residence of the Lord Warden of the Cinque Ports and as a result the Duke of Dorset, Earl Granville and William Pitt, three of the Lords Warden, made considerable alterations. In Pitt's time, Lady Stanhope planned the garden and Granville added the tower by the entrance. On display are 32 pounders, 6 pounders and an impressive stand of early artillery equipment.

The most famous occupant of the castle was the Duke of Wellington who lived here, apart from his wife, in his final years and died in a chair in his room upstairs on 14th September 1852. He was not a believer in comfort and his bed is remarkably small for he believed that 'when it is time to turn round it is time to turn out'. In the upstairs dome landing are pictures of all the Lords Warden, who include W. H. Smith and Winston Churchill. The collection of Wellingtonia is unrivalled, especially since the T. H. Lucas Collection was housed here in August 1966.

Department of the Environment. Open normal times. Closed when Lord Warden is in residence. Admission charge.

WESTENHANGER

On the hill above Hythe and next to the racecourse and railway station, stand the remains of a fortified manor house of the fourteenth century. It was built with nine towers by John de Kiriel on the site of a Saxon palace. Sir Edward Poynings, Lord-Deputy of Ireland, and author of Poynings Law, which attempted to bring law and order to that country, improved the house in Henry VII's reign. After this it appears to have declined although Elizabeth I came here and presented it to Sir Thomas Sackville. In 1648, after the Royalist rising at Maidstone, the castle was used as a prison but 53 years later it was partially demolished and sold for £1,000. Today only three towers remain, including one known as Fair Rosamund's tower, where Rosamund Clifford, mistress of Henry II, was supposed to have lived before her imprisonment at Woodstock. There appears to be no proof for this supposition and it is more likely that the tower is of a later date.

WEST MALLING

Near where the A20 crosses the A228 between Rochester and Tonbridge, St Leonards Tower is the only surviving part of the castle of Gundulf, Bishop of Rochester (Gundulf was responsible for building the White Tower in the Tower of London as well as the abbey at East Malling). The structure dates from about 1080 and is 60 feet high with four Norman-arched windows side by side on the first floor and a larger window above; the top storey is in ruins.

Once used as a gaol, the tower later became a hop store. In the seventeenth century it belonged to the Rainey family who sold it to the Honywoods.

Open to the public at all times. Key at No. 1 Park Cottages. Admission free.

LANCASHIRE

BURY
A drill hall, formerly an armoury, stands on the site of Bury Castle, the remains of which were discovered by workmen in 1865. Licence to crenellate was granted in 1465 and Lord Stanley, of Bosworth fame, lived here.

CLITHEROE
A small Norman keep and part of a wall still remain of Roger de Poitou's castle in the Ribble valley, first mentioned in 1102. He was the son of Roger de Montgomery who commanded the centre divisions of William's army at Hastings. Later it passed to the de Lacys and Alice, last of this family, married a Plantagenet; he was beheaded in 1322 by Edward II, after which the castle became part of the Duchy of Lancaster.

DALTON-IN-FURNESS
Near Barrow-in-Furness, Dalton is a fourteenth-century pele tower, repaired in 1544 and 1856. It has been used as a secular court for the abbot of Furness, as a prison and as an armoury for the Rifle Volunteers.
National Trust. Open at all reasonable times. Key from 18 *Market Place.*

FARLETON
On the Lune river, a mile from Hornby, are a few stones of the Harringtons' castle. Sir William Harrington was killed at Agincourt, and by 1600 the castle was a total ruin.

FOULDRY OR PIEL CASTLE
This island fortress off Roa Island near Barrow, dates from about 1327 but may have been originally a Danish outpost. It is a concentric fortress with the entrance on the west and a keep which is remarkably intact. It was repaired by the Duke of Buccleuch.

GLEASTON
Near Dalton-in-Furness, Gleaston is a fourteenth-century building with four towers connected by a curtain wall, but which may never have been completed. It belonged to the Harringtons and later to Thomas Grey, father of the unfortunate Lady Jane.

GREENHALGH

Near Garstang, Greenhalgh was built by Lord Derby in 1490. It was a rectangular building with four towers but was destroyed by Parliament after its surrender during the Civil War. Today only a portion of one tower remains by the Catholic church.

GRESGARTH

At Caton, Gresgarth Hall was built on the site of a pele tower.

HOGHTON TOWER

An Elizabethan mansion with two courtyards was probably built on the site of an earlier castle here. It was fortified during the Civil War and the gatehouse was used as a powder room; 200 men were killed when this blew up and for many years the house was a ruin.

HORNBY

A much altered castle on the Lune, painted by Turner, was originally built by Roger de Montbegon, who may have built Farleton as his main castle. A later owner moved to this site. It later passed to the Harringtons and Stanleys. Sir Edward Stanley distinguished himself at Flodden and was created Lord Monteagle. The fourth lord was involved in the rebellion of the Earl of Essex in 1601 and was responsible for warning the authorities about the Gunpowder Plot in 1605, after receiving a letter from Sir Francis Tresham, his brother-in-law, telling him not to take his seat in the House of Lords. Partially destroyed during the Civil War, Hornby belonged to Lord Wemyss during the Jacobite Rebellion and part of Lord Elcho's cavalry spent the night here on their march to Derby. The castle then went to ruin until it was restored in Victorian times.

LANCASTER

Originally a Roman fort, probably built by Hadrian, Lancaster then became a Saxon stronghold. The stone castle was built by the Norman Roger de Poitou, who owned a great area of Lancashire at that time. In 1102 he forfeited his land for supporting the barons' rebellion against Henry I and the castle passed to the Crown. King John held court here in 1206 and was responsible for much of the building. In the fourteenth century it belonged to John of Gaunt, but he does not appear to have lived here. His son Henry

Bolingbroke, after deposing Richard II and becoming Henry IV, established the Duchy of Lancaster. The land bestowed on the duchy was deemed a separate inheritance from the Crown and the castle has been part of the duchy ever since.

From the mid seventeenth century the castle has been a prison and criminal court. During the Civil War it remained in Parliamentary hands although besieged by the Royalists in 1648 under Sir Thomas Tyldesley; it held out and was partially demolished by order the following year. In 1715 it was occupied briefly by Jacobites who set the prisoners free. In 1745 the Jacobites again entered Lancaster on their way to and from Derby but do not seem to have occupied the castle. In 1798 the Crown Court was built and in the dock is the branding iron. Prisoners sentenced to be branded had their left hand put in the clamp and a large M pressed on the fleshy part of their hand below the thumb. It was last used in 1801.

The keep is the oldest part of the castle and the upper part was restored in 1585. The first floor contains the old Shire Hall and the ground floor the prison chapel.

The dungeons are on view (five of them were discovered as late as 1931) and the gatehouse, dating from 1400, has the coat of arms of Prince Hal, later Henry V, and, in the niche, a statue of John of Gaunt, put there in 1822.
Open to the public 10.30–12 *and* 2–4 *every weekday except when courts are sitting. Prison area not shown. Admission charge.*

LATHOM HOUSE

Three miles from Ormskirk, only one wing and the recently restored chapel of the eighteenth-century house survive. The original house was built on a low, boggy site and surrounded with a wide moat and a thick wall. It had nine towers and the Earl of Derby armed each with six cannon. Palisades were erected between the moat and the wall, and the gatehouse had two flanking towers. The house itself – large enough to 'receive three kings' – had a high tower known as the Eagle Tower. In 1642 the earl was in the Isle of Man but his wife and children were at Lathom with a strong garrison. Rigby, the local Parliamentary leader, tried to persuade her to surrender and when she refused he turned a large mortar on the house, but the garrison captured this during the night and took it inside. Finally the earl with Prince Rupert relieved Lathom in May 1644 and the countess and her children went to Man. Lathom held out after

Marston Moor until the treachery of an Irish soldier led to its surrender. It was completely destroyed and some of the timbers were used for a scaffold for the execution of Lord Derby after his capture in the retreat from Worcester in 1651. Henceforth the main seat of the Derby family was Knowsley Hall.

Lathom chapel is open at all times.

LIVERPOOL
Roger de Poitou had a castle on the south side of the city with a large keep and a 50 acre bailey. There was also a tower in Water Street used as a prison and demolished in 1820.

MANCHESTER
A castle in Manchester was mentioned in 1184. In King John's reign it belonged to Adam de Yeland and stood on the river bank.

PENWORTHAM
By the church at Penwortham was a Norman castle mentioned in the Domesday book. The Ribble acted as a moat on three sides. There are no remains of it today but excavations in 1856 revealed a circular wooden structure with a central post and a cobbled floor.

PRESTON
A motte and bailey castle at Preston became the property of Furness Abbey in 1123.

RADCLIFFE
A pele tower standing near the church here was joined on to a large hall, 42 feet long, with a fine oak roof. This was later demolished to make room for a row of cottages.

THURLAND
Only the moat remains of this fifteenth-century fortified house, the home of the Tunstalls. The house was completely rebuilt in the 1880s following a fire.

TURTON TOWER
Near Bolton, Turton was a pele tower with a moat.

WARRINGTON
A ringwork and bailey castle near the church is still visible and a coin of Henry III was found during excavations.

WEST DERBY
A motte and bailey castle here was destroyed in the early thirteenth century.

WRAYSHOLME
A pele tower attached to a farmhouse at Flookburgh, it belonged to the Harrington family. The last wolf in England was said to have been shot nearby.

LEICESTERSHIRE

ASHBY-DE-LA-ZOUCH
One of the most famous of England's castles, Ashby-de-la-Zouch was the scene of Sir Walter's Scott's famous jousting tournament in *Ivanhoe*.

At the time of Domesday, Ashby manor belonged to Hugh de Granmesnel, the principal Norman landowner in Leicestershire. In the twelfth century it was acquired by the Beaumonts, the first of them, Robert, being made Earl of Leicester. The castle, however, did not begin to take shape until the twelfth century, when the Zouch family from Brittany built a stone hall and solar. The Mortimers from Shropshire inherited the manor in 1314 and Sir William Mortimer built a new solar, turning the old one into a battery which it remained until the present kitchen was built later in the fourteenth century.

During the Wars of the Roses Ashby belonged to the Earl of Ormond until he was beheaded by the Yorkists after the battle of Towton. His forfeited estates were given to Lord Hastings, a favourite of Edward IV, who lived at nearby Kirby Muxloe. Hastings set about building a large tower at Ashby and also obtained licences to crenellate Kirby and another house he owned at Bagworth. Not wanting to demolish any of the existing buildings, Lord Hastings built a chapel on the end of the solar and connected it to a priest's room. Both these buildings formed, with the new tower, a south courtyard. In the fashion of Tattershall, this tower contained the main living quarters, but unlike Tattershall it had only one small inner doorway and no ground floor windows. The basement walls are over 8 feet thick.

In 1483 Lord Hastings was accused of treason by Richard III and was beheaded. His son escaped to fight for Henry Tudor at Bosworth and Ashby remained in the Hastings family. In 1569 Mary, Queen of Scots, was brought to Ashby after the Northern Rising and in 1617 her son

James I was entertained here by George Hastings, Earl of Huntingdon, who spent so much on the king's seventeen-day visit that he had to sell twenty-four manors and thirty-two lordships to pay for it.

During the Civil War, Ashby was garrisoned by Colonel Hastings, Lord Loughborough, for Charles I. He built Mount House in Leicester Road for his horsemen and connected it to the castle by an underground passage. Another passage, still existing, ran from the Hastings Tower to the kitchen block. In 1644 Lord Grey's Parliamentary forces captured the town but Lord Loughborough held out for Charles. After Naseby in June 1645 the Royalist cavalry arrived with the king, but, although hard pressed at the time it was not until 28th February, 1646 that the garrison surrendered. Two years later Parliamentary commissioners at Leicester reported that the 'great tower is a place of considerable strength' and they gave orders for it to be undermined and blown up with gunpowder. The south wall was destroyed and all the outer part of the rest of the building, so that it is difficult to appreciate the great strength of the castle today.

It has been called 'the maiden garrison' for it was never captured, only surrendered on terms.

Department of the Environment. Entrance in Upper Church Street, Ashby-de-la-Zouch. Open normal times. Admission charge.

BELVOIR

Founded by Robert Todeni, Belvoir Castle was originally a Norman structure. It is situated off the road from Grantham to Waltham-on-the-Wolds on the Lincolnshire border. Part of the Norman keep still exists but the whole structure was completely rebuilt for the Duke of Rutland by Wyatt in 1800.

The Duke of Rutland's ancestors, the Manners and Ros families, owned the castle in the middle ages. During the Wars of the Roses, Lord Ros was an ardent Lancastrian and the castle was besieged by Lord Hastings. It fell to the Yorkists who stripped the lead from its roofs causing it to fall into decay. The thirteenth Lord Ros, created Earl of Rutland in 1525, restored it but the Gothic building today dates from the nineteenth century. It houses the museum of the 17th/21st Lancers and contains many fine paintings by Holbein, Gainsborough and Poussin and other treasures.

Duke of Rutland. Opening times given on enquiry. Admission charge.

101

CASTLE DONINGTON

Nine miles north-east of Ashby-de-la-Zouch, on the Nottingham road, Castle Donington belonged to John Lacy. He was one of the barons who rebelled against King John. Partly destroyed by the latter in 1216, the castle passed to the earls of Kent and later to Lord Huntingdon. The latter, who was driven out of Ashby during the Civil War, incorporated the remaining stones of the castle into Donington House.

EARL SHILTON

Robert, Earl of Leicester founded a castle here which was demolished in the early seventeenth century.

GROBY

The castle of the de Ferrers family stood by Groby Pool. It was pulled down by Henry II.

HINCKLEY

On the present A5, Hinckley had a Norman castle built by Hugh de Grandmesnel, Sheriff of Leicester and later Lord High Steward of England. In old age he became a monk in Normandy and his castle fell into disuse; it was demolished by Henry II (*see* Leicester).

KIRBY MUXLOE

Lord Hastings, favourite of Edward IV, obtained a licence to fortify an old manor house at Kirby in 1474. He had obtained the property from the Earl of Ormond, a Lancastrain who was later killed after the battle of Towton. The old manor's great hall was retained and a fortified wall with a square corner turret and a gatehouse was constructed. The west tower, which remains remarkably intact today, has three storeys with unusual early gunports overlooking the moat, which is fed from a nearby stream.

The accounts for building Kirby Muxloe still survive, and a total of £1,088 17s 6¼d was spent in four years, continuing after 1483, when Hastings was executed for treason. The brickwork is very fine and was probably done by Flemings under Roger Bowlett and their master mason Couper, who worked at Tattershall. The Hastings coat of arms shows a maunch or sleeve and the bricklayers worked this into the pattern of the gatehouse's north-west octagon turret. In 1913 the castle was presented to the Commissioners of Works.

Department of the Environment. Open May–September 9.30–7; November–February 9.30–4; October, March and April 9.30–5.30. Admission charge.

LEICESTER

Hugh de Grandmesnel owned Leicester Castle, a Saxon stronghold, in 1066. Later it passed to Robert de Bellemont, Earl of Leicester. Between 1108 and 1118 the earl built three other castles and his son married a Grandmesnel and inherited Hinckley and Groby. Henry II was alarmed at such baronial strength in the county. The earl supported the Prince Henry as a claimant to the throne and as a result Hinckley, Groby and Leicester were all demolished by the royal army under Humphrey de Bohun. Later Leicester passed to Simon de Montfort. The castle hall was rebuilt and the church of St Mary de Castro served as the chapel. Henry VI held a parliament here, and during the Civil War, when the town was captured by Prince Rupert, the castle armoury was used by the Royalists. The central courtyard was later used as a place of execution and much of the great hall was taken down in 1715 to build the assize courts.

MOUNTSORREL

The Earl of Leicester's castle overlooked the Stour river on a spur near Loughborough. It was surrendered to Henry II in 1173 and later passed to the Earl of Winchester. During the early years of Henry III's reign, the earl brought his army of French ruffians to Mountsorrel and they proceeded to ravage the countryside. In 1217 the royal army under Lord Pembroke defeated the earl and his French troops at Lincoln and then demolished the castle.

RAVENSTONE

There was once a castle here for the earls of Leicester and Cheshire, who made a treaty in 1148 agreeing to destroy the building if it was held against either of them.

WHITWICK

Just off the Ashby-Loughborough road, Whitwick Castle was built by Robert, Earl of Leicester, and like Mountsorrel was acquired by the Earl of Winchester. It was probably demolished by Pembroke at the same time as Mountsorrel but Henry Beaumont obtained a licence to crenellate his house at Whitwick in 1320. Lord Hastings was the owner in 1480.

LINCOLNSHIRE

ASLACKBY

Aslackby is a small village between Sleaford and Bourne. Near the church are the earthwork remains of the early Norman castle of the Wakes.

BOURNE

The Romans are believed to have had a fort here to defend the Carr Dyke. The Saxon leader Morcar lived at Bourne and one of the most famous English heroes, Hereward the Wake, was supposed to have been born here.

Behind West Street are the remains of the Norman castle. Originally covering eight acres, the castle had a large keep with its own moat and another moat round the outer bailey. Two round towers guarded the entrance which had a drawbridge across the moat, which was forty-four feet wide at this place.

The Wake family, who lived in the castle, entertained Edward III here, for Hugh Wake married Blanche Plantagenet, the great-granddaughter of Henry III. In 1397 the Earl of Kent was buried here, as the Wakes were also relatives of the mother of Richard II, the famous 'Fair Maid of Kent'. During the Civil War a Parliamentary garrison was quartered in the castle ruins.

BYTHAM

Eight miles west of Bourne is Little Bytham, where the castle of the Earl of Albemarle stood on a hill overlooking the village. When Albemarle rebelled in 1220, Henry III besieged and destroyed it, granting it to the Colviles who lived there until 1370; it was destroyed completely during the Wars of the Roses.

CARLTON

Six miles south-west of Louth are the castle mound and remains of a wide moat. In the twelfth century the Bardolphs lived here and Sir Hugh Bardolph is supposed to have slain a local dragon.

GAINSBOROUGH

The Earl of Lincoln had a castle here in 1146.

GRANTHAM
There was a castle belonging to Queen Matilda in Castle Gate Street but it has long since vanished.

GRIMSTHORPE
Lincolnshire's finest country house, four miles from Bourne, has a thirteenth-century bastion and a Tudor central core.

HORNCASTLE
Roman remains have been found on the site of Horncastle, which was demolished in 1146.

KINGERBY
A motte inside a square moat stood here. Later the Catholic family of Young built the Hall.

LINCOLN
Built in 1068 on a Roman site; 166 houses had to be demolished to make room for it. Henry II was crowned here in 1155. The east and west gates and wall and Norman shell-keep are still standing.
The keep is open April–September daily 10–6, Sundays 2–7.30; October–March weekdays 10–4. Admission charge.

MOULTON
Thomas de Moulton had a castle here in 1216.

OLD BOLINGBROKE
Near Horncastle, Old Bolingbroke is a tiny village below a small hill with a few stones near the church marking the site of the castle.

In Norman times the manor belonged to William de Roumare who became first Earl of Lincoln. His mother was the heiress of Morcar, Earl of Northumberland, and on her second marriage, Henry I granted the land to William who built the first castle. During the reign of Henry II the castle passed to the de Gaunt family. They died without male issue and in Henry III's reign a famous warrior, Henry de Lacy, lived here. On his death it passed to Edmund Plantagenet, brother of Edward I, whose son Thomas married a de Lacy. At the battle of Boroughbridge the de Lacys were fighting for the rebels and Thomas was captured and beheaded. His brother Henry managed to keep the estate and one of his two daughters, Blanche, married John of Gaunt, Duke of Lancaster. Henceforward Old Bolingbroke belonged to the Duchy of Lancaster. On April 3rd, 1367, John of Gaunt's son, Henry of Bolingbroke was born. He was a friend of Richard II until in 1398 he quarrelled with Thomas Mowbray and challenged him to mortal combat. Richard forbade the fight and both were exiled. The following year John of Gaunt died and Richard seized his property. Gathering a small army Henry landed at Ravenspur in Yorkshire and went south to Bolingbroke. Richard, on a campaign in Ireland, hastened over to Wales. After capturing Bristol Henry moved north to Flint, where at Flint Castle Richard surrendered to him and young Bolingbroke became Henry IV.

The castle was described by Gervase Holles in the seventeenth century. 'The building lies within a square area (the outer bailey) within the walls containing about an acre and a half (outer bailey surrounded by a moat); the building is very uniform. It hath four strong forts or ramparts wherein are many rooms and lodgings; the passage from one to another lying upon the walls which are embattled about. There be likewise two watchtowers all covered in lead. The entrance to it is very stately over a fair drawbridge; the gatehouse a very uniform and strong building.' Holles remarks on the three dungeons or prisons and a ghost – 'a certain spirit in the likeness of a hare'.

During the Civil War the Royalist garrison was isolated, as most of the Eastern counties supported Parliament. In October 1643 the Earl of Manchester ordered the castle to surrender in a rudely worded message. Back came the reply 'Bugbear words must not win a castle nor should make them quit a place'. A few days later Widdrington and Henderson led a Royalist force from Newark to relieve the castle garrison. Manchester, supported by Fairfax and Cromwell with their troopers, met him at Winceby where the Royalists were defeated. Bolingbroke was evacuated and when Manchester's men entered they found 200 horses in the stables, many Royalists having fled on foot to avoid clashing with Cromwell's horsemen.

The castle was abandoned and only the gatehouse remained for some time. In 1815 this too collapsed so that it is difficult to imagine the present fragments as ever constituting a building fit enough 'to entertain a very great Prince with all his train.'

Ruins open at all reasonable times. Admission free.

OWSTON

On the Trent near Gainsborough once stood the twelfth-century castle of Roger de Mowbray. Traces of the moat can be seen near the church.

PARTNEY

A castle was mentioned at Partney in a Charter of 1141.

SLEAFORD

A castle built by the Bishop of Lincoln in 1130 once stood by the river here; it was captured by Stephen in 1139. In 1559 it was already in ruins as Sir Robert Carre bought 'the late fair castle of Sleaford'.

SOMERTON

South of Lincoln on the road to Grantham (A607) is the village of Boothby Graffoe. Two miles west along a small road are the remains of Somerton Castle, now incorporated in a farmhouse.

Built on the site of a Saxon fortress, Somerton was crenellated by Bishop Anthony Bek in 1281 and was a fortified manor house in the same style as Greys Court, Oxfordshire. The quadrangle, 330 feet long and 180 feet wide, was surrounded by a moat and four towers, two of which remain today. A second moat, much wider, enclosed the fortified outer ward so that one had to cross two drawbridges to reach the main living quarters. The south-east tower is 45 feet high and has a projecting corner and three pinnacles with a French style circular pointed roof. The other tower, a ruin in the orchard, has a room with a vaulted ceiling divided into twelve arches. On the walls are the remains of the carved heads of kings.

Two kings are associated with Somerton. Bishop Bek presented it to Edward I and in 1359 the captured King John of France was brought here after the Poitiers campaign. Originally installed at Hertford Castle with his son, John was later placed under the surveillance of Sir Sayer de Rochford, the owner of Somerton, who was paid two shillings a day for the king's food. In 1360, fearing a French invasion, the prisoners were moved to Berkhamsted and then to the Tower of London. Eventually they were ransomed for a sum equal to almost two million pounds today.

Somerton, now a farm, is not open to the public.

SOUTH KYME TOWER

A few miles from Boston on A17 to Sleaford, South Kyme is a small village with a castle keep tower standing beside a Georgian farmhouse. Originally a Saxon island stronghold, South Kyme is named after Philip de Kyme who founded Kyme priory in the twelfth century. Philip took part in the Scottish wars and in 1300 signed a remonstrance against the Pope. His sister married Robert d'Umfraville, who is believed to have built the castle when he inherited the manor after Philip's death. In the fifteenth century the Tallboys or Tailboys family inherited the castle from the Burdons, descendants of the Umfravilles. In 1530 Sir Edward Dymoke inherited it and his family remained there for two hundred years until it passed to the Duke of Newcastle.

The grey square keep is all that remains as the rest of the castle was demolished in the eighteenth century. On the first floor is a room known as the Chequers Chambers because it had a floor of pebbles or chequers. In the centre of the vaulted basement is the coat-of-arms of the Umfraville family. There was a moat round the castle and until the nineteenth century the remains of another tower. There is a brass monument to Gilbert Tailboys in the church.

STAMFORD

Stamford had a Norman castle which was held by Earl de Warrenne for King John and later passed to the Earl of Stamford. It was demolished in the reign of Richard III and the stones used for repairing the Carmelite priory.

TATTERSHALL

Lincolnshire castles tend to have tall towers for lookout posts. Tattershall is no exception and is one of the most remarkable surviving pieces of fifteenth-century brickwork in England.

Situated on the river Bain about thirteen miles from Sleaford on A153 to Horncastle, the great five-storey tower was built by Ralph, Lord Cromwell, in about 1440. It stands on the site of a thirteenth-century castle built by Robert of Tattershall, a descendant of Eudo, the Norman lord of the manor. Ralph inherited the old castle from his father and, using the fortune he made on the Agincourt campaign and later as Treasurer of the King's Exchequer, he built the tower that stands today. Flemish workmen brought their own bricks for the project and Ralph's tower still rises to 100 feet, and to 112 feet to the top of the octagonal machicolated turrets. The walls are 14 feet thick in places, but the large windows made it impractical for defence against cannon. For this reason it had a double moat, the inner moat being supplied by a small channel from the outer moat. Four carved stone fireplaces kept the building warm and on the second floor Ralph had a gallery 38 feet in length with a parapet walk above it lit by loopholes and vaulted like a cloister. Outside the great chamber, also on the second floor, is a wood and plaster dovecote. On the third floor the heraldic glass in the windows includes the arms of Robert of Tattershall. Altogether there are forty-eight separate rooms, with garderobes on each floor and accommodation for a hundred people. Its architect is believed to have been William of Waynflete, Bishop of Winchester, and the cost of Tattershall was recorded by William of Worcester as 'above 4,000 marks'.

After Ralph's death the castle passed to his niece Maud who married Sir Thomas Neville. After his death at the battle of Wakefield, it passed into Lancastrian hands. For a time Henry VII's mother lived here; then in 1520 Henry VIII gave it to the Duke of Suffolk on his marriage to the king's sister. Thirty-one years later it was bestowed on the Earls of Lincoln and descended to the Fortescue family. In 1911 an American syndicate bought the tower and dismantled the fireplaces preparatory to shipping them to the U.S.A. Lord Curzon of Kedleston stepped in, acquired the castle and, rescuing the fireplaces from London, restored them to their original positions and presented the building to the National Trust.

National Trust. Open on weekdays 9.30–7. Sundays 1–7. Close weekdays 1–2. October–March. Admission charge.

NORFOLK

BACONSTHORPE

Situated about three miles east of Holt, off A148 from Kings Lynn to Cromer, Baconsthorpe Hall or Castle, the ancient seat of the Heydon family, is now a ruin. On the same site stood a manor belonging to the Bacons of Baconsthorpe, but early in 1400 the Heydon family acquired the property and William Heydon's son John started to build the castle. He did not obtain a licence to crenellate his house so the date is not exactly known, but it is likely to have been about 1450. The inner gatehouse was the work of John and the outer works were built by his grandson Sir Henry Heydon who was the steward to Cecily, mother of Edward IV. He married the daughter of the Lord Mayor of London, which helped to increase his fortune. He was a keen builder and rebuilt Salthouse church, where the masonry closely resembles Baconsthorpe. Later Heydons took up sheepfarming and Sir Christopher Heydon and his son William had to sell part of the estate to pay off their farming debts. Sir William's son, also Christopher, rebuilt parts of the castle in 1600, narrowing the moat. His two sons were soldiers, the younger one, Sir John Heydon, becoming Lieutenant-General of the Ordinance to Charles I. He was a noted mathematician and fought at Edgehill. After the war he was forced to sell most of the castle for building material. The outer gatehouse became a house and the rest of the castle a walled garden.

The original building with its curtain wall had a single moat round its two courts and a mere on the east side. The southern gatehouse, added in the late sixteenth century, had no moat round it. It has one of its two turrets still standing, built of flint with ashlar cornering and an unusual ogee-shaped cupola. The inner gatehouse has three storeys and is partly of brick. To the south and west the curtain wall remains with a square corner tower containing a keyhole gunport. Two long buildings stand against the east curtain. They are of a later date and were used for wool preparation. The overmantel from the great hall fireplace with its Heydon coat-of-arms is now in the churchyard and in the church is an over-large monument to Sir William Heydon, who died in 1592.

Department of the Environment. Open normal times. Admission free.

BRANCASTER

A Saxon fort once commanded this shore.

BUCKENHAM

At Old Buckenham are earthworks of the old castle used by the Augustine Canons in 1146. A new castle had been built at New Buckenham in 1136. It covered a large area and was similar in design to Castle Acre. A few foundations can still be seen as well as some Norman arches of the church of St Mary in a barn.

CAISTER

Four miles north of Yarmouth off A1064 stand the ruins of Sir John Fastolf's castle built of brick in 1450 out of the ransom money Sir John obtained by capturing a French knight in the Agincourt campaign. The castle passed to John Paston on Sir John's death but the estate was claimed by many others including John Mowbray, Duke of Norfolk. Paston's father, Sir William, was a judge and had been a friend of Sir John's. We know a great deal about the comings and goings of the Pastons through the Paston letters. One of the family fought for Warwick at the battle of Barnet and went to Calais. Another, his brother, defended Caister, when it was attacked by the Duke of Norfolk in 1469. There were less than thirty defenders against an army of three thousand well-armed soldiers. Dame Margaret Paston wrote in haste to her son in London to come with aid: 'Your brother and his fellowship stand in great jeopardy at Caister and lack victuals, Daubeney and Berney be dead, and divers others be greatly hurt, and they fail gunpowder and arrows and the place is sore broken by guns.' Norfolk had to bring in reinforcements from King's Lynn before Caister finally succumbed. For seven years the Pastons gave up the castle and only when Norfolk died suddenly at Framlingham did they return. Sir John Paston died of plague in 1479, worn out by his legal and physical battle to keep Caister. His brother succeeded him and then his brother's son. William, who was present at the Field of the Cloth of Gold. Finally in 1660 Sir William Paston sold the castle, then in a ruinous state, to the Gurney family.

Caister is designed to withstand a siege. It consists of two rectangular outworks surrounded by a moat that was connected with the river Bure. The entrance was by a west drawbridge to the north outwork and thence by another drawbridge to the main building, part of which remains today. The three-storey tower in the south-west corner rises to 90 feet. The great hall, lit by six double square-topped windows butts on to the tower and there used to be a newel staircase in the thin hexagonal turret between the hall and the round tower. The stairs were removed by the Trafford family for their new house at Wroxham. The north outwork contained the Fastolf college and chantry but only two buttressed walls remain intact today.

Alderman P. Hill J.P. Open May–October 10.30–5.30. *Vintage car collection. Admission charge.*

CASTLE ACRE

Situated on the old Pedlars Way track from Holme-next-the-Sea to Brandon, Castle Acre is primarily noted for its fine priory, founded by William de Warrenne in the eleventh century. The castle, of which little remains, was built by de Warrenne on the site of an old Roman fort. It had a motte and bailey with a horseshoe-shaped moat. The north gate still stands at the top of Bailey Street in the village. It is of early English style with two towers on each side. The chapel stood to the east of this gate and until 1800 there was a south gate further down Bailey Street.

William de Warrenne married Gundreda, half-daughter of William the Conqueror, and went on a pilgrimage to Rome. On return they founded the priory, which was subordinate to the Cistercian monastery at Lewes. Gundreda died in 1085 at the castle and William four years later. In the nineteenth century some workmen building a railway line dug up two coffins which were recognised as those of the de Warrennes. The last of this family died in 1347 and the castle has remained a ruin since that day, much of its stone being used to build the village.

Department of the Environment. Castle ruins and bailey gate admission free. Priory, admission charge.

CASTLE RISING

Four miles north-east of King's Lynn, Castle Rising stands on a mound once washed by the sea. The old rhyme goes:

> *Rising was a seaport town*
> *When Lynn was but a marsh;*
> *Now Lynn is a seaport town*
> *And Rising fares the worse.*

The Norman keep which remains today was built by William D'Albini, known as William of the Strong Hand because he was supposed to have pulled out a lion's tongue. He married the widow of Henry I and was created the first Earl of Arundel. His son William inherited the castle and later it passed to the Crown. The Queen Isabella, whose husband Edward II was murdered with her connivance at Berkeley, came to live here after the death of Mortimer, her lover. From 1358, when she died, until 1397 it belonged to the Black Prince and later to Richard II, ultimately becoming part of the Duchy of Cornwall. Henry VIII granted it to Thomas Howard, Duke of Norfolk, and for many years it remained in the Howard family.

In the reign of Henry III there was trouble in King's Lynn.

The Earl of Arundel was entitled to a third part of the customs dues of the port and the garrison of Castle Rising demanded food supplies from the town which were rarely paid for. One year the earl arrived with an armed band to demand his rights despite the gales that had reduced the wealth of the town that year. The citizens captured him and held him in custody. The rest of the garrison fled back to Castle Rising with the mayor's daughter as a hostage. For many weeks the townsfolk besieged the castle. Their leader was Hal Steele, the earl's former armourer, and he was able to make mangonels which breached the walls and yielded the castle to the town. The earl was set free on condition that he no longer claimed his dues and the mayor's daughter was rescued by the brave armourer.

The keep is 50 feet high and is entered on the east side by a flight of steps and three rounded archways; it stands in the middle of earthworks in which there is also a small Norman gatehouse. This brings one to the vestibule. There are two other rooms on the west of the keep but the great hall is open to the sky. A chapel with a two lancet window and a Norman arch is on the first floor with the vestibule. There are also the remains of another chapel and the constable's quarters in the castle ward.

Department of the Environment. Open normal times. Admission charge.

ELMHAM

Bishop Spencer obtained a licence to crenellate his house on the river Wensum in 1388. It was built on an old Saxon earthwork. The inner ward was surrounded by a moat.

GREAT YARMOUTH

The castle was built near the sea front in the reign of Edward I. It was repaired during the Armada and used as a watch and beacon tower. It was completely demolished in 1621.

GRESHAM

The remains of the fourteenth-century fortified mansion of Sir Edmund Bacon stand, surrounded by a moat, opposite The Chequers. Sir William Paston acquired it and, in his absence, his wife was besieged here by Lord Moleyns in 1450. The castle was sacked and fell into decay soon afterwards.

HORSFORD

In this Norwich suburb stood the Norman castle of Walter de Cadamo. It belonged, in succession, to the de Cressys, Uffords and Dacres. Only earthworks and the remains of the moat exist today.

MIDDLETON

Three miles south of King's Lynn stands the gatehouse of Lord Scales' fifteenth-century fortified manor. Lord Scales was killed trying to escape after the battle of Northampton in 1460. His son was beheaded by Richard II at Pontefract. The Victorian wing was added with the name Middleton Tower by Sir Lewis Jarvis of King's Lynn.
Open to the public once a year under the National Gardens Scheme.

NORWICH

Norwich Castle was built as Crown property in the reign of William the Conqueror and probably its first constable was Ralph Guarder. Guarder led a revolt in 1075 against William the Conqueror and was defeated by the troops of the bishops of Bayeux and Coutances. Norwich was captured and Ralph Guarder fled to Brittany. A few years later Roger Bigod, the Earl of Norfolk and Suffolk and the new constable of Norwich, held the castle from William II. In 1549 Kett's Rebellion against the Protector Somerset's government took a serious turn when Kett recruited some 4,000 peasants and threatened Norwich. The Earl of Warwick, with the help of German mercenaries, defeated the rebels at Mousehold Heath and Kett was hanged from the castle battlements. The keep fell into disrepair sometime before the sixteenth century, as was usual with castles which were county gaols. In 1884 it was purchased by the City Council and it now houses the county museum.

The Norman keep (refaced 1834–39), the entrance tower, the bases of the drum towers of the great gate and three underground rooms of the great gate all remain today, as well as the dry moat and both baileys. Somewhat similar to Castle Rising, the entrance was on the east through Bigod's Tower which had a broken flight of steps up to the great hall on the first floor. A well was discovered near the remains of the cross wall during the conversion of the building to a museum. It is over 100 feet deep and still holds water. A wall gallery runs around the keep at different levels and there is access to it from spiral stairs in opposite corners.

The museum comprises good archaeology and natural history collections and a fine selection of paintings from the Norwich School.
Open 10–5 weekdays (5.30 July and August) and Sundays 2–5. Entrance from Castle Meadow. Admission charge.

THETFORD
One of the largest motte and bailey castles in England, Thetford was built by Earl Warenne and destroyed in 1174. The motte was constructed on the site of an iron age fort.

WORMEGAY
There are only grassy remains of the Norman castle of the Bardolphs and Warrennes.

NORTHAMPTONSHIRE

BARNWELL
A few miles south of Oundle, Barnwell Castle was originally built by Reginald de Moine in 1132, and the remains consist of a quadrangular court with circular towers at each corner and a large south-eastern gateway flanked by two further towers. It was rebuilt in 1264 by another de Moine and passed to the Montague family. Today it stands in the grounds of the seventeenth-century Barnwell Castle, home of H.R.H. the Duke of Gloucester.
Open to the public once a year under the National Gardens Scheme.

CASTLE ASHBY
An eleventh-century castle stood where the fine Elizabethan mansion stands today. Lord Compton, who built the first house, used the ruins as a base and there is no sign of the original castle now.
Marquess of Northampton. Open June–August, Thursdays, Saturdays and Bank Holidays as well as Sundays from Easter to September, 2–5.30. Admission charge.

EARLS BARTON
The Saxon church tower stands within the outer ditch of the motte which was north of the church.

FOTHERINGHAY
Nothing but one small stone wall remains of the famous castle by the Nene where Richard III was born (a plaque

records the event) and Mary Queen of Scots was executed. It was built by Simon de Senlis, first husband of Queen Matilda, and was the home of the Earl of Richmond until Edward II granted it to Edmund Langley, Duke of York. Here Mary Queen of Scots was brought from Chartley Castle in Staffordshire, tried, found guilty, and executed in the great hall on 5th February 1587. The castle was demolished by Lord Newport in 1645 and part of it sold to Sir Bruce Cotton who built Connington, Hunts., with eleven of the great arches from Fotheringhay hall. In 1820 an old soldier called Wyatt was removing stones from the ruins and discovered a ring carved with the initials H and M entwined and the Royal coat of arms of Scotland.

LILBOURNE

Just off the M1 on the road to Rugby, Lilbourne was a Roman fort. King Stephen had a castle here which was held by Gerard de Camville.

NORTHAMPTON

The Castle railway station now stands on the site of the castle and the only piece of de Senlis's castle visible today is a postern gate removed to Black Lion Hill. The town walls were once the strongest and most extensive Norman walls of any English fortified town. It was demolished in 1662 and the final wall was pulled down during the reign of Queen Victoria. The castle was the scene of the last meeting between Thomas à Becket and King Henry II.

PRESTON CAPES

A motte and bailey castle once stood here just east of the church and today there is a castle-like cottage in the village, constructed as a folly for nearby Fawsley Hall.

ROCKINGHAM

The most important of the Northamptonshire castles, Rockingham is very close to the manufacturing town of Corby. It was built by William I, who chose a spur commanding the valley between the Nene and the Welland for a shell-keep 100 feet wide. The massive twin towers of the gatehouse date from 1275. King John captured the castle from the Earl of Albemarle and it was used as a hunting lodge up to the fifteenth century.

In the sixteenth century Edward Watson, who had married the daughter of Lord Chief Justice Montagu, altered the great hall. His son, Sir Edward, entertained James I here in 1604. Forty years later the owner, Sir Lewis Watson, was turned out by Lord Grey of Groby, who fortified the castle for Parliament. At first distrusted by the Royalists, Sir Lewis was tried at Oxford but after a period of imprisonment at Belvoir Castle he won his case and at the Restoration he returned to the castle as Baron Rockingham. He built most of the house where his descendants live today, repairing Parliamentarian damage, although two towers and other alterations were made by Salvin in the nineteenth century. Today the motte is a rose garden and the house has some unusual modern paintings and some relics of Dickens who was a frequent visitor.

Cdr. Michael Saunders Watson. Open Easter–30 September on Sundays, Thursdays and Bank Holidays, 2–6 pm. Guided tours. Admission charge.

RUSHTON

Famous for its triangular lodge built by Sir Thomas Tresham, Rushton Castle was captured in 1140. This may have been the motte in Gaultney wood or the Galclint Castle built between 1148 and 1153.

THORPE WATERVILLE

Near Banbury is a large barn once part of the fortified manor of the bishop of Lichfield. It was moated and held by the Lancastrians at the time of the battle of Towton. The Yorkists took six days to capture it and the event is recorded in the Paston letters.

NORTHUMBERLAND

ALNHAM

This is a tower house near the church and opposite the green mound of a castle motte. The village is reached by turning off A697 at Glanton and going through Great Ryle.

ALNWICK

The first Norman owner of Alnwick was probably Gilbert Tyson or de Tesson. He had been William's standard bearer at Hastings, and he was holder of the lands when Malcolm III of Scotland raided the North in 1093. He was ambushed close to the site of the castle by Robert Mowbray, the Earl of Northumberland. But in 1095 Mowbray rebelled against

William Rufus and was joined by Tyson who thereby forfeited his lands. Yvo de Vescy received the site in 1096 and began building. His only daughter married Eustace Fitzjohn. Even though Fitzjohn fought on the side of David I and Matilda at the battle of the Standard in 1138, Stephen allowed him to keep Alnwick and by the time of his death in Wales in 1157 the castle was complete.

Eustace de Vescy, who held the castle during the reign of King John, allied himself with the Barons and was one of the twenty-five chosen to see that the terms of Magna Carta were enforced. Alnwick had already been threatened with destruction by the angry king, and now was burned when John marched on the North. Before the war was over Eustace was was killed by an arrow from a crossbow while besieging Barnard Castle. John de Vescy, grandson of Eustace, continued the feud against the monarchy by supporting Simon de Montfort at Lewes in 1264. But in 1265 at Evesham, when de Montfort was defeated by Prince Edward, John was wounded and captured. Undaunted, he tried to seize back his confiscated estates, was pardoned and joined Prince Edward on crusade before dying in France in 1288. The Scots under Wallace attacked the castle in 1297 and Henry Percy bought it in 1309. In 1402 the Percys captured the Earl of Douglas and other important Scottish prisoners at the battle of Homildon Hill. Angered by Henry IV's demand that he should take charge of the prisoners Harry Hotspur took advantage of the Glyndwr rebellion in Wales to stage his own revolt which led to his defeat at Shrewsbury by the future Henry V.

Alnwick avoided destruction during the Civil War because it was never irrevocably committed to either side. In 1755 Hugh, Duke of Northumberland, hired Robert Adam to gothicise the castle and the lead figures on the battlements date from this period. Two of the five round towers forming the keep were pulled down in 1854 and a larger north-west tower, known as the Prudhoe Tower, and the chapel were built to designs by Salvin.

Duke of Northumberland. Open May–September daily except Fridays and Saturdays 1–5. No dogs. Admission charge.

ANCROFT

Five miles from Berwick, Ancroft church tower is a three storied pele tower added to the church in the thirteenth century. It is approached through a south doorway and has a spiral staircase. It is an unusual example of a vicar's pele.

AYDON

Near Corbridge, Aydon was crenellated by Robert de Raynes of Bolam in 1305. It is a fortified house with an outer bailey and an inner walled bailey. The first floor hall has a solar at one end with a large fireplace. The south wall outside has an unusual chimney with lancets finishing below the battlements. It has been used as a private house so is in excellent condition.

Department of the Environment. Dates of opening to be announced.

BAMBURGH

The most famous of the castles of the eastern seaboard, Bamburgh appears to be enormous because of its immensely thick walls. In prehistoric times it was a stronghold of the Votadini tribe. It was occupied by the Romans and in 547 became the capital of the Saxon King Ida's kingdom. Ida's grandson Ethelfrith married Bebba and it is assumed that the name Bamburgh is a corruption of Bebbanburgh. Oswald, son of Ethelfrith, united the two kingdoms of Deira and Bernicia after the battle of Heavenfield in 633. He was then at the height of his power. It was he who sent to Iona for a missionary, and welcomed Aidan to Bamburgh and Holy Island on which the monastery of Lindisfarne was founded. On 5th August 642 Mercian invaders hung the remains of King Oswald on three wooden stakes and Bamburgh never regained its prominence as capital of the largest British kingdom. The Vikings sacked the fortress in the ninth century. The Normans recognised the military value of the site, and the rock was fortified, probably with a wooden structure. In 1095 the fortress was held by Robert Mowbray against William Rufus. In attempting to escape while under siege, Mowbray was captured and paraded before his wife who was still in the castle. She surrendered on receiving a message that her husband would lose his eyes if resistance continued. In King Stephen's war the Scots invaded Northumberland and pierced the outer bailey, capturing and killing a hundred defenders. Henry II built the massive keep and strengthened the defences; King John spent money on the construction and installed a constable, who made himself an evil reputation by robbing passing ships. Henry III built the King's Hall (which was restored completely by Ferguson in about 1900). It has a dais and hammerbeam roof.

The most famous constable was Hotspur who led out his army to defeat the Scots at Homildon Hill and then plotted with them against the king and lost his life at Shrewsbury in 1403. After the battle of Towton in 1461, in which the Lancastrian forces of Henry VI were defeated by the newly proclaimed king Edward IV, the North and Bamburgh became the centre of the great struggle. Henry and his Queen, Margaret, escaped to Scotland pursued by the Earl of Warwick. The castle was surrendered to Edward, but it was immediately re-taken and occupied by Queen Margaret. She escaped on hearing of the approach of Warwick's army and left the castle under Sir Ralph Percy's command. In December the siege began and the defenders were soon eating horse-meat. On Christmas Eve they surrendered, but broke the treaty and filled the castle with reinforcements. Henry joined the defenders and the cat and mouse affair ended when in June 1464, after the battle of Hexham, Bamburgh became the first English castle to surrender to gunpowder.

Bamburgh was a ruin when it was purchased by Lord Crewe in 1704. Lady Crewe's nephew, Thomas Forster, the Jacobite general at Preston in 1715, spent much of his life at Bamburgh. In 1722 Lord Crewe died and it passed to a charity administered by Dr Sharp, who set up a school and a life-boat station there, restoring the building with his own money. Over a hundred years later the charity continued until the first Lord Armstrong of Vickers Armstrong took over the property when the functions of the charity devolved upon public authorities. Apart from the Great Hall already mentioned, the ruins were restored to contain eight flats for public tenants, two for staff and accommodation for the Armstrongs. No other British castle, with the exception of Windsor, houses so many people.
Open to the public every day except Saturdays, Easter–September, 2–8. Guided tour. Admission charge.

BASTLES

This guidebook does not list the border country bastles – defensive houses built by small farmers or country families who put their beasts in the ground floor and lived on the top floor. Entrance was by an outside ladder, replaced later by stone steps, and the ground floor door was closed by internal wooden bolts. The man who locked up the animals had an internal ladder to reach the floor above and there was a first floor fireplace and usually two or more windows set in the walls. The complete bastle usually measured about 25 feet by 35 feet and had a steeply pitched roof, tiled or thatched. Fine examples can be seen at Hole, near Bellingham,

Northumberland, and Tarset, near Greenhaugh, Northumberland.

BELLISTER
Near Haltwhistle, Bellister is a square tower attached to a Victorian house standing on a low motte once surrounded by a moat. It was the home of the Blenkinsop family.

BELSAY
In a field behind the nineteenth-century mansion stands Belsay tower, three storeys high with four bartizans. It is well preserved, with a modern roof and was the home of the Middletons. The topmost bartizan has a small chamber fitted out during the last war as a radio room for reporting on enemy aircraft.

BERWICK-ON-TWEED
Once a very important castle, only the water tower by the river and some of the Elizabethan walls, best seen on the north side of the town, remain. Berwick changed hands many times before the union of the English and Scottish crowns in 1603.

BLENKINSOPP
Near Haltwhistle, Blenkinsopp was crenellated in 1349. Stones from the Roman wall were used to build the tower. A farmhouse was added at a later date. There are two ghosts at Blenkinsopp, one of a white lady who searches in vain for treasure which she hid and thereby lost her husband's love; the other is a black dog which appears when someone in the house is going to die.

BOTHAL
Near Morpeth, Bothal was crenellated in 1343. The gatehouse remains in the form of a keep. On the parapet are stone figures of knights as at Alnwick and the battlements were equipped with shutters. Little remains of the bailey. *Duke of Portland. Not open to the public.*

BURRADON
Near Seghill six miles north of Newcastle, Burradon Tower dates from the sixteenth century and, although in ruins, has a brattice above the entrance. It was formerly connected to two buildings since destroyed.

121

BYWELL

Close to Prudhoe but on the other side of the Tyne, Bywell is a fifteenth-century tower, built by the Nevilles as the gatehouse to a castle never completed. Part of a curtain wall goes to the old gun house, which has been modernised. There was a Roman bridge over the river here but the castle was not built to defend a river crossing.

Duke of Portland. Not open to the public.

CALLALY

The first castle was built in the reign of Henry II and was sited 600 yards north-east of the present building but the lady of the house determined to have it in the more sheltered valley. The house is seventeenth-century with nineteenth-century additions, and the south-west tower is a fifteenth-century pele tower. This was built by the Claverings, a Royalist family, who in 1715 fought for the Jacobites at Preston. There is a portrait of General Forster, the inexperienced commander at Preston, in the hall.

Major A. S. C. Brown DL. Open to the public weekends May–September and Bank Holiday Mondays 2.15–6. No dogs allowed. Admission charge.

CARTINGTON

One of the most unusual and interesting ruins in the county, Cartington stands in farmland two miles from Rothbury on the Thropton–Wittingham road, and was probably a thirteenth-century tower but it has been drastically altered. In 1494 it passed to the Radcliffes and during the Civil War it was used as a Royalist armoury. In 1648 it was besieged and held out for two hours before surrendering to the Parliamentarians. In 1660 it was rebuilt by the Widdringtons who built the imposing gateway. Further repairs were carried out by Lord Armstrong in Victorian times but now it is very decayed. The field below the tower has signs of a rampart wall probably built during the Civil War.

CHILLINGHAM

Originally this was a fourteenth-century tower built by Sir Thomas de Heton, added to in the fifteenth century. Now there is a quadrangular house with a deep dungeon in the north-west tower. It is empty at the moment and not open to the public although the famous wild cattle can be visited every day from April to September.

CHIPCHASE

Easily seen from the Chollerton-Wark road, Chipchase is a Jacobean house with a tower dating from 1350. It belonged to the Herons, one of whom was High Sheriff of the county and was killed by the Scots in the skirmish at Reidswire in 1575. It is not open to the public.

COCKLAW TOWER

Near Chollerton, Cocklaw was built by the Erringtons and had two storeys.

COCKLE PARK TOWER

Just south of Earsdon off the A1 north of Morpeth, this is one of the latest towers built in the county, being mid-sixteenth century. It has bartizans and is oblong in shape. It is used as a students' hostel and can be visited with permission from the director of Newcastle University experimental farm.

CORBRIDGE

The vicar's pele in the churchyard is one of the best preserved towers in the county.

COUPLAND

Near Millfield, this is a late tower house which belonged to the Akeld family.

CRASTER TOWER

Just outside the little port, Craster is a fifteenth-century tower with eighteenth-century additions and still belongs to the Craster family.
Open to the public by written permission only.

CRESSWELL

This small tower on the coast was built by the Baker-Cresswells. It is in excellent condition.

DALLEY

A small ruin near Tarset, this was probably a bastle house to which turrets were added later. Now it has only a few stones and a blocked-up slit window.

DILSTON

On a hill above the Hexham-Corbridge level crossing, Dilston consists of a rectangular tower house with a chapel

123

and archway probably dating from the seventeenth century. The famous Earl of Derwentwater lived here. On 6th October, 1715, at the age of 26, he rode off reaching Preston in November with about 2700 men. After one day's gallant resistance he surrendered to General Carpenter and was executed in London. His brother inherited Dilston but lived abroad until he was captured on board a French ship in 1745 and he, too, was executed. The castle estate was sold to Greenwich hospital and today the house on the site is a children's home. Traditionally, the aurora borealis is supposed to be clearly visible every 24th February, the anniversary of Lord Derwentwater's execution.

DUDDO

Between Berwick and Ford, a small portion of Duddo tower remains on a knoll. It belonged to the Stirlings and later the Claverings.

DUNSTANBURGH

On the site of a Saxon burh or fortified settlement, the gaunt remains of Dunstanburgh are accessible only on foot. They stand on the Great Whin Sill and it is easy to imagine the site surrounded by sea. The site belonged to the barony of Embleton and in the thirteenth century to Simon de Montfort. At his death it passed to the earls of Lancaster, and Thomas, the second earl who became High Steward of England, built the castle. In 1313 work was started and the licence was granted three years later when most of it was finished. It is doubtful whether it was ever impregnable as it covers such a large area.

Earl Thomas was beheaded at Pontefract after the battle of Boroughbridge in 1322 and the castle passed in 1324 to Henry, Duke of Lancaster, and then to his granddaughter Blanche, John of Gaunt's wife. John altered the great gatehouse, which was blocked and turned into a keep. The new entrance on the south-west had a mantlet and additional tower with a drawbridge as extra protection. The inner ward was made at the same time.

Dunstanburgh became a Lancastrian stronghold during the Wars of the Roses and sheltered many who escaped from the great defeat at Towton. After the Lancastrian defeat at the battle of Hexham in 1464 the castle surrendered to the Earl of Warwick who occupied it for Edward IV. It was repaired in 1436 and again in 1470, but in 1524 the lead was stripped off and used to repair the castle at Wark-on-Tweed because the Scots could bypass Dunstanburgh but Wark, being on the border, was more important. Elizabeth I had Dunstanburgh surveyed but decided it was not worth repairing and for many years it belonged to the earls of Tankerville before becoming ministry property.

The castle is best approached from Craster harbour and the path crosses the harbour once used by the castle; but the old route ran across the low-lying land on a causeway. The approach from Embleton golf course is longer but in many respects more dramatic.

Department of the Environment. Open at normal times. Admission charge.

DUNSTAN HALL

Near Craster, this is a house with a tower dating from the fourteenth and fifteenth centuries. It was probably more of a fortified house than a pele tower.

EDLINGHAM

Between Alnwick and Rothbury, Edlingham tower stands in a field near the church. It belonged to the Swinburnes. The entrance leads into the first floor hall, which was vaulted. The basement is now filled with earth.

ELSDON

The Umfravilles built the vicar's pele at Elsdon which is inhabited and is not open to the public. On the road to Thropton there is a fine motte and bailey castle.

EMBLETON

Not far from Dunstanburgh, the vicarage at Embleton has a pele tower attached to it.

ETAL

This unusual castle near Norham was crenellated in 1342 and consists of a massive gatehouse and an equally massive keep with a piece of connecting wall. It belonged to the Manners family and was knocked down by the Scots before Flodden.

FEATHERSTONE

Near Haltwhistle stands Featherstone, a pele tower with two watch-towers at one time surrounded by a moat. It was built by the Featherstonehaugh family. One of them raised

125

a troop of horse to fight for Charles II at Worcester, but was captured and later executed in Lancashire. The Wallaces added to Featherstone in 1812.

FORD

This large quadrangular castle stands on the Till near Etal. William Heron obtained a licence to crenellate his manor at Ford in 1338. It was attacked and burnt by the Scots in 1513 in spite of Lady Heron's efforts to persuade the English commander, the Earl of Surrey, to come to her aid. It must have been efficiently repaired for in 1549 the Scots again attacked it, this time with four guns. The French general Esse was beaten off by young Thomas Carr, son of the governor of Wark, who was besieged in the north-west tower. The young man married a Heron heiress and inherited the castle much to the resentment of the other Herons. It passed to the Blakes and Delavals and in 1861 it was extensively rebuilt by the Marchioness of Waterford. It is now a field study centre belonging to Northumberland County Council and is not open to the public.

GREAT TOSSON

This ruined tower house, with very thick ashlar walls, is near Whitton. It was used as a watch-tower from which the watchkeeper would sound the alarm by blowing a sheep-horn.

HALTON

The de Haltons built this picturesque tower which has Jacobean and seventeenth-century additions. It passed to the Caranbys, who were Royalists and suffered after Marston Moor. The castle was bought by John Douglas in 1706 and then passed to the Blacketts.

HARBOTTLE

Inland from Rothbury, the small village of Harbottle on the Coquet river is dominated by the ruin of a large castle. Built by Robert d'Umfraville between 1159 and 1160, it had a shell-keep and two baileys. It was captured by the men of Galloway in 1174. In 1515 it belonged to Lord Dacre, Warden of the Middle March. Queen Margaret, widow of James IV of Scotland, came here with her second husband, the Earl of Angus. Her daughter, born in the castle, was a grand-

126

mother of James I of England. In 1584 Harbottle was repaired and the two oillets now visible in the keep probably date from this time. Garrisoned by 100 soldiers, it was an important Crown fortress commanding the road from Jedburgh over the Cheviots. An extra garrison of part-time soldiers from neighbouring villages could be mustered if required.

HARNHAM

The Babingtons owned this tower near Belsay which stands above a sixteenth-century house. Dame Katherine Babington, a dissenter, was buried in the garden and the inscription remains on her tomb.

HAUGHTON

This impressive castle is best seen from the main road between Chollerton and Wark-on-Tyne. It is similar to Langley but larger, with five towers dating from 1373 when the Widdringtons fortified it. Once it was surrounded by a curtain wall and there was a chapel in the grounds. Salvin had a hand in the Victorian alterations in 1876. Though not open to the public, Haughton is visible from the public footpath leading from the village.

HEATON

Very little remains of the fortified manor of Sir Thomas Grey, which was once large enough to hold 300 horsemen. It stands on the river Till and is part of Newcastle.

HEPPLE

Near Harbottle, Hepple tower stands in the garden of a modern house. It has a bastle with a gable staircase added to it and much of the tunnel vaulting survives. It belonged to Sir Robert Ogle and once had a garrison of twenty men.

HORTON

Nothing remains of de Charron's thirteenth-century castle near Seaton Delaval. It once had a double moat but the site was levelled to build a farmhouse.

HOWTEL TOWER

Near Flodden, Howtel is a fifteenth-century tower, the south wall of which is three storeys high. It was destroyed by the Scots in the fifteenth century.

LANGLEY

Near Haydon Bridge, Langley Castle is a well restored tower house dating originally from 1350. It was built by Sir Thomas Lucy, one of the commanders at Crecy and Neville's Cross. It was Lancastrian during the Wars of the Roses and Lord Montague captured it in 1464. For a time it belonged to the Radcliffes, but after their involvement in the Jacobite rebellion of 1715, it was settled on Greenwich Hospital. The Governor sold it to a Mr Cadwallader Bates, whose family owns it today.

Langley is oblong in shape with four protruding towers and an entrance at ground-floor level defended only by a portcullis. The south-west tower has a spiral stone staircase and on each floor there are two fireplaces and a tunnel-vaulted guardroom.

Open to the public on Wednesdays only, May–September, 2–7. Admission charge.

LINDISFARNE

Lindisfarne or Holy Island Castle, a landmark crowning the highest point on the island, was originally a Tudor fort built in 1542 when the harbour was used as an advance base for an expedition against the Scots organised by Lord Hertford. During the early part of the Civil War Captain Rugg held Lindisfarne for the King. It fell into Parliamentary hands in 1645 and when Langdale captured Berwick a strong force was stationed there. In 1675 another fort was built covering the sea approaches.

In 1715 a Jacobite, Laurence Errington, with his nephew captured the fort for one night when only two of the garrison of seven were on duty. The Berwick garrison soon recaptured it and Errington was marched back with his nephew to Berwick jail. Later they escaped, obtained a pardon, and opened an inn in Newcastle.

During the Napoleonic Wars, Lindisfarne continued to be garrisoned and when the guns were withdrawn in 1819 it became a coastguard station and centre for the Northumberland Artillery Volunteers. In 1902 it was purchased by the owner of *Country Life*, Edward Hudson, who commissioned Edwin Lutyens to turn it into a home. Today it has four living-rooms and nine bedrooms with a magnificent view from the upper battery windows. Inside, the simple furniture, much of it designed by Lutyens, makes it one of the most intriguing inhabited castles in the country with a setting second to none.

*National Trust. Open April–September 1–5 daily except
Tuesday. Open Wednesdays only 24 June–25 July. Closed
Good Friday. Admission charge. Before visiting the castle,
visitors should check the tide timetable in the local newspaper
or on the noticeboard at the A1 junction with the road to
Beal and Lindisfarne.*

LITTLE HARLE

Near Kirkharle, the Victorian mansion incorporates a pele
tower. It belonged to the Fenwick and Aynsley families.

LITTLE SWINBURNE

The Middletons of Belsay owned this ruined pele tower
near Thockrington. It was once surrounded by a barmkin.

MITFORD

On the junction of the Wansbeck and the Font, Mitford
ruins stand in a field opposite the church. The castle was
erected in 1150 for William Bertram, brother of Balliol,
founder of Barnard Castle. It has a ruined five-sided keep
with two baileys. By Leland's time it was uninhabitable, which
probably explains why the Mitfords built a seventeenth-
century fortified house next to the church. The porch tower
of this house remains. Nearby is the nineteenth-century
Mitford Hall.
Not open to the public.

MORPETH

William de Merlay's castle at Morpeth dates from 1095.
It passed to the Greystokes and William Greystoke built the
fifteenth-century gatehouse with its peaked tower roof. The
motte and bailey castle was once surrounded by a strong
curtain wall. During the Civil War, it was held by Parliament
until attacked in 1644 by Montrose who battered it into
submission.
The gatehouse is not open to the public.

NAFFERTON

Near Prudhoe, Nafferton was an adulterine castle built
by Philip de Ulecote during King John's reign and the
remains of a large keep and two baileys stand on the bank
of Whittle Dene near the A69 bridge. Richard d'Umfraville
at Prudhoe obtained a writ from the Crown restraining
Philip from completing Nafferton. The timber tower was
transported to Newcastle and in revenge Philip tried to
restrain Richard from completing Harbottle.

NEWCASTLE

The Romans first fortified the Tyne at Newcastle where Hadrian built the first bridge. The Normans had a fort here and then Henry II constructed the new castle 1172-7, but now only the keep, the Black Gate and a part of the curtain remain.

The Black Gate was built in 1247 and houses the Bagpipe Museum. It consists of a vaulted passage and twin towers. It was the main entrance of the castle leading to a drawbridge across a ditch and the North Gate.

The massive keep, dating from 1172, has walls 15 feet thick and an entrance through a forebuilding to the second floor. During the Civil War the Scots captured Newcastle but the mayor and Sir John Marley held out for a further three days in the keep. After that it was used for many years as a gaol. It has a hall and king's chamber, and battlements restored in 1809 by William Dobson. The chapel is below the hall and has a fine zigzag frieze. It now houses a museum. *Open to the public Tuesdays to Saturdays 10–5, Mondays 2–5, April–September; October–March 10–4 Tuesdays–Saturdays, Mondays 2–4. Admission charge. Closed winter, Bank holidays and Good Friday.*

NORHAM

One of the strongest of Northumberland's castles, Norham lies on the Tweed halfway between Wark and Berwick. It was part of the Durham palatinate and the castle was built to command the ford and had a constable appointed by the bishop of Durham. The motte and bailey erected by Bishop Flambard in 1121 was destroyed in two Scottish raids. The existing castle was built by Bishop Hugh in Henry II's reign. It was finished in 1174 and in the same year surrendered to the King, Bishop Hugh being suspected of treason.

In 1215 Alexander II of Scotland besieged it without success. King John visited Norham and in 1217 it was restored to the bishopric. During Edward I's campaign in Scotland, his queen lived there. In 1318 Bishop Lewis appointed Sir Thomas Grey as constable. For a year the castle was under Scottish attack and desperate fighting took place. A Lincolnshire knight, Sir William Marmion, in a spirit of chivalry, charged the Scots single-handed to honour his lady. He was only rescued from death by Grey and others of the garrison who rushed to his help when he was unhorsed.

In Edward III's reign Norham was finally captured by the Scots but did not come to much harm. Soon restored to the bishops it was repaired and during the Wars of the Roses was besieged by the Lancastrians, holding out only to fall by treachery in 1464. In 1497 Bishop Fox was present during another siege. He was responsible for building the aqueduct and for the water tanks in the moat which were probably used as an extra water supply.

Shortly before Flodden in 1513 James IV captured Norham with the help of Mons Meg, the mighty cannon of Edinburgh Castle. The castle was repaired and gunners from Portsmouth were added to its garrison. After the Scottish victory at Ancrum Moor in 1545 Norham was immediately repaired and garrisoned by the Earl of Hertford. In 1559 Norham became Crown property and gradually decayed when the borders became peaceful.

The gun ports on the north-west wall are of interest and the arches by the Sheep Gate are very different to any other in the castle. According to the Ministry these form the substructure of the curtain wall.

Department of the Environment. Open at normal times. Admission charge.

OGLE

Not far from Belsay, Ogle is a fourteenth-century tower house, now a farmhouse. The wounded King David of Scotland was brought here after being captured at Neville's Cross in 1346. The Ogles have always been Royalists and the Duke of Newcastle, who fled abroad after his defeat at Marston Moor, was also Earl of Ogle. Ogle once had a semicircular towered curtain wall surrounded by two moats with a drawbridge entrance.

OTTERBURN

The tower house at Otterburn is now a hotel. It belonged to the Halls of Redesdale.

PRESTON TOWER

Near Ellingham, in the grounds of modern Preston Tower, Preston had four corner turrets only two of which are now standing. It was built by the Sheriff of Dunstanburgh, Robert Harbottle. It was restored by the Baker-Cresswells in 1864 for use as a clock-tower.

PRUDHOE

On the Newcastle to Hexham road, Prudhoe Castle is at Low Prudhoe, near the Tyne. The river course has altered since the castle was built and the steep bank and river obviously formed one solid defensive barrier with a ditch on the other three sides. The stone castle was probably built in the reign of Henry II by Odinel d'Umfraville. In 1174 the Scots failed to take it in a three-day siege. It remained with the d'Umfravilles for nearly four hundred years before passing to the Percys when Henry Percy married the widow of the last of the d'Umfravilles.

The castle is of great interest because of its unusual gate-house and barbican, and its old keep. The main entrance has a chapel above it with an oriel window. The barbican was added in the fourteenth century with a drawbridge and an outer gatehouse; a mill-pond was sited at the entrance. The nineteenth-century owner who built the house near to the keep filled in and levelled the outer bailey with several feet of earth.

Department of the Environment. Opening times to be announced shortly.

ROCK HALL

Near Preston, Rock Hall incorporates a Norman pele tower which was considerably altered in Tudor times. It was burnt down in 1752 and restored by the Bosanquets.

RUDCHESTER

Near Heddon-on-the-wall, Rudchester Tower is a Georgian house incorporating a late tower house which belonged to the Catholic family of Rutherford.

SEATON DELAVAL

A Norman castle stood where Sir John Vanbrugh's mansion now stands. Only the chapel remains of the old castle and this has been considerably altered.

Lord Hastings. Open May–September, Wednesdays, Sundays and Bank Holidays 2–6. Admission charge.

SHILBOTTLE

Not far from Alnwick, this is a vicar's pele adjoining the church, dating from the fourteenth century and much restored.

SHORTFLATT HOUSE

Robert de Raynes built this tower in 1305. It had a house added to it in the seventeenth century and is still inhabited.

According to tradition, in 1715 a dog used to take provisions from the tower to nearby Shafto Crags, where Lord Derwentwater had a hiding place.

SIMONBURN

A very attractive village off B6320, Simonburn has a fine bastle house and a short distance to the north-west is a ruined thirteenth-century tower built by the Herons of Chipchase and restored in 1766 as an eyecatcher. In the sixteenth century it was the home of the Keeper of Tynedale.

STAWARD

Near Langley Castle, high up over the West Allen, little remains of Staward, which dates from the fourteenth century.

SWINBURNE

Near Haughton, Swinburne ruins stand near the eighteenth-century house.

TARSET

Now a large green mound on the Upper Tyne not far from Dalley ruins, Tarset was built by Black Comyn, a Scot, during Henry III's reign, at a time of comparative peace in the borders. It was completely destroyed when the Fenwicks lived there, and its stones were dispersed.

THIRLWALL

Built of stones from the Roman wall near Greenhead, it was inhabited by John de Thirlwall and at one time stood in Scotland. It had a yett and an east tower.
Ruins open at all times.

TWIZELL

Near Flodden, Twizell bridge is fifteenth-century and above it on the Till bank is a ruined castle. On the site of a pele tower destroyed by the Scots, it is a folly built by Sir Francis Blake in 1770 and never completed.

TYNEMOUTH

In the grounds of the Priory at Tynemouth, Robert de Mowbray built a wall and ditch with a strong gatehouse. Licence to crenellate dates from 1296 and the gatehouse dates from the early fifteenth century. It had bartizan towers like Belsay and was protected by a barbican.

Foundations of the curtain wall and a square tower known as Whitley Tower remain, but there was never a keep. It was used as a prison in the sixteenth century and fortified by the Marquess of Newcastle in 1642. It was captured by the Scots and the deputy governor, Colonel Lilburne, changed sides releasing all the Royalist prisoners. Hazelrigg recaptured it and Lilburne and others were executed. In 1783 it was used as a barracks and various extra buildings were erected.

Department of the Environment. Open normal times including Sunday mornings May–September. Admission charge.

WALLINGTON

The Fenwicks had a tower house here, dating from the fourteenth century, which was destroyed and the foundations are incorporated in Wallington Hall, one of the finest showplaces of Northumberland. The painted hall, depicting incidents in the history of Northumberland, should not be missed.

National Trust. Open April–September, daily except Tuesday 2–6. Admission charge. Garden opposite open daily 10–6, weekends 10–7.

WARK-ON-TWEED

Only the motte remains of one of the most important border castles. It was built early in the twelfth century, destroyed by King David of Scotland in 1138 and rebuilt by Robert de Roos between 1158 and 1161. In 1519 the castle was repaired and the keep enlarged by the Greys. It had two baileys and, when enlarged, the keep was three times the size of Alnwick.

WARK-ON-TYNE

The remains of a motte and bailey castle are visible on the road to Humshaugh.

WARKWORTH

Near Alnmouth on the Coquet river, Warkworth was once the property of the monks of Lindisfarne. It then passed to the rulers of Northumbria. The castle was built after 1139 by Henry, Earl of Northumberland, son of David I of Scotland. It was in a very weak condition when it was granted by Henry II to Roger Fitz-Richard, constable of Newcastle, in recognition of his bravery in a campaign against the Welsh.

His son Robert retained the property on payment of 300 marks to King John in 1199. He built the gatehouse and probably the keep. Robert's son John succeeded in 1214 and on his death in 1240 Roger, the next in line, succeeded. He was killed in a tournament and during the minority of his heir, Robert, Earl of Pembroke was in charge of the castle. After Robert's death in 1310 his son John of Clavering succeeded. During the war with Scotland in 1322–23 Warkworth held out against Bruce's army but the high cost of equipping the garrison obliged the Claverings to leave and when John died in 1332 the castle passed to Lord Percy of Alnwick. The history of the castle henceforward is similar to that of Alnwick.

After the Percy rebellion in 1403 further conspiracy obliged Henry IV to take Warkworth which he gave to his son John, Duke of Bedford. Henry V restored it to the Percys but the Wars of the Roses saw it pass to Warwick the Kingmaker. Repaired in 1480 it became once more Percy property and the Lion Tower dates from this period. The sixth earl repaired it, rebuilding the gateway and south wall. He left it to Henry VIII, who granted it to Lord Grey, his Lieutenant of the Borders. Sir Thomas Percy was restored to Warkworth by Queen Mary in 1557. He took part in the Rising of the North in 1569 and forfeited his property and his head. It then fell into decay and when the Greys of Chillingham owned it in the seventeenth century it ceased to be habitable. The gates were left open and cattle grazed in the bailey. After the Scots occupied it during the Civil War it was demolished by the Percy estate and used to build a house at Chirton.

The fourth Duke of Northumberland restored the keep in the nineteenth century and today the look-out tower is still in good condition but is not open to the public. Warkworth is a maze of complicated buildings and the visitor needs a plan to understand them. The medieval bridge and the Hermitage nearby should also be visited.

Department of the Environment. Open at normal times. Admission charge.

WEST BEECHFIELD

This tower, attached to a seventeenth-century house, stands in an isolated position near Belsay. It belonged to the Fenwicks.

WHITTON TOWER

Overlooking Rothbury, on the bank of the Coquet river, Whitton dates from the fourteenth century and has vaulting on two storeys. Until recently it was Rothbury vicarage; it is now the Ethel Satson Children's Home.
Gardens open to the public with permission from the Sister-in-charge.

WILLIMOTESWICK

Near Bellingham, two towers remain together with a strong gatehouse. It dates from the fifteenth century and was the home of the Ridleys, the most famous of whom was the martyr Bishop Ridley, burnt at the stake in Oxford during Queen Mary's reign.

NOTTINGHAMSHIRE

BLYTH

The Norman castle of Roger de Builli once stood here but it fell into disuse after the building of Tickhill in Yorkshire.

CUCKNEY

On the opposite hill to Bolsover, Derbyshire, and separated from it by the M1, Cuckney once belonged to a Saxon, who was granted a horse from the king if he could shoe the royal horse without laming or pricking the foot. The castle stood by the church and was built by Thomas de Cuckney, the founder of Welbeck Abbey.

GREASLEY

Near the Derbyshire border, and not far from Byron's resting place at Hucknall Torkard, are the remains of a wall and moat of the fourteenth-century castle of Lord Cantelupe. It is incorporated into a farmhouse.

HAYTON

Not far from Retford, the de Hayton family had a castle of which only a portion of the moat remains.

NEWARK

One of the most important castles in the north, Newark-on-Trent lies on the Roman Foss Way and on the Great North Road where it crosses the river Trent. The castle that stands today was built by Alexander, Bishop of Lincoln, who also built Banbury and Sleaford castles.

King John held the castle until the close of his reign when it was seized by the barons. In October 1216, the weary King spent the last three days of his life here. When he died his body was moved, as he wished, to Worcester where his monument stands in the cathedral. The barons held the castle against Henry III and for eight days Lord Pembroke battered it with his siege engines before it surrendered. In 1480 Bishop Rotherham altered the Great Hall, adding an oriel window, and in 1547 the castle reverted to the crown. Later it was leased to Sir Francis Leeke at an annual rent of 53s 4d. James I stopped here on his way to the throne of England and was so horrified at the state of the prisoners that he freed them all.

During the Civil War the town of Newark was a Royalist outpost. Well defended by the rivers Trent and Devon, with the earthwork cannon platforms known as the King's Sconce and the Queen's Sconce protecting the Foss Way, it was a difficult position to attack. The first siege was beaten off in 1643 but in 1644 Sir John Meldrum arrived with a force of over 8,000 men. Prince Rupert with 6,000 men came to the rescue in the early hours of 21st March and, before all his men had arrived, attacked the Parliamentary horse on Beacon Hill. Meldrum moved into the 'island' and Sir Richard Byron attacked him across the river from the castle. Surprised, and alarmed at his lack of provisions, Meldrum surrendered. A further Parliamentary attack was defeated by Langdale's Horse and after Naseby Charles came to Newark twice, for it was his only safe refuge in the north-east. On the second occasion there occurred the quarrel with Prince Rupert after which the Prince virtually ceased to play any further part in the struggle. John Belasyse, the new governor of the castle, held out against the Scots under Leslie, as well as against the English, until May 1646 when he was summoned to surrender by Charles himself. The king had walked into the Scots camp at Kelham and no one was more surprised at the command than the unfortunate Belasyse, a veteran of Edgehill, who escaped to France where he was killed in a drunken brawl.

The castle's north gateway dating from 1170 is the largest of any castle in England. In the north end of the structure is an undercroft which was below the state apartments. Today Newark Castle is seen best from the Trent bridge for, although slighted in 1646, the ruins are well preserved.

Newark Corporation. Grounds open at all reasonable times.
Parties of six or more shown round by guide on application
to the Curator, Newark Museum, Appleton Gate. Admission
charge.

NOTTINGHAM

The castle today is very different from the medieval building. It was built by William I in 1068 above the river Leen
and in the late fifteenth century had three baileys with three
gateways and two large towers. The keep was built in 1213,
as were numerous smaller towers and living quarters.

King John called it his favourite castle but it was in 1330
that the castle earned its real fame. Three years before this
Mortimer and Queen Isabella had contrived the murder of
Edward II at Berkeley castle. Edward III, urged by his
supporters to dispose of Mortimer, organised a party with
Sir William Eland the deputy constable and a few others to
enter the castle at night, possibly by way of an underground
passage known as Mortimer's Hole, still visible today. Mortimer was dragged out of his chamber in the inner ward and
taken to London where he was given a mock trial and
hanged at Tyburn.

Richard III raised his army here against Henry Tudor and
in 1642 the Royalist standard of Charles I was raised on a
hill to the north of the castle. The street is now called
Standard Hill Street. It was a dreadful day and the wind
blew the flag down during the night which many considered
an ill omen for the war. From 1643 Colonel Hutchinson
was the Parliamentary governor in the 'very ruinous and
uninhabitable' castle, and it was his wife, Lady Hutchinson,
who wrote the famous memoirs. After the war Colonel
Hutchinson instigated the demolition of the structure and
the Duke of Newcastle, who acquired the site, built an
Italian style house. This was burnt during the Reform Bill
riots in 1831. The present art museum, the first provincial
one in England, houses exhibitions of fine lace, sixteenth
to eighteenth-century costume, silver, local archaeology
and medieval alabasters as well as a collection of paintings
by artists like Kneller, Bonington, Sandby and Richard
Wilson.

Nottingham Corporation. Open weekdays 10–6.45 (5.45 on
Fridays) in summer, and 10–dusk in winter. Sundays 2–4.45.
Admission free except Sundays and Bank Holidays when there
is a charge. Grounds open weekdays 8–dusk. Sundays 9–dusk.
Limited parking.

WIVERTON

Nine miles east of Nottingham, Wiverton Castle was built by Sir Thomas Chaworth in 1446. It was destroyed during the Civil War but the gatehouse was incorporated into Wiverton Hall which was built in 1814.

WORKSOP

The castle stood on Castle Hill on the north-west side of the town and was built in the twelfth century by the founder of the Priory, William de Lovetot.

OXFORDSHIRE

ASCOT D'OILLY

Between Burford and Chipping Norton off A361 stood a Norman tower believed to have been built by Robert D'Oyley, the builder of Oxford Castle. The site was excavated in 1946 and arrow heads, nails, glass and a horseshoe were discovered.

BAMPTON

Now part of a farmhouse, Bampton Castle was built in 1315 by Aylmer de Valence. It passed to the Talbot family and later to Jesus College, Oxford.

BANBURY

The gatehouse of this Norman castle stood by the north-east end of the market place and it was protected on one side by the river Cherwell. It formed the headquarters of the Royalists under Compton who finally surrendered it to Whalley in May 1646. It was then slighted and the owner Lord Saye and Sele received £2,000 as compensation.

BEAUMONT

At Mixbury near the Buckinghamshire border, Beaumont Castle was built by Roger d'Ivry and in 1194 it was one of the five official tournament grounds in England. Excavations in 1954 revealed a deep well together with an underground passage in the north-west corner.

BROUGHTON

Broughton Castle, three miles west of Banbury, dates from the thirteenth century. The original house at Broughton was built by John de Broughton and much of it remains. A later owner, Thomas Wykeham, heir to William of Wykeham, obtained a licence to crenellate. He built the gatehouse and the wall round the manor house and constructed the wide moat, once crossed by a drawbridge. His granddaughter married William, Lord Saye and Sele, who rebuilt the old manor. The castle was greatly enlarged in the sixteenth century, turning it into the Elizabethan manor that stands today.

The most famous Lord Saye and Sele was William, the first Viscount, who held secret meetings in his upstairs room with his fellow Parliamentarians, including Pym, Lord Brook, John Hampden and Henry Vane. The Viscount and his four sons all went to fight at Edgehill in Sir John Meldrum's brigade of foot. They were well equipped and today one can still see their swords neatly lined up in the castle hall. All returned home but not for long, because Prince Rupert occupied the castle after the battle. His troopers must have been too exhausted to do any damage, and after the Restoration Charles II honoured Lord Saye and Sele by making his old enemy Lord Privy Seal.

The house contains many fine pictures, including a Gainsborough and a portrait by Mirevelt of Nathaniel Fiennes in his yellow coat and scarf. He was a Parliamentary colonel, condemned to death for surrendering Bristol to Prince Rupert, but later pardoned. His daughter Celia wrote an account of her journeys round England – a book that remains today one of the best descriptions of life in the eighteenth century.

Open April–September; Wednesdays and Bank Holidays only 2–5.30 1st and 2nd Sundays June–September. Admission charge.

DEDDINGTON
The vast outer bailey earthworks now enclose a football field. From here 'The Black Dog of Arden', alias Guy of Warwick, carried off Piers Gaveston, friend of Edward II, to his death at Warwick.

GREYS COURT
Unlike Broughton, Greys Court, a few miles north of Henley, is a castle without a moat. It was built by the second John de Grey, a favourite of Edward III, who obtained a licence to crenellate in 1348. The manor had been obtained by the Greys in the reign of King John, the first Grey,

Walter, being Archbishop of York. The last Grey died in 1387 and the estate eventually passed to his granddaughter Alice, the wife of Viscount Lovell of Minster Lovell. Lord Lovell, the friend of Richard III, was attainted after the battles of Bosworth and Stoke, escaping from the latter by riding his horse across the Trent (*see* Minster Lovell, Oxfordshire).

Greys Court was given to Jasper, Duke of Bedford, by Henry VII, and Henry VIII presented it to Robert Knowles, whose family lived here for many years. Under Elizabeth, Francis Knowles, Treasurer to the Household, possessed it and his son William became Earl of Banbury. In 1622 the Earl of Somerset and his wife came here to live with William, who married the countess's sister. They were involved in the strange murder of Sir Thomas Overbury and were sent to Greys Court as prisoners. They hated each other so much that they lived in separate towers at the castle. William's two sons, born when he was over eighty, were disinherited by the House of Lords and the resulting lawsuit continued until the reign of George III.

During the Civil War the castle was held for the King and guarded the approach from Henley. It was captured and badly damaged, the Elizabethan house having to be pulled down, making way for the Restoration building with a Georgian garden front we see today. The old castle had four towers and a large curtain wall. Within the bailey is a well with a donkey wheel. (When the donkey was retired recently it returned to work the wheel on its own.) Only three towers remain: the south-west and the north-east are octagonal, the south-east tower is square shaped with oillets. The brickwork of the small building attached to the south-east tower is very fine and some of the towers have herringbone flint and brick mixed.

Inside the Cromwell Room, opposite the house, is a large chest where Lord Lovell's young bride is supposed to have hidden while playing on her wedding day. No one found her until it was too late and she had suffocated. The sad affair was attributed to the fact that mistletoe was hanging inside the castle although it was not Christmas week. A poem *The Mistletoe Bough* by Thomas Haynes Bayley describes the event and is on display in the room.

National Trust. Open April–September, Mondays, Wednesdays and Fridays 2.15–6. Grounds open April–September, Mondays–Saturdays 2.15–6. Admission charge.

HANWELL

Here stood a late medieval brick castle, part of which is now a house near the church. It belonged to the Copes, a Royalist family, and was partly pulled down in 1770.

MIDDLETON STONEY

A motte and bailey castle was mentioned here in 1215.

MINSTER LOVELL

One of the most picturesque ruins in the county, Minster Lovell Hall and church lie on the banks of the Windrush just off A40 between Witney and Burford. Originally the village was called Minster after the church and the name Lovell was added at the end of the thirteenth century, the manor having been in the Lovell family since the reign of Henry I. The manor was granted to William Lovell by his mother Maud in about 1180 and later the church was given to Ivrey Abbey, thus becoming a small priory.

The Lovells seem to have been soldiers for three centuries. William was one of the English knights in the Third Crusade. In the thirteenth century John Lovell was Marshal of the Army in Scotland. His son was killed at Bannockburn. In 1408 John the sixth Lord Lovell inherited Minster Lovell and on his death it passed to his son William, who obtained possession in 1423 on the death of his grandmother. His wife Alice Deincourt was heiress to the baronies of Deincourt and Grey of Rotherfield. These Lovells were wealthy and William built the hall on his return from the French wars in about 1435. The south-west tower and river wall make it a fortified manor and were added in the fifteenth century.

William Lovell, whose tomb can be seen in the church, was master forester of Wychwood Forest and a Lancastrian, but his son Francis, the last and most famous of the Lovells, was a Yorkist. He was a man of some ability and during the reign of Richard III he became a viscount, Chamberlain of the Household and Constable of Wallingford Castle. A contemporary saying went: 'The cat, the rat and Lovell our dog ruled all England under the Hog'.

At Bosworth, Lovell was one of the few Yorkist leaders to escape with his life. He fled to Flanders but returned a year later with Lambert Simnel. At Stoke near Newark their army was defeated by the Earl of Oxford and Henry VII. Lovell was last seen swimming his horse over the Trent. His death was a mystery until 1708 when some workmen erecting a new chimney on the hall found a large vault. A letter of

142

1737 written to Francis Peck, a local historian, describes the scene: 'where was the skeleton of a man . . . sitting at a table which was before him with a book, paper, pen, etc.; in another part of the room lay a cap all moulded and decayed. Which the family took to be this Lord Lovell whose exit hath hitherto been so uncertain'.

The manor went to the Crown until 1602 when it was purchased by Sir Edward Coke. Thomas Coke, Earl of Leicester, lived here for a time but in 1734, when his new house had been built at Holkham in Norfolk, the hall fell into decay. It was finally demolished in 1747 and a print of 1775 shows it in much the same state as it is today.

Department of the Environment. Open normal times. Admission charge.

OXFORD

In New Road near the railway station is the rectangular keep of Oxford Castle. Built by Robert D'Oyley it was once used as a prison and originally had four towers. Queen Matilda, dressed in white, escaped from here with three companions by walking over the frozen river to Abingdon.

RADCOT

A castle here was captured by King Stephen. Radcot Bridge was the site of a skirmish during the Civil War.

SHIRBURN

Near the pleasant old town of Watlington and just off B4009 Shirburn is one of the few inhabited small castles in England.

At the time of Domesday Shirburn belonged to Robert D'Oyley who had built both Oxford and Watlington castles. He may well have built an early wooden structure at Shirburn. In the twelfth century D'Oyley's castle belonged to Henry de Tyeis who held it for the Earl of Cornwall, brother of Henry III. Alice, the daughter of de Tyeis, inherited it in 1307 and it passed to her husband Warine de L'Isle. Here Thomas, Earl of Lancaster, came to see de L'Isle and they plotted to overthrow Edward II, whose army had been routed at Bannockburn. The rebel lords gathered at Borough-bridge in Yorkshire where in March, 1322, they were defeated by a force of men-at-arms and archers under Sir Andrew Harcla. Both Earl Thomas and de L'Isle were executed and the castle passed to a grandson, also Warine de L'Isle. It was he who obtained a licence to crenellate and built the present

143

building in 1378. When he died, his granddaughter inherited the estate and she married the twelfth Earl of Warwick. In 1426, however, it was in the possession of a local family, the Quatremaynes of Thame. Richard Quatremayne left it to his servant Thomas Fowler, but the Fowlers were always in debt and Richard Fowler married his daughter Sibyl to Richard Chamberlain, giving them Shirburn in exchange for enough money to pay his creditors.

During the Civil War Shirburn escaped destruction due to the common sense of the Chamberlains, who were Royalists, but remained neutral. One of the Chamberlains married a Gage and in 1716 it was sold to Lord Parker, Lord Chief Justice, who was created Earl of Macclesfield by George I. The same family own it today.

Built of brick originally, in the nineteenth century the castle was covered in plaster stucco. The windows were modernised and a real drawbridge was built at this time over the wide moat.

Shirburn belongs to the Earl of Macclesfield and is not open to the public.

SOMERTON

Lord Lovell, Richard III's admiral, had a castle here, which was demolished in 1580 to make way for a parish school.

SWERFORD

Between Banbury and Chipping Norton, the earthworks of Swerford Castle are still visible.

RUTLAND

ESSENDINE

South-east of the village stood the moated castle of Gilbert de Gand. It had a Norman chapel, today the parish church of St Mary, in which there is some early Norman sculpture.

OAKHAM

Originally the property of Earl Ferrars, Oakham Castle, of which only the great hall remains, was described in 1340 as 'a castle well walled with 1 hall, 4 chambers, 1 kitchen, 2 stables, 1 grange for hay, 1 house for prisoners, 1 chamber for the porter, 1 drawbridge with chains and within the walls by estimation 2 acres of land'.

Several owners were killed in battles. Earl Ferrars died fighting in the Crusades; the Duke of Rutland, the youngest son of the Duke of York, who owned the castle in 1415, was killed at Agincourt; finally the Duke of Buckingham inherited it through his mother but he too was killed in battle, at Northampton, in 1460. In Tudor times it belonged to Thomas Cromwell and, under Elizabeth, to Sir John Harrington. Later it passed to George Villiers, Duke of Buckingham, who sold it to the Earl of Nottingham, whose family possessed it until living memory.

The curious habit of sticking horseshoes on the wall of the great hall dates back to the earliest owner, Earl Ferrars, who was a royal farrier. The owner of Oakham has always had the right to stop peers who visited or passed through the town for the first time and demand a horseshoe. This was returned for a sum of money and a horseshoe, large or small according to the money received, was fixed on the wall to record the event.

Open daily 9.30–8.30 April–September; 9.30–4 October–March. Admission free.

SHROPSHIRE

ACTON BURNELL

About four miles from Shrewsbury towards Wenlock Edge is the small village of Acton Burnell with its four-sided ruined castle standing next to the church. It was built by Edward I's Lord Chancellor, Edward Burnell, who was Bishop of Bath and Wells. King Edward came here in 1283 and it was in the great barn, the gable ends of which still remain, that the first Parliament was held when the Statute of Acton Burnell was passed dealing with the collection of business debts.

The castle was built the following year (the date 1284 is the date of the licence to crenellate but the castle may well have been nearly complete when Edward held his Parliament). Of red sandstone, Acton Burnell is one of the earliest fortified mansions in the country and was never built to withstand a siege.

After the death of Bishop Burnell the family lived on here until the marriage of Maud Burnell with John Lovell in 1315 whose famous descendant was Francis, Lord Lovell (*see* Minster Lovell, Oxfordshire). Henry VII acquired the castle in 1486 after the battle of Stoke and Henry VIII presented

it to the Earl of Surrey for his services in leading the success-
ful Flodden campaign. During the reign of Charles II, Sir
Richard Lee's heiress married Sir Edward Smythe and the
Smythe family still own the property today.
Open to the public at all reasonable times. Admission free.

ALBERBURY
To the west of Shrewsbury on B4393 are the remains of
the castle of the Fitzwarines. It had a small keep with massive
walls and a curtain that extended to the church.

APLEY
One mile north of Wellington, Apley had three castles.
The first was a fourteenth-century crenellated manor erected
by John Charlton: the second, which was built for £6000 by
Thomas Hammer, who married a Charlton, was demolished
by the Parliamentarians during the Civil War. The third
castle, built in 1780 and enlarged during Victoria's reign,
was demolished recently.

BISHOP'S CASTLE
Just north of Clun on the Welsh border, a few stones of
the shell-keep remain behind the Castle hotel. It was the
home of the bishop of Hereford, was known as Lydbury
Castle and was partly destroyed by Sir John Fitzalan who
captured it during the Baron's War. In 1618 it belonged to
the Earl of Arundel but seems to have become a ruin shortly
after this date.

BRIDGNORTH
Earl Robert de Belleme, a Norman baron and a supporter
of Robert, brother of Henry I, built the castle at Bridgnorth
on the edge of a cliff. The keep, which stands today at an
angle of 17 degrees, was erected 'in a great hurry' when
Henry I came to besiege Belleme at Shrewsbury and stopped
first at Bridgnorth. Belleme surrendered and Henry granted
Bridgnorth to Hugh de Mortimer, who later supported
Stephen. Henry II besieged the castle when Mortimer held
out for Stephen and one of his archers nearly killed the king:
only the quick action of Hubert St Clair saved Henry. He
jumped in front of the king and thereby lost his own life.
The castle became Crown property and Edward II was
captured here by Roger Mortimer.
During the Civil War Colonel Howard garrisoned Bridgnorth for the king and in 1646 the castle was besieged for

three weeks. Mines were driven through the cliff and Howard, running out of ammunition, was forced to surrender. The castle was slighted and the keep, undermined, toppled to its present extraordinary position. Lavington's Hole, as the mine is called, is still visible and when it was explored at the beginning of the century, some old candles were discovered.

The entrance to the grounds is at the end of East Castle Street on the right of St Mary's church, which once stood within the bailey. A terrace walk round the old walls overlooking the river starts to the left of the church and takes one round the castle hill.

Bridgnorth Town Council. Open every day 9–dusk.

BRONCROFT

On the Clee Hills near Tugford, the present Broncroft castle is Victorian but the tower on the right of the entrance is part of the fourteenth-century structure built by Sir Simon Burley, tutor to Richard II. It is the only inhabited castle in the county.

CAUS

Ten miles west of Shrewsbury, the Norman Roger Fitz-Corbet built his castle, calling it after his home in the Pays de Caux in France. It had a massive rectangular wall round the keep with a circular tower in each corner, the whole structure covering six acres. It was destroyed during the Civil War and its Royalist owner Henry Thynne was imprisoned and heavily fined.

CHARLTON

Not far from the Wrekin, only the mound of a fourteenth-century castellated manor remains.

CLUN

On A488 near the Herefordshire border are the remains of the twelfth-century castle of the de Says, who were granted the land by Roger de Montgomery, Earl of Shrewsbury. Clun has three baileys connected by narrow causeways and on the motte are a rectangular keep and two semi-circular towers. The river acts as a moat to what must have been a formidable fortress.

ELLESMERE

Between Oswestry and Whitchurch, nothing remains of the castle built by the Peverels and later owned by the Strange family from 1276. The site is now a bowling green.

HOLGATE
Off B4868 the fourteenth-century tower of the castle is joined on to a farmhouse. There is also a motte and bailey visible by the church. At one time Holgate belonged to Lord Lovell.

HOPTON
The twelfth-century keep of Picot de Say's castle still stands. In 1644 it was owned by Henry Wallop who garrisoned it with thirty-one men, the commander, in the absence of Wallop, being Samuel More. Sir Michael Woodhouse with 500 Royalists captured it after a fierce fight and according to one report had the garrison tied back to back and cast into the nearby pond. The Parliamentary commander Milton repeated this barbarous method of disposing of prisoners when he captured Conway Castle.

KNOCKIN
Six miles from Oswestry, Knockin Castle belonged to the Strange family and was demolished during King John's reign.

LUDLOW
Built by Roger de Lacy at the time of Domesday, Ludlow is the principal castle of the thirty-two that guarded the Welsh Marches. It is an ideal site for a fortress, perched on a cliff overlooking the rivers Teme and Corve. Roger de Lacy was exiled after rebelling against William Rufus and the property passed to his brother and, on the latter's death, to the Crown.

During the reign of Henry I, Ludlow was granted to Pain FitzJohn who was killed by the Welsh in 1136. His successor, Sir Joyce de Dinan, was responsible for building the circular chapel and for digging the double moat – the inner moat surrounded the keep. In 1138 Gervase de Paganel captured Ludlow on behalf of Queen Matilda and in the ensuing siege King Stephen personally prevented the young Prince Henry of Scotland from being dragged off his horse by a grappling iron. The window from which the iron was thrown is still pointed out today.

Joyce de Dinan was virtually a prisoner in his own castle after 1150 when de Paganel was ousted. Hugh de Mortimer threatened him and Joyce, by a clever ambush, captured Hugh and imprisoned him in the highest tower of the castle, ever since called Mortimer's tower. Mortimer obtained his freedom by paying 3,000 marks in ransom. In 1166 Joyce died and the castle was seized by Hugh de Lacy. King John then acquired it for himself until restoring it eventually to Hugh's brother, Walter de Lacy. This was a period of incessant war against the Welsh, and Ludlow remained fully garrisoned. The de Genevilles, relations of the de Lacys, inherited the property and Joan de Geneville married Roger Mortimer, first Earl of March and virtual ruler of England during the minority of Edward III. He finally became a threat to the young King and was captured at Nottingham in 1330 and hung at Tyburn for treason (*see* Nottingham Castle).

During the Wars of the Roses, Ludlow was the property of Richard, Duke of York, who was nephew to the fifth Earl of March. The battle of Ludford Bridge was fought over the Teme when Henry VI and his army closed in on Ludlow and Richard decided to attack the Lancastrians early in the morning before they had time to get to arms. His scheme was foiled however by the treachery of Sir Andrew Trollope who deserted Richard in the night and took his experienced troops over to the King's side, forcing York to flee to Ireland. The castle was sacked and the Lancastrians were in temporary command until the position was reversed at the battle of Northampton in 1460. After Richard had been killed fighting against the Lancastrians at Wakefield, his son Edward of March was proclaimed King Edward IV in 1461.

During the ten years 1472–1483 the young Prince of Wales and his brother lived in the castle until they went to London and eventually met their death in the Tower, a murder mystery that has never been solved. Edward IV had instituted a prince's council in Ludlow for administering justice in Wales. This Court of the Marches was carried on by Henry VII whose son Arthur lived at Ludlow. Under Elizabeth I Sir Henry Sidney was governor for twenty-seven years. He built the gatehouse (inscribed 1581) into the middle ward and repaired the keep, which was used as a prison. The Court of the Marches continued until 1689 when it was abolished by William III, and the castle thereafter declined in importance.

Milton's *Comus* was first performed at Ludlow and Butler wrote *Hudibras* in a room over the gateway. The original entrance – through the keep by a drawbridge – was replaced in Sidney's time by a gateway to the right of the keep. The building was not seriously damaged during the Civil War, when it was mostly held by the Royalists. It was during the reign of George I that it suffered most, when the lead was stripped off the roof of the main hall, bringing about the decay of what was once one of England's proudest castles. *Open daily* 10.30–1, 2–7.30 *April–September; weekdays only October–March* 10.30–1, 2–4.30. *Admission charge.*

MORE
Near Bishop's Castle, More had a motte and two baileys dating from c. 1215.

MORETON CORBET
North of Shrewsbury off A53, the ruins of the Elizabethan manor stand close to the older ruins of the castle. It is believed to have been built by the Turret family in the late twelfth century. One of the Turret heiresses married Richard Corbet of Wattlesborough. Roger Corbet, who had travelled in Italy, built the Elizabethan house in 1579. It was never completed, as Corbet died of the plague and his cousin Sir Richard did not live much longer, dying in 1606. Sir Vincent Corbet who succeeded was an ardent Royalist and garrisoned the castle with eighty foot soldiers and thirty horsemen. The Parliamentary army at Wem, commanded by Colonel Rinking, attacked the castle during the night and captured it. The roof was removed and when the Corbets regained their property they moved to Shawbury Park so the castle and its magnificent Elizabethan house fell rapidly into ruins. The Corbet crest, an elephant and castle, can be seen on the screen in the church. Moreton ranks with Kirby Hall, Northamptonshire, as one of the finest Elizabethan architectural ruins in the country.
Department of the Environment. Open weekdays 9.30–dusk, Sundays 2–dusk. Admission free.

MYDDLE CASTLE
On the A528 north of Shrewsbury, Myddle Castle was built by Lord Le Strange in 1307 and all that remains is a stair turret. The last Strange owner was George Stanley, who was held by Richard III as a hostage at Bosworth until his father Lord Stanley joined the battle. He narrowly escaped execution. Myddle was inherited by his son Lord Derby. It was a small structure with two baileys and was partly destroyed by an earthquake in 1688, which knocked down one tower.

OSWESTRY
Built in 1085 by Reginald de Ballieul Oswestry was enlarged by Alan Fitzalan. His son William, lord of Clun Castle, inherited it and King John made the castle his headquarters during his war against Wales. Young Edmund, Earl of Arundel, who held the castle during Edward II's reign, was killed because of his friendship for the king. The castle

passed to the Howards in 1580 and Thomas Howard lost his life supporting the cause of Mary Queen of Scots. Captured by the Parliamentarians under Lord Denbigh during the Civil War, the castle was destroyed and only the mound remains, although the outer bailey is still called Baily Head.

QUATFORD
Before Bridgnorth Castle was built Roger de Montgomery had a castle down the river at Quatford. It was demolished by Robert Beleme and the stones were used for the higher and more easily defended castle. Today there is a nineteenth-century sham castle here.

REDCASTLE
In the grounds of Hawkstone Park, once the seat of the Hills, was a towered castle perched on a hill. Built by Lord Audley in 1228, it consists today of a few stones.

ROWTON
A few miles west of Shrewsbury, Rowton Castle was built in the nineteenth century on the site of 'the most ancient of Shropshire castles' which once belonged to the de Says. It was flattened by Llewellyn in 1282 and rebuilt by the Lyster family.

RUYTON OF THE ELEVEN TOWNS
Between Shrewsbury and Oswestry is the village which was once eleven different townships. By the church stands the ruins of the castle built by Edmund Fitzalan in the fourteenth century. A nineteenth-century castle, Ruyton Towers, stands on the road to Knockin.

SHRAWARDINE
To the west of Shrewsbury off A5 on a hill commanding a crossing over the Severn, once stood an important castle built by order of Henry I. It passed to the Fitzalans and in the fifteenth century to the Bromleys, one of whom presided over the trial of Mary Queen of Scots. During the Civil War Colonel Vaughan held the castle for the king and carried out many damaging sallies from here. On one occasion he was captured and was led with twelve of his officers back to Shrawardine by Colonel Mytton, the local Parliamentary officer. The castle defenders, seeing their leader in enemy hands, prepared to surrender but Vaughan gave Mytton the slip and ran over the drawbridge as it was being

raised. Although his officers remained in captivity the castle held out until 1645 when it was completely razed to the ground. In 1760 the land belonged to Lord Clive.

SHREWSBURY

Roger de Montgomery built Shrewsbury Castle on a loop of the Severn in about 1080. Roger's successor extended the walls to the other side of the river and in the twelfth century the town walls were built. Much of the wall was constructed of wooden stakes. Even in Edward I's time the main keep was built of wood, although the fine hall and Norman gatehouse were originally built of stone.

In 1138 Shrewsbury was besieged by Stephen and captured after four weeks resistance. The garrison were all ruthlessly hanged, except William Fitzalan, the owner, who escaped. Henry II used Shrewsbury, now a royal castle, as a springboard for his attacks against the Welsh and in 1283 Edward I witnessed the execution of David, the Welsh king, in the castle yard.

Henry IV garrisoned the castle against Hotspur before the battle of Shrewsbury in 1403, when young Prince Hal helped his father defeat the rebel army. During the Civil War Shrewsbury was an important Royalist training centre and the castle was strengthened. In February 1645 Colonels Boyer and Mytton with 1,200 Parliamentary troops attacked it at night and, with the loss of only two men, took it by climbing over the east wall.

In the eighteenth century the crumbling ruin was bought by Sir William Pulteney MP, who wanted a town house large enough for receptions. His architect was Thomas Telford who carried out many repairs including the construction of a Gothic room in the south-west tower and Laura's tower on the mound. Further modernisation was carried out by Sir Charles Nicholson in 1926. Today it is well looked after and the grounds are a park and garden.
Open weekdays 9–12 and 1.30–5; June–August 9–5; Sundays 2–5 (March–end October only). Admission charge.

STOKESAY

Without doubt the best preserved fortified manor house in England, Stokesay lies in a secluded position not far from Craven Arms. It was the Norman home of the de Say family – hence the name (the word 'stoke' means dairy farm) – and the castle was built by Lawrence Ludlow, a wool merchant, who obtained a licence to crenellate in 1291. The only known parts of the old Say home are the lower two storeys of the north tower, in one of which is a medieval fireplace.

Lawrence built the great hall. It is of cruck construction and the timber markings are still visible. There used to be an open fire in the centre of the floor and the black timbers are an indication that the usual louvres in the roof to let out the smoke never existed. The large windows are very unusual, indicating that the house was not really built with defence as the main object.

In 1497 Anne Ludlow married Thomas Vernon and their family lived here until the sixteenth century when Stokesay was sold to Sir George Mainwaring. Later it was sold to Dame Elizabeth Craven and her son, the Royalist Lord Craven. He surrendered the castle in 1645 and, although the neighbouring church was damaged, very surprisingly the only damage to the castle was the lowering of the east wall. The next inhabitants were the Baldwyns who leased it from Lord Craven and then sub-let it to local farmers until, in 1814, it was rapidly becoming a ruin. Lord Craven added the hall buttresses and in 1869 Stokesay was sold for the fifth time. The new owner Mr J. D. Allcroft preserved it and the present owner, his granddaughter, Lady Magnus Allcroft, has carried on with the work, still incomplete.

The castle hall and solar, with its carved overmantel, the south tower with its magnificent view, and the gatehouse with its seventeenth-century wooden superstructure form a part of a rural scene without equal in Britain.

Open every day except Tuesday, 9–6 summer, 10–4.30 winter. Admission charge.

TONG

An eighteenth-century castle built by Capability Brown and demolished in 1964, Tong was once the home of the Vernons who are buried in the remarkable fourteenth-century church across the road. The gate remains and on it is carved a picture of the old Tong Castle that Brown demolished.

WATTLEBOROUGH

Near Rowton, this castle keep still stands next to a Georgian farmhouse. It was built by Roger FitzCorbet of Caus and later passed to the De la Poles and Leightons.

WHITCHURCH

A Norman castle once stood by the old mill.

WHITTINGTON

Two miles to the east of Oswestry, the gatehouse, ditch and tower stand on a bend of A5 by the railway station. Fulk de Warenne paid Henry III £262 and two chargers for the manor with a licence to crenellate it in 1219. Defended by a system of flooded ditches with a bog on one side, Whittington had five towers until 1790 when one fell and another was demolished for repairing the road.

SOMERSET

BRIDGWATER

Only the water gate remains of Bridgwater's thirteenth-century castle. The town was built by Walter de Douai when he constructed a bridge over the Parret. It was known as Walter's bridge and later became Bridgwater. The land passed to William de Briwere who obtained a licence from King John to build a castle. The Royalists fortified the town in 1645 and when it fell to Fairfax's artillery, the castle was demolished.

BRISTOL

Nothing remains of Robert Fitz-Hamon's castle between the Avon and the Frome, built in about 1120 of Caen stone. In 1534 Leland described it as having 'two courts, in the upper court . . . a great dungeon tower, a pretty church, a stone bridge and three bulwarks'. Second World War bombs destroyed St Peter's church nearby and excavations revealed a very large keep.

CASTLE CARY

Two grassy mounds on a hill are all that remain of Henry de Tracy's twelfth-century castle, which had a tower keep. The Lords Cary were supporters of Stephen in the war with Matilda. In 1586 one of the family, Richard Perceval, Lord Cary, translated the Spanish letters which forewarned of the Armada. Charles II spent a night at Castle Cary manor, now demolished, during his escape after the battle of Worcester.

CASTLE NEROCHE

In the Blackdown Hills not far from the village of Buckland St Mary, Neroche is a collection of three banks and ditches. The inner one is the largest and has an entrance leading to a farm. The motte to the north is from a twelfth-century motte and bailey castle built on the site of a much earlier hill-fort.

Forestry Commission. Nature trail and picnic area. Car park. Open at all times.

DUNSTER

Just outside Minehead, Dunster Castle stands high on the western edge of Exmoor, dominating the valley and the small village. William de Mohun built a castle here on a Saxon site after the battle of Hastings. King John appointed Hubert de Burgh custodian when the owner, Reginald de Mohun, was still a minor. In 1376 the last male heir of the Mohuns died and the castle was sold to Elizabeth, daughter of the Earl of Devon. She was a widow and was outlived by Lady Mohun but her son, Hugh Luttrell, gained possession of Dunster on Lady Mohun's death in 1404, and the Luttrell family have owned it ever since. In spite of legal proceedings against him Hugh found the money to strengthen the gatehouse and to carry out other improvements.

The Luttrells were Lancastrians. James was killed at the battle of St Albans in 1461. The next three Luttrells were all knighted. During the Civil War Thomas Luttrell, originally for Parliament, became a Royalist, so that in 1645 Blake besieged and mined the castle. Colonel Wyndham, the governor, finally surrendered in April 1646. Fortunately the usual slighting did not take place and George Luttrell took up residence again in 1651 on payment of a fine. During the Monmouth Rebellion some of the Luttrell retainers went to the Duke's support and there is a halberd in the castle supposed to have been made there for use in the rising.

Inside is a magnificent staircase dating from 1681, and the dining room has panelling of the same date. Among the famous pictures are one of Oliver Cromwell and Bower's *The Cavalier*. There is much more of interest in what is one of the very few privately owned, inhabited castles in England.

Lt Col G. W. Luttrell. Open Bank Holidays; Wednesdays 2.15–4.30. Admission charge.

ENMORE

A few miles west of Bridgwater, Enmore belonged to William Malet, a Norman soldier who fought at Hastings, but the present building, dating from the eighteenth century, was constructed by John Perceval, Earl of Egmont.

FARLEIGH HUNGERFORD

On the Wiltshire border, near Trowbridge, Farleigh Hungerford was built by Sir Thomas Hungerford on the site of a small Norman manor belonging to the Montforts. Sir Thomas was Speaker of the House of Commons in 1377 and made money in the war with France. He fortified his manor without a licence but received royal consent later. His son Walter, also Speaker and a soldier, enlarged the outer court of the castle and on his death in 1449 his widow built a chapel.

In 1462 Richard, Duke of Gloucester, acquired the castle and gave it to the Duke of Norfolk. But at Bosworth Norfolk was killed and Sir Walter Hungerford, a supporter of Henry VII, regained the family property in 1486. The castle was the birthplace of the Countess of Salisbury, one of the last of the Plantagenets, who was executed at the age of 70 on a trumped-up charge of treason. Colonel John Hungerford garrisoned the castle for Charles during the Civil War but later surrendered it to his half-brother, Sir Edward, and this probably saved it from slighting. The last Hungerford to live in the castle was Sir Edward who was knighted by Charles II. He became a Whig and was involved in the Rye House Plot; this and his spendthrift ways forced him to sell Farleigh to a Mr Baynton, brother-in-law to the Earl of Rochester. Later, in 1730, it was sold again to the Houltons of Trowbridge and remained in their hands until 1891 when it was bought by Lord Donington. Later it was sold to Lord Cairns who placed it under the guardianship of the Ministry of Works in 1915.

The gatehouse and the chapel are virtually complete and the latter houses an interesting display of armour, mostly of the Civil War period.

Department of the Environment. Open normal times. Admission charge.

MONTACUTE

Built by Robert of Mortain and in existence in 1069, Montacute was finally destroyed when the Elizabethan house was built.

NETHER STOWEY

Ruins remain of a Norman keep built on Castle Hill in the Quantocks by William Fitzodo. It was the home of Lord Audley who fought with the Cornishmen at Blackheath in 1497.

NUNNEY

John de la Mare obtained a licence to crenellate his house near Frome in 1373. He was interested in French castles and his building is unique amongst English castles. The four towers are very close together and are surmounted by machicolated parapets and round turrets that once had conical roofs. It has a wide deep moat and for two days in 1645 it held out against Fairfax until a 36 pdr. cannon knocked down one wall and the garrison under Colonel Prater surrendered. The slighting was inefficiently done and much of the building remains today.

Department of the Environment. Open normal times. Key from caretaker's cottage. Admission charge.

RICHMONT

Once an important castle of the Gournays, there are only a few remains of this Norman structure, near East Harptree church. It was destroyed by Sir John Newton, Chief Justice to Henry VIII, who built a manor-house with the stone.

STOGURSEY

Near Bridgwater, the castle of the de Courcys was held for King John in 1215 and destroyed the following year. A few walls and the moat remain. One of the de Courcys subdued Ulster and became its first earl.

TAUNTON

In the centre of the town and now the County Museum, the castle hall was built on a Saxon site by William Gifford between 1107 and 1129. The keep was added by Henry of Blois between 1129 and 1171 and further buildings were added in 1207.

The castle was a ruin by 1490 and had to be repaired by Bishop Langton of Winchester. During the Civil War it was captured and held by Blake for Parliament. The inner moat was filled in by Sir Benjamin Hammet who carried out other alterations so that Taunton castle today has lost most of its character.

Open Monday–Friday 9–12, 2–5, Saturday 9–12.

WALTON

Near Clevedon, Walton was a hunting lodge built in 1615 by Lord Poulett; it was an octagonal tower surrounded by an embattled wall.

157

STAFFORDSHIRE

ALTON

Near Uttoxeter on B5032 from Cheadle, Alton Towers is a ruined nineteenth-century mansion designed by Pugin and built on a hill. The gardens are magnificent and the shell of the mansion imposing. During Stephen's reign there was a castle here that belonged to the Verdon family. William Verdon's daughter married Lord Furnival in whose hands the castle remained until it passed to the Talbots, Earls of Shrewsbury. It was demolished during the Civil War.

Alton Towers. Open daily from Good Friday to October. Admission charge.

CAVERSWALL

Near Cheadle, Caverswall is a seventeenth-century castellated mansion built on the site of Sir William de Caverswall's thirteenth-century castle.

CHARTLEY

Off A518, between Stafford and Uttoxeter, the ruins of this castle of the earls of Derby stand above the present mansion. During the reign of Henry III it was seized by Robert de Ferrars, whose family had owned it since Norman times. When the king's son Edmund led the attack against it, Robert held out against all odds. Finally forced to surrender, he was pardoned by the king for his bravery. In a wooden house nearby lived the unfortunate Mary Queen of Scots for a short time before her final journey to Fotheringhay.

ECCLESHALL

On A519 from Newport to Newcastle-under-Lyme stood the fortified mansion of the bishops of Lichfield. Built originally by Bishop Muschamp in 1200, it was rebuilt in 1310 and was a Lancastrian stronghold during the Wars of the Roses. From 1645 to 1646 it was held by the Royalists against the Parliamentary forces of Sir William Brereton and after the Civil War it had to be rebuilt again. Today it is a private house and only one tower remains of the original structure.

LICHFIELD

A castle stood here in 1129, but no trace of it can be seen today.

NEWCASTLE-UNDER-LYME

Built by Edmund Crouchback during the reign of Henry III, Newcastle was built in a lake to take the place of a wooden castle at Chesterton. It was a well made structure according to an account of 1610: '150 paces from N to S and near 200 from E to W, 2 trancepts and 4 bays, with a donjon tower 20 paces square, 2 storeys in height and 70ft. high the whole more fit as a stately comfortable dwelling than as a fortress because of the rising lands S and E.'

STAFFORD

There were once two castles at Stafford, both built by Ethelfleda, builder of Warwick Castle, one inside and the other outside the town. William I also built two castles on the same sites. In 1348 Randolph de Stafford obtained a licence to crenellate the outer castle on the Newport road. The Stafford family suffered more than most from executions and death in battle during the Wars of the Roses. In the Civil War Lady Stafford was besieged by Brereton who 'spent much time' trying to persuade the 'ould Lady . . . to admitte some of our men to secure the castle'. He finally succeeded and the castle was later demolished. Sir George Jerningham rebuilt part of it in 1817.

STOURTON

On the road from Bridgnorth to Stourbridge, Stourton is a modern house incorporating part of the fifteenth-century castellated mansion of the Poles. Twice elected to the papal chair and twice refusing to accept the honour, Cardinal Pole was one of Queen Mary's leading advisers and a grandson of the Duke of Clarence. He died shortly after his queen in 1558, having tried unsuccessfully to reconvert England to the old religion.

TAMWORTH

One of the most important Midland castles, Tamworth lies just off A5 not far from Lichfield. It was first fortified by Ethelfleda, who constructed a fifty foot motte that covers an area a hundred feet in diameter. The shell-keep was built in Norman times by the Marmions, Royal Champions of England, but has been much altered since, principally in Elizabethan times. The remarkable herringbone stone wall that crosses the moat is believed to date from the reign of Henry I.

159

The Marmions held Tamworth during the twelfth and thirteenth centuries. The Ferrers of Groby inherited it during the Wars of the Roses and the family lived there for over two hundred years. During the Civil War the owner, John Ferrers, was a minor and the castle escaped serious damage, although it was garrisoned by both Royalists and Parliamentarians.

Today it belongs to the Borough of Tamworth and contains some fine carved chimney pieces, doorways and an important heraldic frieze. The Castle Museum houses one of the best collections of Saxon coins in England and there is a local history collection. The grounds contain two modern swimming pools, a children's playground and a roller-skating rink.

Borough of Tamworth. March–September, open weekdays 10–8, Sundays 2–8; November–February, open weekdays except Friday 10–4, Sundays 2–4.

TUTBURY

Three miles north of Burton on Trent on A50, Tutbury Castle stands on a bend of the Dove and was once a Saxon stronghold. Much of the ruin remains standing although the keep is a sham nineteenth-century structure erected by one of the Vernon family. The castle was originally granted by William I to Henry de Ferrars, later made Earl of Derby, but when a Ferrars supported Simon de Montfort in 1266, the castle was forfeited to the House of Lancaster.

Thomas, second Earl of Lancaster, who lived here in 1322, was driven out by Edward II and lost his treasure in the Dove during his escape. Some of the coins were discovered in 1831 and are now in the British Museum. In 1350 John of Gaunt inherited Tutbury and spent a great sum of money on its repairs, as well as introducing the sport of bull-running to the town. Later Tutbury was one of the castles used to imprison Mary Queen of Scots. She was allowed a retinue of 47 people, ten horses and a guard of thirty soldiers. Her custodian, Sir Richard Sadler, took her hawking and was afterwards censured for his kindness.

During the Civil War Tutbury was garrisoned for the King by Lord Loughborough. It surrendered and was reduced to its present state by Brereton who was the scourge of the Midlands in 1646.

Open summer, 10–6; Winter 10–4. Admission charge.

SUFFOLK

BUNGAY

The Norfolk-Suffolk boundary follows the river Waveney and on a double loop of the river about twelve miles west of Lowestoft is the small town of Bungay. It was a natural place for a castle and Roger Bigod, owner of Framlingham, built the first castle here. It was in occupation during Stephen's reign when Hugh Bigod supported the cause of Matilda. The king captured it and made terms with Bigod, but the unrepentant baron later joined the Earl of Leicester's rebellion against Henry II and in 1174 Bungay again came under attack. Although defended by 500 men, the king's sappers excavated a mine under the south-west corner. Many men deserted and Bigod had to pay a fine of a thousand marks.

For a hundred years the castle remained a ruin until Roger, fifth Earl of Norfolk, who obtained a licence to crenellate in 1294, built the present building, the remains of which can be seen behind the King's Head Hotel. It consisted of a 70 foot high square keep, with the thickest walls of any castle in England, surrounded by a polygonal curtain wall. On the west the gatehouse had two semi-circular towers. In the eighteenth century there was a cottage between the towers in which Mrs Bonhote wrote her book *Bungay Castle*. In 1891 excavations carried out here revealed the mine constructed in 1174 which runs from the west wall to the prison beneath the forebuilding. Another gallery had been started but not finished. The castle well in the north-west corner and the pit in which the drawbridge was manipulated were also discovered.
Open at all times. Admission free.

BURGH

The Roman camp at the junction of the Waveney and Bure rivers has three impressive walls of flint and brick. The Normans built a motte and bailey castle in one corner of the five acre court. One of the best Roman remains in Britain, Burgh was known as *Gariannonum*. Later it became a Saxon shore fort like Brancaster.

CLARE

The Saxons built a large earthwork at Clare which, having once been occupied by a railway station, is now the centre of Clare Castle Country Park and is the site of the Warden's

161

house and information centre. At the time of the Norman conquest, Clare was one of the ninety-five lordships given to Richard FitzGilbert. Richard's son Gilbert de Clare annexed the little chapel of St John to the Abbey of Bec in Normandy and was probably responsible for building the castle, of which very little stonework remains, although the ramparts and parts of the moat are visible.

The de Clares also owned Tonbridge Castle in Kent, where they usually lived. Another Gilbert, known as the Red Earl, married the daughter of Edward I. Their son, the Earl of Gloucester, was killed leading the vanguard of the English king at the battle of Bannockburn in 1314 and the male branch of the de Clare family died out. The castle was inherited by Elizabeth, the dead earl's sister, who, with her husband John de Burgh, founded Clare College at Cambridge. In Charles II's reign the castle came into the possession of Sir Gervase Elwes and it remained in his family until 1829 when it was sold to John Barker of Clare. The present owner of Clare castle, A. L. de Fonblanque, is a descendant of Barker.

Open at all times. Clare Priory, founded 1248, is open from Easter to October 10–12, 3–6. It stands in the north bailey.

EYE

A Saxon motte and bailey castle stood in the centre of the village. After the conquest it belonged to William de Malet and later passed to the Crown. There are no signs of William's stone keep but the motte rises to 60 feet and has a modern tower on its summit.

FRAMLINGHAM

Framlingham is probably the most important castle in Suffolk. The town of Framlingham is about four miles west of A12 from Wickham Market and the castle still presents an impressive aspect. Once a Saxon stronghold associated with St Edmund, in the twelfth century it consisted of a timber house surrounded by a ditch and rampart and belonged to Roger Bigod. Roger's second son Hugh was created Earl of Norfolk by Stephen, and in 1173 joined the Earl of Leicester in his rebellion against Henry II. Henry, returning from France, captured Ipswich, Walton and Bungay castles, all possessions of Hugh, and Framlingham surrendered. It was dismantled and the ditch filled in, but in 1189 Bigod bought back the site and rebuilt the castle.

Today it consists of three wards, the inner one surrounded

SUFFOLK

by a 44 foot wall with thirteen towers, mostly intact, surrounded by a moat and the outer bailey, now containing most of the town, which itself had a moat. To the west was the small lower court protected by an artificial marsh. The earl's son, Roger II, built the walls and erected a chapel and great hall against the eastern curtain between 1190 and 1210. He copied the style of Dover and Windsor castles in dispensing with a keep and relying upon the towers in the wall as the main places of defence. This idea was copied from the Crusaders' castles based upon the Roman idea of a defensive wall interspaced with bastions.

Roger II rebelled against King John whose army captured Framlingham in 1215. In 1306 the last of the Bigods died and the castle passed to the Crown. In 1312 Edward II presented it to Thomas Brotherton, Marshal of England, and on his death it was inherited by the Countess Marshal, his widow. Later his two sisters inherited it one after the other and the youngest, Margaret, married to Lord Seagrave, had a daughter Elizabeth who married Lord Mowbray. Their son Thomas Mowbray was a favourite of Richard II and became hereditary Earl Marshal of England and the first Duke of Norfolk. He was banished in 1399. Henry IV seized Framlingham when he came to the throne. The new Thomas Mowbray, Earl Marshal, being a supporter of Richard II, also rebelled, and was captured and beheaded at York in 1405.

The Mowbray line died out and the Howards inherited the castle in 1476. The first Howard duke was the famous 'Jockey of Norfolk', who was killed fighting for Richard III at Bosworth. His son, the Earl of Surrey, was captured and sent to the Tower. This young man became the military genius of his time and led the English army to victory at Flodden in 1513. Henry VIII created him Duke of Norfolk and allowed him to add the 'Flodden augmentation' to his coat-of-arms. The next duke was also Earl Marshal but incurred the displeasure of the king and was imprisoned. His son, the poet Earl of Surrey, was executed.

Once more Framlingham became Crown property. Edward VI left it to his sister Mary and in 1553, when the attempt was made to crown Lady Jane Grey, Mary gathered an army of 13,000 supporters here and marched on London, where she was proclaimed Queen of England in spite of her Catholic religion. The old duke, restored to his property, lived on for a year and his grandson Thomas inherited the castle. But in 1572 he was sent to the block by Elizabeth,

163

who suspected him of supporting Mary Queen of Scots.

James I restored the castle to the Howards but shortly after this it was acquired by Sir Robert Hitcham, whose tomb is in Framlingham church. By his will in 1636 it was left to Pembroke College, Cambridge, and the inner buildings were all demolished to make a large poor-house, later used as a court room.

The wall walk, not recommended for those afraid of heights, commands an excellent view of the town and takes one round nine of the thirteen towers. The strange Tudor chimneys, added by the later Howards, are dummies except in the eighth and ninth towers. The drawbridge was of the counter-weight variety and the present bridge dates from 1524. To the west is a postern leading to the Prison Tower and lower court. To the east are the remains of a stone bridge over the moat near the seventh tower.

Department of the Environment. Open normal times. Admission charge.

HAUGHLEY

A very strong motte and bailey castle stood here until it was captured by the Earl of Leicester in 1163. It was demolished in 1173 and a royal manor built in its place, inhabited by the Sulyard family in the sixteenth century. Two moated enclosures and the 80 foot motte are still visible.

IPSWICH

Hugh Bigod had a castle here which was captured by King Stephen. It had a ditch dug in 1204.

METTINGHAM

Sir John de Norwich obtained a licence to crenellate his house in 1342. He was governor of Angoulême in France and made a fortune in the French wars. An ecclesiastical college moved here in 1392. Only the original twin-towered gatehouse remains plus a few stones of Kate's Tower, which collapsed in 1839. Six bells were found in the moat when it was cleaned out in the nineteenth century.

ORFORD

On the Suffolk coast south of Aldeburgh (but best approached via Woodbridge) stands one of the most unusual castles in England. The keep, which is all that remains, is polygonal on the outside and circular on the inside. It has three square projecting towers and a forebuilding between the south turret and the main structure. According to the Pipe Rolls, which are remarkably complete for this part of Suffolk, Orford Castle was built between 1166 and 1172 by Henry I when Orford was a busy port on the river Alde and it was completed in time to put down the rebellion of Hugh Bigod, the Earl of Norfolk who owned the castles of Bungay, Framlingham, Walton and Thetford. Supplied by sea, Orford was a useful base and the revolt was soon crushed. In 1217 during the Barons' War the French occupied the castle but, although it changed hands on more than one occasion, at no time was the keep damaged and in 1277 two of the towers were further protected by lead roofs.

There are no traces of the bailey walls today. Originally the curtain enceinte had bastions protecting the intermediate walls but the walls gradually vanished, the last piece falling down in 1841. No doubt the strategic importance of the castle declined in the fourteenth century and the keep was strong enough to act as a castle in itself. In 1336 Edward III gave it to Robert Ufford, Earl of Suffolk, and it remained in private hands until its presentation to the Ministry of Public Building and Works in 1962.

Inside Orford, reached by a second storey door as at Castle Hedingham, there is a large, well-lit chamber, with a spiral staircase in one tower and chambers in the others. In the basement is a deep well with a ladder cut into the stone, most of which is dressed and came from Caen, like most of the castle. The pointed windows and the chapel vaulting in the forebuilding are among the earliest known examples of Gothic architecture in England.

Department of the Environment. Open normal times. Admission charge.

WALTON

Built on the cliff near Felixstowe, it was destroyed by Henry II and recently, more completely, by the encroaching sea.

WINGFIELD

Wingfield was built by Michael de la Pole in 1384. He married Katherine, daughter of Sir James Wingfield, the companion of the Black Prince. A later de la Pole was Duke of Suffolk and Lord Chamberlain to Henry VI. He was banished by the Yorkists and murdered at sea. Most of the building is Tudor but the south front and gatehouse are original.

SURREY

ABINGER

A Norman motte stands near the church. Excavations recently revealed that it supported a wooden tower house.

BETCHWORTH

Richard FitzGilbert owned this castle near Reigate but it soon passed to the earls of Arundel, then through the female line to Sir Thomas Browne, Henry VI's Lord Treasurer, whose family lived here until 1690. The next owner, William Fenwick, demolished most of it and turned the rest into an ordinary house. What remains of Sir Thomas's castle is at the end of an avenue of lime trees at Deepdene.

BLETCHINGLEY

Richard FitzGilbert, Earl of Clare, had a castle here in Norman times. When Gilbert de Clare revolted against Henry III the king's army destroyed the castle. In 1541 Henry VIII gave it to Anne of Cleves who lived at the manor house built near the site of the old castle, the moat of which is still visible. Bletchingley passed next to Sir Thomas Cawarden, who supported Lady Jane Grey. Queen Mary's troops searched the castle and removed a great store of arms including sixteen cannon. The next owner was Lord Howard of Effingham. During the Civil War his Royalist son, Lord Peterborough, was fined £10,000 and was thereby forced to sell the estate in 1665 to Sir Robert Clayton, Lord Mayor of London. One of the Claytons served under Wellington and his monument is in Bletchingley church. Nothing remains of the manor but a gatehouse at Place Farm.

FARNHAM

Between 1129 and 1171 Henry of Blois, Bishop of Winchester, built a castle on the road from Winchester to London. The first keep was a square tower on a 30-foot mound and two of the wooden piers are still preserved in the great hall. During the thirteenth century a chapel was added and stone replaced wood.

During the Civil War of John's reign, the Dauphin captured Farnham in 1216 and held it for ten months. It was retaken by the Earl of Pembroke after a short siege. Food was stored in the keep in case of siege during the Barons' War of 1264–5. During the fourteenth century Bishop

166

William of Wykeham enlarged the bishop's quarters and Bishop Waynflete added the brick entry tower. It must have been impressive because both Henry VII and Henry VIII stayed at Farnham.

In the seventeenth century James I used Farnham as a hunting seat. It was strengthened by Parliament during the Civil War, but after Edgehill, the commander, George Wither, abandoned it to the Royalists. Charles placed Sir John Denham there with a small force but this was not strong enough to hold out against Sir William Waller in December 1642 and for a time it was used as a prison for captured Royalists; in 1648 it was slighted. After the Restoration Bishop Morley of Winchester regained what was left and spent £8,000 rebuilding the domestic quarters. More alterations and improvements were made in the eighteenth and nineteenth centuries and from 1927 to 1955 it was the home of the bishops of Guildford.

In 1958 excavations revealed the base of the square keep and a deep well shaft. The visitor today can examine the foundations and see the original ground level. The tower must have been about 70 feet high.

Department of the Environment. Keep open weekdays 9.30– dusk, Sundays 2–dusk. Overseas Training College (Bishop's building) open Wednesdays 2–4. Admission charge.

GUILDFORD

The fine Norman keep of Guildford's castle, once used as a gaol, stands in a public garden off Quarry Street, dating from Henry II's reign although the surrounding walls are older. The castle was a favourite royal residence in the thirteenth century.

Garden open at all times. Keep normally open Easter–end of September 2.30–6.30. Admission charge.

REIGATE

The mighty castle of the de Warennes once stood on the hill near the railway station. The site is now a public park. There are caves under the castle where the barons are reputed to have conferred before the signing of Magna Carta. During the second Civil War of 1648 Reigate was seized by the Royalists and held for a day before the Parliamentary horse drove them to Kingston where there was a short skirmish in which Lord Francis Villiers was killed. Lord Peterborough of Bletchingley Castle took part in this episode and was fortunate to escape to the Continent.

STARBOROUGH

Three miles east of Lingfield, Starborough Castle was founded by Reginald de Cobham in 1341. It was rectangular with four round towers surmounted by strange domes. After distinguishing himself at Poitiers, Reginald became a knight of the garter and was made Lord High Admiral. His son Reginald fought at Agincourt and was entrusted with the captured Duke of Orleans (who later became Louis XII) at Starborough. Louis spent twenty years here before being ransomed. After the Reigate affair of 1648 the castle was demolished by Parliament so that nothing remains of it today.

SUSSEX

AMBERLEY

The castle lies south of Pulborough on B2139 and was a manor house belonging to the bishops of Chichester. In 1377 Bishop Rede obtained a licence to crenellate from Richard II and built the high walls that stand today. The outer wall was probably started several years earlier to safeguard the village against a probable peasants' revolt. Rede added a great hall, connected by the solar to the main house. A water gate was constructed in the west wall so that boats could come in when the castle was flooded. There does not appear to have been a moat on this side. The main entrance on the south was guarded by twin drum towers which were protected by a south moat. Bishop Sherburne restored the Queen's Room above the Dining Hall in about 1530. Nine panels of classical scenes were painted by Lambert Bernard at this time. They were recently removed for restoration.

Held by John Goring during the Civil War, Amberley fell to Parliament shortly after the capture of Arundel. The castle, then belonging to the Lewknors, was stripped of valuables and the roof of the Great Hall was removed; the contents were sold to James Butler for over £3,000. In succeeding years the castle passed to the Peachey, Harcourt and Zouche families until 1893 when it was purchased and restored by the Duke of Norfolk. Most of the existing battlements date from this time.

Baroness Emmet of Amberley. Garden only open occasionally under the National Gardens Scheme.

ARUNDEL

The Duke of Norfolk's large castle is mostly a Victorian restoration in Gothic style, and its history and contents are really of more interest than its architecture, although from the south especially it presents a magnificent spectacle.

Earl Roger de Montgomery was originally granted the keep and land after Hastings and he constructed the Norman arch and walls which form the inner gateway. Today there are the remains of the buildings which consisted of a motte and two baileys. Robert de Beleme, who inherited Arundel from Earl Roger, sided with the Duke of Normandy against Henry I. The castle was besieged, the defenders surrendered and Beleme was later captured and imprisoned at Wareham. Arundel was settled on Henry's wife Adela of Lourain, who married, after Henry's death, William d'Albini, a supporter of Matilda in the war against Stephen. For a second time (1139) Arundel was besieged; this time it did not surrender and Stephen's army withdrew.

In 1243 the last of the Albinis died and Arundel passed to his daughter Isabel, who married John Fitzalan, son of the lord of Clun Castle. The Fitzalans lived here until 1580 when the last, Henry, Earl of Arundel, died. His daughter succeeded to the property with her husband Thomas Howard, Duke of Norfolk. It has remained Norfolk property ever since. During the Civil War the third and longest siege took place. The constable, Sir Edward Ford, held out bravely for eighteen days but on 6th January 1644 he surrendered to Sir William Waller after the walls had been battered by cannon placed in the tower of St Nicholas Church. A few Royalists escaped but most were taken prisoner.

For nearly 150 years Arundel remained a ruin until the eighth duke began restoring it in 1716 and this work was continued by the tenth duke in 1789. One of the rooms added was the library with its mahogany panelling which was completed in 1801. The fifteenth duke finalised restoration work from 1890 to 1903. A total of £600,000 was spent on its restoration. The Well Tower, which defended the keep, is basically thirteenth century and contains a well (76 feet) and a chapel. Below the Victorian Great Hall is a Norman undercroft with two windows that once formed the outside wall of the Norman hall, which was half the size of the present structure.

The Duke of Norfolk. Open mid-April–mid-May, Monday–Thursday 1–4.30. May 14–June 15 Monday–Friday 1–4.30. June 18–September 28 Monday–Friday 12–4.30. Sundays only in August. Entrance at Lower Lodge, Mill Road. No dogs. Admission charge.

BODIAM

Situated just off the A229 Hastings to Hawkhurst road, Bodiam was built in 1385 by Sir Edward Dalyngrigge to protect the river Rother from French raiding parties which frequently attacked the coast at Rye and Winchelsea. During the wars in France, Dalyngrigge had made a fortune. His wife was the heiress of the Wardeux family who owned Bodiam and by the terms of the licence dated 21st October 1385 he was entitled to 'strengthen his manorhouse with a wall of stone and lime'. The castle is rectangular with a wide moat and two entrances, the main one having three drawbridges and fortified bridge heads. The apartments inside are remarkably comfortable. The Lord's Hall and the Lord's Kitchen are at the south end, the chapel and main apartments at the east end. The retainers, soldiers and servants had their kitchen on the west side, with special vents in its chimney to heat their hall behind. The rectangular mid tower leads up to the retainers' dormitory, separated from the lord's quarters. The only means of communication with these is over the central courtyard. In the north range there is a replica of a bombard or siege gun which was capable of casting a stone ball weighing 150 lb.

Within defensive range of the castle a harbour was built for ships sailing up the Rother. In 1483, during the reign of Richard III, Bodiam was held for Henry Tudor by one of the Lewknors. He was attainted and the Earl of Surrey was ordered to take the castle. No damage appears to have been done at that time. It was reduced to ruin by Sir William Waller after his capture of Arundel in 1643. The later owners were Tuftons, Powells, Websters, Fullers and Cubritts and, in 1917, Lord Curzon. He enabled the National Trust to acquire in 1925 what is unquestionably their finest ruined castle and one of the architectural gems of the period. A museum at the custodian's cottage contains items found during excavations, including remains of Dalyngrigge's tomb.

National Trust. Open to the public every day April–October 10–7. October–March, weekdays only 10–dusk. Admission charge.

BRAMBER

William de Braose built a castle here, of which there remains only a tall wall of one side of the keep. It was

170

garrisoned by Captain Temple in 1644 and blown up when captured by the Parliamentarians. At one time ships came up the Adur and there were salt pans beneath the walls and a moat on the south and north-west sides.
Open at all times.

CHICHESTER
Earl d'Alencon built a castle here in Priory Park. It was destroyed by Philip d'Albini in 1217 and for a time the remains served as a prison.

COWDRAY
The magnificent remains of Cowdray manor are near the centre of Midhurst. About 1273 John Bohun built the original moated house. Sir David Owen's quadrangular building of 1520 was crenellated under licence in 1535 by Sir William FitzWilliam and the gatehouse was added. Sir William became Earl of Southampton and Lord Privy Seal. He was succeeded by his half-brother Sir Anthony Browne whose son Viscount Montague added the large Tudor windows in about 1554. The sixth Lord Montague built the gates at the park entrance and added more large windows.

In 1552 young Edward VI visited Cowdray where Sir Anthony Browne saw that he was 'marvelously, yea rather excessively, banketted'. In 1591 Elizabeth I came here and shot four deer, rivalling Lady Kildare who could manage only one. The following year Viscount Montague died and his tomb can be seen in Midhurst church. The second viscount was involved in the Gunpowder Plot but was pardoned after a year's imprisonment, on payment of a heavy fine. The third viscount was a Royalist whose estate was sequestered and Parliamentary troops were quartered here until 1660.

In 1793 the eighth viscount was drowned attempting to shoot the rapids of Laufenburg on the Rhine; a few weeks earlier, on 24th September, a workman had left a charcoal pan burning in the north-west corner tower. The house was gutted by fire and many valuables were destroyed, including the Roll of Battle Abbey. The estate passed to the Poyntz family who lived in the Keeper's Lodge and a second tragedy occurred in 1815 when their two sons were drowned at Bognor Regis. Thus the saying of one of the Battle Abbey monks at the time of the Dissolution came true, that Sir Anthony Browne's family 'by fire and water should come to an end'.

171

In 1908 Sir Weetman Dickinson Pearson bought the estate and was made Viscount Cowdray in 1916. The ruins were repaired and later a small museum was opened.

Viscount Cowdray. Open at all reasonable times. Admission charge. Tickets from the Round Tower.

CROWHURST

Walter de Scotney had a fortified manor at Crowhurst. He was executed for attempting to poison his master, Richard de Clare, in 1259. Part of the first-floor hall remains near the church.

EWHURST

The Peverels and Wests had a castle here, the gatehouse of which was still standing in Victorian times.

HARTFIELD

A castle of the barons of Pevensey once stood here and its site is called Castle Field today.

HASTINGS

The original castle at Hastings is in the sea. The ruins seen today are mostly of the chapel of St Mary and date from the thirteenth century. In about 1069 Robert, Count of Eu, was granted this land, William the Conqueror's first English possession, and replaced the king's wooden castle, brought over from Normandy as depicted in the Bayeux tapestry, with a stone one. The first tournament in England was held at Hastings, William's daughter Adela representing the Queen of Beauty. The castle was often held by the king. The French landed in 1339 and 1377 and destroyed part of the town which was not fortified. The last owners were the Pelhams and today it stands in a small park. There are two underground 'dungeons' of unusual interest.

Open daily 10–5.30, Easter–mid-October.

HERSTMONCEUX

One of the most remarkable and least accessible castles in England, Herstmonceux lies in a valley off A271 between Lewes and Battle. It was originally a Norman manor belonging to the Herst family from Monceux, near Bayeux in Normandy. Their last heiress married Sir John de Fiennes in 1320 and her great-grandson, Sir Roger, obtained a licence in 1441 and built the castle. He was a veteran of Agincourt,

172

Treasurer of the Household to Henry VI, and became Lord Dacre. Of a similar age to Tattershall, Lincolnshire, Herstmonceux was also built of Flemish bricks and the original structure had 365 windows and 52 chimneys. There were three courts: a large Green Court, a smaller Pump Court, and a tiny Chicken Court; also a strange chamber for the gardener known as Drummer's Hall where a French gardener used to beat a drum to distract the family's attention from smugglers.

The Dacres lived here until the end of Elizabeth's reign, when the castle passed to the Leonards, who assumed the title of Dacre. A Dacre married the illegitimate daughter of Charles II and the Duchess of Cleveland but his extravagance forced him to sell the castle to a Mr Naylor for £38,215. Mr Naylor died without issue and the castle passed to Dr Hare, Bishop of Chichester, whose second son Robert was responsible in 1777 for commissioning Samuel Wyatt to build nearby Herstmonceux Place out of much of the interior brick of the castle. The tapestries, furniture and sculptures were all auctioned. The castle remained a ruin until Colonel Claude Lowther rebuilt it with one courtyard in 1913 and it was further restored by Sir Paul Latham in 1933.

Royal Observatory. Gardens open to the public 2–5, Mondays to Fridays, April–October. Admission charge. Enter by Wartling Road.

KNEPP

On the main Horsham-Worthing road (A24), Knepp Castle keep stands 30 feet high on a motte. It is ruined but two windows remain and a modern Gothic castle stands nearby, once the home of Sir William Burrell, the Sussex historian. The old castle belonged to the de Braose family and was forfeited to King John, who used it as a hunting lodge.

LEWES

Earl William de Warenne, whose wife Gundrada is believed to be the daughter of William the Conqueror, built the castle in the late eleventh century. During the fourteenth century it passed to Richard Fitzalan, 13th Earl of Arundel, who was the son of Alice, the sister of the last de Warenne.

Lewes Castle is remarkable in having two mounds, the one on the north-east being the present Brack Mount. An elliptical shell-keep was raised on the western mound; the projecting polygonal towers, of which two remain, were

173

added in the thirteenth century. The fine Barbican, or outer gatehouse, was erected in the fourteenth century in front of the Norman gateway.

John, the seventh earl, fought under Henry III at the battle of Lewes, fleeing to France on defeat. The following year he returned and took part in the battle at Evesham, where Simon de Montfort was killed.

In the castle grounds are iron railings made in Sussex for St Paul's Cathedral, an Armada cannon, a Russian gun captured in the Crimean War, two prehistoric canoes and other interesting items. Barbican House museum, opposite the castle entrance, houses the Prehistoric, Roman, Saxon and Medieval collections of the Sussex Archaeological Society.

Open weekdays 10–1, 2–5.30. Sundays (April to October) 2–5.30. Admission charge.

PETWORTH

The Percy family obtained a licence to crenellate their manor at Petworth in 1309. Only the chapel walls and the undercroft remain of the old manor, which was incorporated into the new house built in 1688.

National Trust. Open Wednesdays, Thursdays, Saturdays, and Bank Holiday Mondays April–October, 2–6. Admission charge.

PEVENSEY

Pevensey Castle once stood beside the sea but with the gradual alteration of the coast line, it now lies about a mile inland on A259 between Eastbourne and Bexhill. One of the nine Saxon shore forts, Pevensey was formerly the Roman city Anderida and the ten acres of the outer bailey enclose an oval surrounded by most of the original Roman walls. The Normans landed near here and there is a small monument to William the Conqueror by the main gate. The Norman castle has five towers and a moat with a keep constructed about the year 1100 by Count Robert of Mortain and his son William. It is 55 feet by 30 feet inside and uses the east wall of the Roman fort for its outer wall. The main entrance was from the west gate, but the visitor now enters by the east gate which once probably led to the harbour. Inside the keep are some interesting ballista missiles, a dungeon, an oulbiette, remains of a chapel and an Elizabethan cannon probably used to defend the castle during the Armada alert.

174

Pevensey has several times been besieged. In 1088, after the death of the Conqueror, Bishop Odo supported the claims of Robert, the Conqueror's brother, against William Rufus who besieged the castle until it was starved into surrender. In 1147 the castle was besieged by Stephen and again the hungry garrison, under the Earl of Clare, was forced to surrender. It withstood a siege by Simon de Montfort and another in the fourteenth century when Lady Pelham, in her husband's absence, held out for Henry Bolingbroke against Richard II. It was then held by the Crown until bestowed by William III on the Bentincks who sold it to the Earl of Wilmington from whom it passed in 1782 to the dukes of Devonshire. After this it was used as a quarry and decayed into ruin. During the last war, however, it was fitted with several ingenious machine-gun positions, the one on the north-west bastion looking like part of the Norman building. Observation troops and the U.S. Army Air Corps were residents as well as Canadians and the Home Guard. The west gate was fitted with a blockhouse containing anti-tank weapons and a new tower was added to the eastern wall. In 1945 it was restored by the Ministry of Public Building and Works who removed the blockhouse and carried out some internal excavations.

Department of the Environment. Open at normal times. Admission charge.

RUDGWICK

Near Horsham, a few stones remain of the de Sauvage castle. It had two moats and was circular in plan with a well outside the outer moat. It was excavated in 1923 but today the remains are hard to find.

VERDLEY

Near Eastbourne a hunting lodge surrounded by a moat was built in the thirteenth century by the de Bohuns. Camden described it as 'a lonely and romantic place known only to those that hunt the marten cat'.

YPRES TOWER

Rye, one of the most attractive towns in Sussex, was attacked by the French on more than one occasion. The tower was built to orders of Henry III by the Constable of the Cinque Ports, as part of the fortification of Rye, and in 1377 was burnt to the ground. It is a small building and

was used as a prison in the nineteenth century. Today it is a museum.
Open weekdays 10.30–1, 2.15–5.30, *Sundays* 11.30–1, 2.15–5.30 *Easter–mid October. Admission charge.*

WARWICKSHIRE

ANSLEY
Nothing remains of the former house of the Hastings family who fortified it after obtaining a licence from Edward I in 1300.

ASTLEY
A few miles from Nuneaton off B4102 stands the sixteenth-century castle of the Grey family. Originally built at the time of Edward I by the Astleys, the estate passed to Reginald Grey through marriage in the fifteenth century. Lady Jane Grey spent much of her early life here, where her father was betrayed by his park-keeper and taken to London and beheaded for his part in the Wyatt rebellion. The castle that stands today was built during the reign of Queen Mary. In 1674 it was bought by the Newdigates of Arbury Hall.
It is now a restaurant with lounge bars.

BAGINTON
Just outside Coventry on A444 stood a fourteenth-century tower that belonged to the Bagots. Henry Bolingbroke stayed here the night before his intended duel with Thomas Mowbray at nearby Gosford Green. Richard II was told of the plan and banished both lords from the country. Henry returned in 1399 to become Henry IV.

BEAUDESERT
On the other side of the Alne from Henley is the Mount at Beaudesert where the de Montforts had a castle built by 1141 when Thurstan de Montfort had a charter for a market in the castle. It was a ruin by 1547.

BRINKLOW
On the Foss Way, where it crosses the Rugby and Coventry road, stood a castle that belonged to the Mowbrays and later to the de Stutevilles.

CALEDON

Three miles north-east of Coventry stood another castle that belonged to the Mowbrays. From here Thomas Mowbray, Duke of Norfolk, set out to duel with Henry Bolingbroke (*see* Baginton above). An Elizabethan house was built on the site but in 1800 Lord Clifford demolished this and built a farmhouse with the material.

CASTLE BROMWICH

Slight traces of a motte and bailey, that gave this part of Birmingham its name, can be seen north of the church.

COLESHILL

Here stood a castle that belonged to the Clintons and later the Mountfords. Sir Simon Mountford supported Perkin Warbeck's revolt in 1487 and was led to his trial by Simon Digby, Deputy Constable of the Tower, who was granted the castle after Mountford's execution.

COVENTRY

A priory here was converted into a castle by Robert Marmion in 1143 and the Earl of Chester built a siege castle or malvoisin in front of it in 1147.

FILLONGLEY

On the Nuneaton to Solihull road, Fillongley was a fortified manor known as Castle Yard. It belonged to Sir Henry Hastings, one of the supporters of Simon de Montfort. Faint traces of the moat remain.

FULBROKE

On a hill between Stratford and Warwick stood a castle that once belonged to Warwick the Kingmaker. It was 'an eyesore to the earls that lay in Warwick' and as a result was demolished in the reign of Henry VIII. The stones were used by Sir William Compton to build his remarkable house Compton Wynyates.

HARTSHILL

Hugh de Hardreshall built a castle here in 1125 and the walls were strengthened in the fourteenth century. The castle was still intact in 1790; parts of the chapel and the walls remain.

KENILWORTH

The only lake fortress in England, Kenilworth was granted to Geoffrey de Clinton by Henry I. The first building was probably a motte and bailey castle but the first stone structure was the massive twelfth-century keep, which was built by Geoffrey's son. Between 1212 and 1216 Kenilworth was the property of King John who had exchanged it with the Clintons for Swanbourne manor in Buckinghamshire. The Lunn's Tower and Water Tower were constructed at the king's expense and many other improvements were carried out.

Henry III's sister Eleanor married Simon de Montfort, Earl of Leicester, and the castle was granted first to Eleanor and in 1254 to them both for life. With its wide meres and moat Kenilworth made an ideal centre for de Montfort's rebellion. Successfully defeating the king at Lewes in 1264, Simon sent Henry's brother Richard and his youngest son Edmund to Kenilworth as prisoners, the king and Prince Edward being held at Hereford. The following year Prince Edward escaped and attacked Simon's son, who was camping with his soldiers outside the castle. Young Simon was nearly captured but escaped into the castle which, following the elder Simon's defeat at Evesham, was besieged for six months. The defenders dressed up one of their men as a priest to excommunicate the attackers, but finally disease and hunger forced the surrender and young Simon fled abroad.

In 1279 the castle was in the possession of the Earl of Lancaster and a great three-day tournament was held at Kenilworth. Roger de Mortimer, organiser of the tournament, started the 'Round Table', a new military game, outside Mortimer's tower. In 1326 Edward II was brought here as a prisoner by the Earl of Lancaster and detained until he abdicated in favour of his son. The fourth earl's daughter Blanche married John of Gaunt, fourth son of Edward III, and the latter, on taking possession of the castle, built the Lancaster Buildings including the Great Hall with its two huge fireplaces. Much of the stone fabric of this massive building remains today.

No further permanent building was carried out until Elizabeth's reign when the castle was in the possession of Robert Dudley, Earl of Leicester. He erected the gatehouse with its four corner towers, part of which is now the caretaker's house and is closed to the public. In July 1575 Queen Elizabeth visited Kenilworth and stayed for seventeen days. Every kind of festivity took place including fireworks on the mere and the cost to Leicester was £1,000 a day, an enormous sum for those days.

During the Civil War the castle was used as quarters for Parliamentary troops but the owner, Lord Monmouth, was unable to prevent the unnecessary slighting that took place in 1649, when the keep was destroyed and huge gaps were made in the outer walls. Colonel Hawksworth, who carried out the demolition work, then occupied the inhabitable part with ten other officers. He drained the mere and ignored decaying stonework.

Charles II granted Kenilworth to Laurence Hyde whose son became the Earl of Clarendon. It remained in their family until 1958 when it was presented to the people of Kenilworth and came under the guardianship of the Ministry of Public Building and Works.

Department of the Environment. Open normal times. Admission charge.

MAXSTOKE

One of the most perfectly preserved private castles of the fourteenth century, Maxstoke stands in a large park near Coleshill. To reach it take the A47 from Birmingham towards Nuneaton and turn right at the village of Shustoke, or alternatively, go into Coleshill and take the B4117. In either case it is not necessary to go into Maxstoke village which is some three miles from the castle.

The licence to crenellate Maxstoke is dated 1346 and was granted by Edward III to William de Clinton, Earl of Huntingdon. From the Clintons it passed in 1438 to Humphrey, Earl of Stafford. The four octagonal towers guarded the curtain wall which is surrounded by a moat and the entrance has iron and wood doors. Maxstoke was more a residential castle than a military one. Richard III is supposed to have spent a night before Bosworth at Maxstoke. Sir Thomas Egerton, Lord Keeper of the Great Seal, subsequently lived there. Edward Stafford, Lord High Constable of England, lived here during Henry VIII's reign but due to Wolsey's influence, fell out of favour and was beheaded in 1521 whereupon the castle passed to Sir William Compton. It was later purchased by the Dilkes of Kirkby Mallory, whose descendants still live there.

Capt. C. B. Fetherstone-Dilke, R.N. Open to organised parties by written appointment only.

STUDLEY
Where the river Avon joins the Arrow once stood the Norman castle of William de Corbucion. Peter Corbucion later founded a priory, the remains of which can still be seen at Priory Farm.

WARWICK
Originally a Saxon town, Warwick was one of the places selected by Ethelfleda, daughter of King Alfred, for a defensive mound to be built by the Avon to keep out the Danes. With Stafford and Tamworth she blocked the Foss Way and Watling Street so that Mercia could be protected from the north. At the time of the Norman Conquest the largest landowner in Warwickshire was the Saxon thegn Turchil, who had not supported Harold, and was allowed by the Normans to keep his estates. The Normans similarly looked at Warwick as a suitable spot for a castle, and William the Conqueror ordered a new and enlarged castle to be built there on the site of the Saxon fortifications. Henry de Newburgh was made its constable, and later, on the death of Turchil, was created Earl of Warwick and given most of Turchil's lands.

The castle remained Crown property and the earl was merely the custodian. During the Barons' War the earl was forcibly removed to Kenilworth by John Gifford and held to ransom. In 1265, perhaps due to the shock of his imprisonment, he died and the title passed through his daughter to the Beauchamp family.

The two successive Thomas Beauchamps, Earls of Warwick, were responsible for building most of the castle that stands today. Both Guy's and Caesar's towers were constructed at this time. Guy's tower is twelve-sided and rises to 128 feet; Caesar's tower is like three towers squashed together with an inner stage and rises to 147 feet. In 1356 French prisoners captured at Poitiers were accommodated in Guy's tower.

The famous Richard Neville, Earl of Warwick, inherited the castle from the Beauchamps and it remained in Yorkist hands. After Warwick's death at the battle of Barnet in 1471 the title of Earl of Warwick went to the unfortunate Clarence, his son-in-law, who met his death by drowning in wine. Clarence is said to have had grandiose schemes for enlarging and improving the castle, but did not carry them out. The unfinished Bear and Clarence towers are in fact the remains of the artillery fort started, but never finished, by Richard III, which originally consisted of four towers. The Bear tower contains a pit which is thought to have been a bear pit. Richard III's nephew Edward was beheaded by Henry VII on a trumped-up charge, and for sixty years there was no earl of Warwick. Henry VIII bestowed the earldom on John Dudley, a relation of the Beauchamps, and it was this earl, later made Duke of Northumberland, who tried to put his daughter-in-law Lady Jane Grey on the throne and lost his life in the attempt. His son Ambrose inherited the title and when he died childless in 1589 it reverted to the Crown.

James I bestowed the title, but not the castle, on Lord Rich of Leighs and in the eighteenth century the title passed to the Greville family in whose hands it remains today.

In 1604 Fulke Greville had obtained a grant of the castle and had repaired it at great expense until it became 'the most princely seat within the midland parts of this realm'. Fulke, a man of letters and a courtier, was stabbed by his servant in 1628 and his cousin Robert, Lord Brooke, inherited the castle. Robert was a Parliamentary supporter and took part in the battle of Edgehill. For three days Warwick was besieged by the Royalists under Lord Northampton. Sir Edward Peto, in charge of the garrison, refused to surrender. Robert was killed at Lichfield by a musket bullet in the eye and his successor was a Royalist who was responsible for the fitting up of the present magnificent state apartments. The collection of armour in the great hall, the pictures in the state rooms, the Warwick vase and the Italian castle garden are only some of the attractions of Warwick; the dominant spectacle is of the magnificent battlements of one of the best preserved and maintained castles in England.

Earl of Warwick. Open daily Good Friday to mid-September 10–5.30; weekdays (except Saturdays) mid-September, October and March 12.30–4.30. Closed November–February. Admission charge.

WEOLEY

Recent excavations have uncovered the footings of Roger de Somery's thirteenth-century castle near Birmingham. It had six towers and replaced a wooden structure on the same site.

WOLSTON

Between Rugby and Coventry, earthworks remain of the thirteenth-century Brandon Castle, which had an oblong keep.

WESTMORLAND

APPLEBY

Founded like Brough, Brougham and Pendragon by Ranulf de Meschines, Appleby changed ownership frequently between the Viponts and Morvilles before becoming a Clifford castle. The keep is mostly twelfth-century and was probably built by Henry II who took over the castle in 1157 and again in 1173. The gatehouse was built by John Clifford in 1418 and the eastern part – hall, chapel and great chamber – was built by Lord Thomas Clifford in 1454. He was killed at St Albans in the Wars of the Roses.

In 1651 Lady Anne Clifford restored the castle and used it as her home. Her son-in-law, the Earl of Thanet, rebuilt the east wing with stone from Brough Castle and further repairs were done in the nineteenth century.

It is not open to the public.

ARNSIDE TOWER

On Morecambe Bay, Arnside is a ruined three-storey pele tower which belonged to the Stanleys. It was badly burnt in 1602 and never restored.

BEETHAM HALL

Beetham stands near Milnthorpe, on the site of a four-teenth-century fortified house. It has a large curtain wall and chapel and belonged to the Stanleys.

BEWLEY

This is a ruined castle at Bolton on the Eden. It belonged to the bishops of Carlisle.

BROUGH

William Rufus built the Norman castle on a Roman site at Brough in about 1095. It was destroyed by William the Lion of Scotland in 1174 and rebuilt by the Cliffords. Lady Anne carried out restorations in 1659–62 and her son-in-law used it as a quarry for repairing Appleby in 1695.

Department of the Environment. Open at normal times.

BROUGHAM

Between Penrith and Clifton, where the river Eamont joins the Lowther, was a Roman fort called Brocavum which could accommodate a thousand troops. On this site a keep was built in Henry II's reign, probably by Hugh d'Albini, and it passed to the Vipont family until the death, at the battle of Evesham, of Robert de Vipont, a supporter of Simon de Montfort. His daughter Isabella succeeded to the estate with her husband Roger Clifford. Robert Clifford, who constructed the massive gatehouse, was killed at Bannockburn. In the seventeenth century Lady Anne Clifford, who also owned Appleby, Brough, Pendragon and Skipton, repaired the castle. After her death in 1676 it fell into decay once more. Her grandson Lord Tufton pulled down much of the interior and parts of it were sold in 1708 as building material.

The inner and outer gatehouse are linked by a court and a walled walkway that has arrow loops. The castle had a postern gate at the south-west corner leading to a causeway over the moat. There is also a causeway across the moat at the junction of the fourteenth-century chapel on the first floor and the kitchen. There seems to be no reason for this and it is assumed that it was built at a later date, perhaps to allow Lady Anne's masons to get their stones to that side of the castle.

There are Roman gravestones inside the gatehouse and an old tablet to Lady Anne.

Department of the Environment. Open normal times. Admission charge.

BURNESIDE HALL

North of Kendal, Burneside is a fourteenth-century hall house with a north wing that was originally a pele tower. It has a fine ceiling in one of the upstairs rooms.

CLIFTON

This impressive pele tower is on a farm between the main road and the railway south of Penrith. It had a hall range which was taken down. Nearby is the site of the last battle on English soil, Clifton Moor (1745).

HARTLEY

Near Kirkby Stephen, Hartley belonged to Andrew Harcla, who was beheaded in 1322 for signing an independent treaty with Robert Bruce. Only part of the old wall survives and the house is eighteenth-century.

HAZELSLACK

This fourteenth-century pele tower near Beetham Hall is now in ruins, it was once similar to Arnside.

183

HOWGILL

At Milburn, Howgill is mostly seventeenth-century but was originally built by the de Stutevilles in the fourteenth century. It was a very strong structure, consisting of a rectangular hall between two towers, each 64 feet by 33 feet with walls nearly 10 feet thick.

KENDAL

To reach Kendal Castle one should stay on the south side of the town and park up one of the side streets towards the park. The climb up to the de Taillebois castle is worthwhile although only parts of the curtain wall and the keep remain. In 1513 Catherine Parr, fortunate widow of Henry VIII, was born here and it is probable that the Norman keep was altered by her family. There is a separate motte and bailey at Castle How near the hospital.

KENTMERE

This is a ruined fourteenth-century pele tower with a later hall attached.

KIRKBY LONSDALE

A motte and bailey castle can be seen near the vicarage.

LAMMERSIDE

Near Pendragon is a ruined pele tower with a corridor running across from north to south inside and the usual tunnel vaulting.

PENDRAGON

This late Norman pele tower was burnt by the Scots in 1341 and was restored by the redoubtable Lady Anne Clifford. There was a bridge here over the Eden.

PRESTON PATRICK HALL

Not far from Beetham, this is a fifteenth-century house built on the site of an earlier pele tower. It is similar in many ways to Burneside.

SIZERGH

The Stricklands' castle lies close to A6 between Kendal and Milnthorpe, and is a fine example of a pele tower with a hall attached. In 1239 Elizabeth Deincourt, whose family had owned Sizergh, married Sir William Strickland. Sir Walter Strickland built the tower about 1340. His sister

184

Jean married Robert de Wessington, ancestor of George Washington. In 1415 a Strickland carried the royal banner at Agincourt. They were Yorkists in the Wars of the Roses and provided troops for the Earl of Salisbury. In Henry VIII's reign they were brought into court life having intermarried in Edward IV's reign with the Parrs of Kendal. Walter Strickland was one of Elizabeth I's captains on the border. He had an armed retinue of 290 men and during his lifetime Elizabethan additions with fine panelling and alterations to the fifteenth-century Great Hall were made. Sir Robert Strickland was a Royalist and lost much of his fortune during the Civil War. Sir Thomas, his son, was a supporter of James II and followed him into exile. Many Stuart relics can be seen in a little room on the top floor.

In Victorian times Sir Gerald Strickland was an M.P., prime minister of Malta, and later was created Baron Strickland of Sizergh. The estate passed to his daughter and her husband, Henry Hornyold-Strickland who, with their son, presented it to the National Trust in 1950.

Sizergh has avoided destruction by siege or fire although, apart from the pele tower and a three-sided moat, it was never constructed as a place of great strength.

The castle contains some interesting pictures of the family and in the old Pele Tower with its adzed floor is a massive James I table and a very large sword as old as the pele tower. The gardens are very neatly laid out.

National Trust. Open Wednesdays 2–5.45 April–September. Gardens only. Admission charge.

TEBAY

There is a motte and bailey castle of two acres here.

WHARTON

The fortified manor-house near Kirkby Stephen belonging to the Whartons is now mostly in ruins. The first Lord Wharton was partly responsible for the rout of the Scots at Solway Moss in 1542, but later Whartons preferred to live in the south at Upper Winchendon near Aylesbury.

YANWATH

This is the finest fourteenth-century pele tower in the north and was built by John Sutton. It was altered in Elizabethan times and one room has the royal arms over the fireplace. It was sold to the Lowthers in 1654. The gateway is modern but the original is supposed to have had a chapel above it similar to that at Prudhoe castle.

WILTSHIRE

CASTLE COMBE

The attractive village of Castle Combe, near Chippenham, has a few remains of its castle behind the manor house. It belonged to the Dunstanvilles, Montforts, Badlesmeres, Tiptofts and Scropes and the keep was standing in the seventeenth century. Saxon coins have been found on the site.

CASTLE EATON

Near Cricklade, William of Dover had a castle built here in 1142; it was a ruin by the fifteenth century.

DEVIZES

One of the more important castles of England once stood here and its outer bailey is marked by the curve of Bridewell Street, Sheep Street, Market Street and New Park Street. It was built by Henry I's friend, Bishop Roger of Salisbury, and in Leland's time it had 'divers goodly towers' and the main gate had 'places for seven or eight portcullises'. The main hall was 70 feet long and in the eighteenth century one of the surviving towers was capped by a windmill. The castle changed hands many times in Stephen's war with Matilda. It passed to the Crown in 1157 and was often included in the dowry of English queens. Henry III imprisoned his former favourite Hubert de Burgh here. The Royalists garrisoned it during the Civil War. In 1643 Royalist success at the Battle of Roundway Down secured the relief of Lord Hopton who was trapped with his army in the castle. Two years later it was captured by Cromwell and slighted. A castellated building of 1842 hides any trace of the old structure.

DOWNTON

Henry de Blois built a castle here on the Avon in 1137 but nothing remains today.

LUDGERSHALL

Earthworks and part of the flint keep remain of Henry III's castle. The well water was fit for drinking until Victorian times.

186

MALMESBURY

Bishop Roger had a castle here which was dismantled in 1216 to add to the abbey. The site is occupied by the Castle Hotel.

MARLBOROUGH

William I built a castle here and established a mint. His motte can still be seen in the college grounds.

MEMBURY

Near Ramsbury, this was a twelfth-century keep which was converted into a fortified manor house.

MERE

Richard, Earl of Cornwall, built a castle on a mound in 1253 which recent excavations have revealed to have been rectangular with six towers, the two middle ones being round.

OLD SARUM

In 1070 the Conqueror reviewed his victorious army in Old Sarum, and it was at this time that the great circular earthwork was constructed in the centre of a magnificent Iron Age fort. The outer fortifications were increased to their present dimensions. The cathedral church, whose remains can still be seen, was consecrated in 1092 and improved by Bishop Roger of Salisbury between 1107 and 1139. By 1447 the castle was in decay and the town was abandoned in the fifteenth century. However, the site was to become famous amongst schoolboys as the classic 'rotten borough' which returned two members to Parliament, amongst them the Pitts, until the Reform Act of 1832 finally abolished this practice.

Department of the Environment. Open at normal times.

SHERRINGTON

A small motte and bailey castle built by the Giffords stood next to the church. The site is now an island in a large pond of remarkably clear water.

SOUTH CERNEY

Captured by Stephen in 1139, the castle site may be the earthworks at Ashton Keynes.

STOURTON

Sir John Stourton built a castellated house in the fifteenth century out of ransom money received in the French wars and the site is now occupied by Stourhead. It was the scene of a double murder in 1557 when Charles, seventh Lord Stourton, quarrelled with his servant Hartgill and put him and his father to death. He was tried, and hanged at Salisbury, with a silken cord as befitted his rank. The house was demolished in 1720. The present house was built in 1722 in the Palladian style and the landscape garden is historically important as an example of 'le jardin Anglais'. *Garden open daily all year. House open daily April–September, and on Wednesday, Saturday and Sunday afternoons in March, October and November.*

TROWBRIDGE

The de Bohuns had a castle here which was demolished in 1814. The main street in the town curves because it follows the line of the moat.

WARDOUR

This fourteenth-century castle, shaped like a keyhole with the main entrance facing east, was built by John, Lord Lovell, who obtained a licence to crenellate in 1393. The daughter of Lord Lovell married Lord Dynham and their granddaughter married an Arundell. Sir Matthew Arundell's coat of arms and the date 1570 are above the door and his successor Sir Thomas, the first Lord Arundell, distinguished himself fighting against the Turks in 1595. The second Lord Arundell raised a troop to fight for Charles I and left his wife Blanche, the daughter of the Marquess of Worcester, at Wardour with a small garrison. In May 1643 Colonel Strode attacked it with 1300 men and for five days the garrison held out. Two mines under the fabric did little damage but Lady Blanche decided to surrender as food and ammunition supplies were short. Colonel Ludlow now put in a Parliamentary garrison. After the death of the second lord at Lansdowne, the third lord raised a small army to regain his castle. In March 1644 he succeeded after blowing up the corn store and killing three of the garrison. The colonel surrendered and the Arundells returned to live in an outhouse, for the main structure had been too damaged to be habitable. The eighth lord built the new castle nearby, between 1769 and 1776. This is now a girl's school.
Department of the Environment. Admission charge.

WILTON

   Stephen converted a monastic building near Salisbury into a castle in 1143.

WORCESTERSHIRE

DUDLEY

   Dudley Castle was probably built by William Fitz-Ansculf, who held it at the time of Domesday. Later it passed to the Paganels and when in 1173 Gervase de Paganel joined the revolt against Henry II, the latter demolished it. In 1264 Roger de Somery, a relation of the Peverels, obtained a licence to crenellate the manor of Dudley and erected the castle, part of which we see today. Captured by de Montfort at Lewes, Somery was imprisoned and when released died shortly after his king. The castle then passed to his son-in-law John Sutton, whose grandson Sir John Sutton was a Lancastrian during the Wars of the Roses. Captured at Blore Heath, he was imprisoned in Ludlow and after the accession of Edward IV changed sides. During the reign of Henry VII, Lord Dudley, his descendant, became penniless after the misdeeds of his namesake, John Dudley, Duke of Northumberland. When the duke was executed on the accession of Queen Mary, Dudley was restored to his castle and it remained in his family until 1621 when it descended to Queen Henrietta Maria's goldsmith Humble Ward. The latter married the granddaughter of Lord Dudley and became Lord Dudley and Ward. His descendants have held the castle from that date.

   The castle keep had four round towers, and the one ward was guarded by a strong gatehouse with walls 9 feet thick. The outer bailey was surrounded by a moat. During the Civil War Dudley was garrisoned for the king and held out until May 1646 when Colonel Levison surrendered to Sir William Brereton. It was slighted in 1646 but, like Newark, the job was not carried out completely for in 1750 a gang of counterfeiters, who set fire to the surviving woodwork, did more effective and long-lasting damage.
Dudley Castle and Zoo. Open daily 10–dusk or 6 pm. Admission charge.

ELMLEY

   A quiet village off A435 between Evesham and Cheltenham, the original castle at Elmley Castle was built by Robert

D'Abitot in 1086. It was extended by Robert's heir Urso and by his son Roger. In the middle of the twelfth century Roger's daughter Emmeline married Walter de Beauchamp, who also possessed Worcester castle. It was the decline of the latter that made Elmley important as the main seat of the Beauchamps.

Inside the church today is a matchstick model of the castle built by a local historian and based on an early drawing. It shows a castle of unusual design with high walls and a circular keep. After the last Beauchamp died in 1269 his daughter married the Earl of Warwick and it was the latter's famous descendant, Warwick the Kingmaker, who was killed at the battle of Barnet in 1471. The castle fell into decay and the stones were carried off to build Pershore bridge and the fine manor house of the Savages, pulled down quite recently and still partly visible behind the new housing estate. Sir John Savage commanded the left wing of Henry's victorious army at the battle of Bosworth Field and the church contains two fine Savage monuments as well as an interesting booklet on the village by the Rev. R. H. Lloyd.

HANLEY

Near Upton-on-Severn, Hanley Castle was once the seat of the Clares and Beauchamps (earls of Gloucester and earls of Warwick). Only the moat remains today near the river Severn and a farmhouse stands on the site.

HARTLEBURY

Near Kidderminster on A449, Hartlebury is a seventeenth-century house with some fine rococo interiors and a chapel with fan vaulting by Henry Keene. There is no sign of a castle, but on the site of the house was once the moated home of the bishops of Worcester. Bishop Walter de Cantelupe started the building in 1255 and Bishop Giffard obtained a licence to crenellate it in 1268. Parts of one tower and a blocked up window above the hall, together with the moat, are the only remaining parts.

During the Civil War Hartlebury was held for the king until 1646 when Colonel Morgan besieged it and the governor, Captain Sandys, surrendered it without firing a shot, due possibly to the fact that there were many women among the garrison. The London committee sold it to Thomas Westrowe for £3,133 and it was demolished; Westrowe presumably paid such a high sum for both the building materials and the contents.

The Lord Bishop of Worcester. Open Easter–September 1st Sundays only and Bank Holidays 2–6. Admission charge. The north wing contains the Worcestershire County Museum.

HOLT

Between Worcester and Stourport stand the ruins of the fourteenth-century castle of the Beauchamps. One tower of four storeys remains beside the Elizabethan hall. During the Civil War Colonel Bromley fortified Holt for the king and spent £30,000 on the Royal cause.

MADRESFIELD COURT

Near Great Malvern, Madresfield means 'field of the mowers'. The Court is the home of the Lygons, who became earls of Beauchamp. It is mostly Victorian and only the moat wall remains from the fifteenth-century castellated manor.

WORCESTER

The Norman castle once stood south of the cathedral on a high mound which was levelled in 1848. There was a priory between castle and cathedral. The dungeons were once very extensive and were used as a prison. In one of them Henry III was kept for some time by Simon de Montfort after the battle of Lewes.

YORKSHIRE

AUGHTON

Once a Norman motte and bailey castle stood by the church near Bubwith off A163. It was the home of Robert Aske, the leader of the Pilgrimage of Grace in 1536, whose story has been well told by H. F. M. Prescott in *The Man on a Donkey*.

BARDEN TOWER

Henry Clifford of Skipton built this Wharfedale hunting lodge, now a ruin. It was restored by Lady Anne Clifford in 1659 and a chapel was added. The Listers, who lived for many years in the cottage nearby, have on display a family halberd that was used at Flodden.

BARWICK IN ELMET

A motte and bailey castle that once belonged to Henry de Lacy stands here.

BEDALE

The Fitzalans had a castle here near the church in which is the fourteenth-century tomb of Sir Brian, Viceroy for Scotland during the reign of Edward I.

BOLTON

Four miles from Middleham, Bolton is the fourteenth-century castle home of the Scropes. Lord Scrope was Richard II's Lord Chancellor and obtained a licence to crenellate his house in 1379. The cost of crenellation came to 1,000 marks and took eighteen years to complete. The castle has one entrance from the east, a quadrangular courtyard, and four towers, one of which collapsed in 1649. As the castle had no moat or outbuildings the defenders had to rely entirely on the strength of the fabric.

Lord Scrope left three sons – the Earl of Wiltshire, who was executed at Bristol in 1399 for treason, Stephen, the Deputy Lieutenant of Ireland, and Roger, who inherited the castle but died shortly after his father. During the Wars of the Roses the Scropes supported the Yorkist cause. In 1513 Henry, ninth Lord Scrope, fought with distinction at Flodden. After her defeat at Langside in 1568, Mary Queen of Scots was brought to Bolton for about six months before being moved to Tutbury. She was closely guarded but managed to escape one evening and reached the Queen's Gap on Leybourne Hill before she was recaptured.

During the Civil War Bolton held out under the 20-year-old John Scrope. The defenders surrendered after a year's resistance (they had been reduced to eating their horses) and young Scrope was fined and taken to London where he died. The castle was slighted and does not appear to have been inhabited since. In the Great Hall is a museum which includes a collection of Wensleydale lead-mining tools.

Open to the public every day except Mondays, other than bank holiday Mondays, 10–dusk, Sundays 9–5.30. Admission charge. Dales Museum inside.

BOWES

In the North Riding, not far from Barnard Castle, Bowes stands on the Roman site of *Lavatrae* commanding the road from York to Appleby. It was built between 1170 and 1187 by the Earl of Richmond, and consists of a large square Norman keep, although it once had two baileys.

Department of the Environment. Open normal times. Admission free.

BURTON IN LONSDALE
A motte and bailey that belonged to the Crown is visible here.

BUTTERCAMBE
A few miles east of York, William de Stuteville obtained a licence to fortify his castle here in 1201. A large motte can clearly be seen in the grounds of the manor.

CASTLETON
This is the site of a motte and bailey overlooking the Esk, near Cleveland. It once belonged to the Norman Robert de Brus.

CAWOOD
This surprising gatehouse, now part of a farm, dates from the fifteenth century and was constructed by Archbishop Kempe on a site believed to have been occupied by a palace of King Athelstan. The adjoining barn has a magnificent fireplace high up one wall. Wolsey spent time here after his fall from power and caught dysentery from which he died at Leicester on his way south to his trial for treason. During the Civil War, Cawood was garrisoned for the king and troops from here helped defeat Fairfax at Adwalton Moor in 1643. When the garrison surrendered to Meldrum the following year many of the men changed sides. It is not open to the public, but is visible from the road.

CLIFTON
Near Masham the Scropes had a castle here by the Ure. It is now ruined and the modern Clifton Castle was built in 1802 a few miles away.

CONISBROUGH
One of the most important of the Yorkshire castles, Conisbrough is in the middle of an industrial area between Doncaster and Rotherham. The first owner was William de Warenne, Earl of Surrey, who probably erected a wooden structure. In 1163 his grandson's daughter Isabel married Hamelin Plantagenet, the half-brother of Henry II. There is a written reference to an endowment of 50 shillings a year for a chapel in the castle and it is generally presumed that Hamelin built the famous keep with its six massive buttresses rising to 86 feet. The keep has three chambers, one of which was an oratory.

The castle later belonged to the Duke of York who died at Agincourt, and after his brother's execution in 1415 the castle passed to Richard, Duke of York, father of Edward IV and Richard III. After 1446 the castle was neglected and later passed to the Carey family. By the sixteenth century it was so ruinous that during the Civil War it was not fortified and so escaped slighting.

In England there are no other keeps of quite the same magnificence and one has to go to Houdan and Etampes in France to find anything comparable of the same age. Little remains of the main castle gate, which turns towards the gatehouse. The inner bailey curtain, in parts 35 feet high, is of a slightly later date than the keep which abuts the north-west wall.

Department of the Environment. Open normal times. Admission charge.

COTHERSTONE

Near the Durham border, Cotherstone was built in about 1200 for the Fitzhughs. It was destroyed during a Scottish raid and only the motte now remains.

COTTINGHAM

William de Stuteville obtained a licence to fortify his manor here and there are remains of his motte and bailey castle.

CRAYKE

The Bishop of Durham built Crayke, which stands square and forbidding on top of a hill near Easingwold. There are two buildings, presumably once connected, and the earlier one, built in about 1441-42, is inhabited; the other is in ruins. The gatehouse and curtain wall have long since vanished. During the Civil War there was a minor engagement here and after 1648 it was slighted but this did not prevent its repair by a Mr Waite in the eighteenth century.

DANBY

In the middle of the north Yorkshire moors is a late fourteenth-century castle, built by William Latimer, and which later passed to the Nevilles of Raby. Lady Latimer was Catherine Parr, who outlived her later husband, Henry VIII.

DRIFFIELD

A motte and bailey castle existed at Driffield. King Aldfrid of Northumbria is supposed to have died here in 705.

GILLING

On a hill beside B1363 between York and Helmsley is Gilling Castle, now a school. It was once a Norman castle belonging to Roger de Mowbray. At the end of the twelfth century it belonged to the de Etton family and in the reign of Edward II Thomas de Etton constructed a fortified house with a large square tower that forms the base of the present structure. In Henry VII's reign Thomas Fairfax married Elizabeth Etton and Gilling passed to the Fairfaxes. It was Sir William who built the famous Jacobean chamber with its wooden panelling, heraldic glass dating from 1585, and a frieze incorporating the arms of local gentry and the 21 wapentakes of Yorkshire.

Abbot of Ampleforth. Open daily (except Sundays) 10–12, 2–4. Gardens open from July to September.

HAREWOOD

This fourteenth-century castle was built on the site of an earlier one which once belonged to Earl Rivers. Later it passed to the de Lisles and over the entrance are the arms of Sir William Aldburgh who married Elizabeth de Lisle and built this castle. He was a messenger of John Balliol, King of Scotland, and he left the castle to his two daughters. It was partially dismantled during the Civil War and in 1657 was purchased by Sir John Cutler, a London merchant. It is rectangular in shape with two angle towers and has the main entrance on the north. The great hall was used as a court-room and above it are the solar and the chapel.

HARLSEY

At East Harlsey not far from Northallerton there is a large enclosure marking the sight of Harlsey Castle. This belonged to the Strangeways and Hotham families. Only portions of the keep undercroft remain.

HELMSLEY

Helmsley Castle stands between Thirsk and Scarborough. It is large and, in its complexities of ditch and rampart, could be called a Yorkshire Caerphilly. After the Conquest, Helmsley was granted to Robert de Mortain, half brother of the Conqueror. William Rufus confiscated the lands in 1088 after the barons' uprising and granted them to William l'Espec. In 1154 Helmsley passed by marriage to the de Roos family and between 1186 and 1227 the present castle walls and three towers were built. The barbican was added in the thirteenth century. At the end of the sixteenth century, Edward Manners, Earl of Rutland, added the oak panelling in the living quarters, some of which survives.

The castle was fortified for the King in 1644 after Marston Moor. It held out for three months against Fairfax, who was wounded and forced to retire to York. Colonel Jordan Crosland finally surrendered on 22nd November 1644 and the castle was slighted. After the Restoration it was claimed by the Duke of Buckingham, whose father had inherited it shortly before his death. The duke lost his money and died penniless in Kirbymoorside in 1688, and the castle was sold to a London banker, Sir Charles Duncombe, for £95,000. In 1718 Duncombe Park was built nearby.

'Helmsley, once proud Buckingham's delight,
Slid to a scrivener and a City Knight.'
Department of the Environment. Open normal times. Admission charge.

HORNBY

Four miles from Bedale, Hornby was built in the fourteenth century by the St Quentins and altered in the fifteenth by Lord Conyers. The castle was again altered in the eighteenth century and only the south range bears any resemblance to the original.

HULL

The city of Hull had two blockhouses and a central fort built at the time of Henry VIII in similar style to his south coast forts. It was used as a prison for many years and has long since been demolished.

HUTTON CONYERS

Earl Alan built a castle here about 1140 with two baileys. Traces of it are still visible.

KILTON

Near Loftus in the North Riding, Kilton stands in a wood. Strongly constructed in Norman times, on a semi-circular plan, it had a great hall and one tower. The owners, the Lumleys, were involved in the Pilgrimage of Grace in 1536, after which it passed to the Crown.

KIRKBY MALZEARD

Earthworks to the east of the church mark the site of Roger de Mowbray's castle, which was destroyed about 1174.

KNARESBOROUGH

Once a Saxon stronghold, Knaresborough was granted by William I to Serlo de Burgh, whose grandson Eustace Fitz-John built the castle but lived mostly at his other, more magnificent castle at Alnwick. Knaresborough sheltered three of the Becket murderers for a time in 1170, for one of them, Hugh de Morville, was the constable; later the unfortunate Richard II was brought here on his way to Pontefract from Flint. Apart from a twelfth-century pillar all the ruins date from the fourteenth century when the eleven-towered castle belonged to John of Gaunt.

During the Civil War Knaresborough was a Royalist stronghold; with the Nidd on three sides and a 30-foot wall on the other, it proved a difficult fortress for the Parliamentarians to capture. The Royalists surrendered when they ran out of supplies and the castle was slighted in 1648. Cromwell had a particular reason for demolishing it thoroughly, as his son was killed in a skirmish outside its walls.

The large rectangular keep is almost all that remains and it contains a museum in the ground-floor room with armour worn at Marston Moor, catapult balls and early chests. Beneath is a dungeon whose central pillar is 9 feet in circumference. In its walls are traces of iron staples. There used to be an underground passage leading to the Nidd ravine at St Robert's Cave.

Knaresborough Council. Keep open to the public during the summer 2–5. Guided parties only. Admission charge.

LECONFIELD

In the East Riding, not far from Beverley, the Percys had a castle which was crenellated in 1308. After the ninth earl had been fined £30,000 for his part in the Gunpowder Plot, the castle fell into decay and was demolished.

LEEDS

Nothing remains of Leeds castle, which stood in an area surrounded by Bishopsgate, Boar Lane and Millhill. It is supposed to have been demolished by King Stephen. In the nineteenth century excavations at Lydgate revealed part of the gatehouse.

MALTON

Nothing remains of Eustace Fitzjohn's castle at Malton. It was converted into a house in James I's reign by Lord

197

Eure but his granddaughters quarrelled about the inheritance and it was demolished, with the exception of the lodge in Old Maltongate.

MARKENFIELD

This is one of the oldest and most beautiful of inhabited houses, and is on the road between Harrogate and Ripon. It was crenellated in 1311 by John de Markenfield. The Markenfields forfeited their estates for their part in the Rising of the North in which Richard Norton, uncle of young Markenfield, was the standard-bearer. The castle has a chapel and great hall, which was partly rebuilt by the Egertons in Elizabethan times. In the mid-eighteenth century the house was bought back by the family (Fletcher Norton, Lord Grantley). The moat is still complete.

Lord Grantley. Open to the public Mondays, 10–3, May–September. Admission charge.

MIDDLEHAM

The home of Warwick the Kingmaker, Middleham is one of the most famous castles in the country. It stands at the entrance to Wensleydale on A6108. The builder of Richmond Castle, the Count of Penhievre, gave the land to his son Alan who passed it to his brother Ranulph. His grandson Ralph Fitzranulph built the first keep in 1170. When he died his daughter married Robert Neville of Raby. Richard Neville, Earl of Warwick, lived here in the stormy years of the Wars of the Roses and Edward IV was imprisoned here for a short period. After Warwick's death at the battle of Barnet in 1471 the castle was given to Richard, Duke of Gloucester. After the battle of Bosworth Middleham became Crown property until James I gave it to Henry Lindley in 1604. During the Civil War it was slighted by the Roundheads. Thereafter it passed through several hands before becoming the property of the Commissioners of Works in 1925.

The first castle at Middleham was a motte and bailey 500 yards south-west of the existing ruin. The curtain walls date from the end of the twelfth century. The rectangular keep – one of the largest in England – originally had corner towers and battlements, and a first floor entrance. Unusually, it incorporates the great hall. The keep has a three-storey chapel, the basement having been used as a vestry and the middle room as a priest's chamber. There are two-storey towers in the south-east and north-west corners. The gatehouse is to the north-east and the round Prince's Tower to the south-west. The castle had a moat, most of which has now vanished, and an east bailey.

Department of the Environment. Open normal times. Admission charge.

MORTHAM TOWER

Not far from Rokeby, North Riding, Mortham is a fourteenth-century tower house with fifteenth-century additions and a small courtyard. The entrance is crenellated and the arch is held up by diagonal buttresses. The top of the tower has tourelles in place of battlements; these were probably added in the eighteenth century by Sir Thomas Robinson for the Rokeby family.

MULGRAVE

Near Whitby, the new Mulgrave Castle is some distance from the ruins of the old one, which was the thirteenth-century home of the de Mauleys. The entrance tower on the west has a large arch and the keep is square with a round turret at each angle. The Duchess of Buckingham built the new castle in the eighteenth century.

NAPPA HALL

This fourteenth-century fortified manor with two towers and connecting hall belonged to the Metcalfes. It is not open to the public.

NORTHALLERTON

West of the church is a motte and bailey castle built by Henry I's Chancellor, Bishop Rufus.

PICKERING

The ruins of Pickering Castle stand on a hill above the river. The first records indicate that building took place between 1179 and 1180 and most English sovereigns between 1100 and 1400 visited Pickering to hunt wild boar and deer. In 1267, the castle passed to Edmund Crouchback, son of Henry III and Earl of Lancaster. His son, Thomas, was created Steward of England in 1308, and became virtual ruler of the kingdom after Edward II's disastrous engagement at Bannockburn. However, Edward struck back, and defeated the barons at Boroughbridge in 1322. Thomas was executed at Pontefract, and the king took possession of the castle. However, after Edward's death in 1327 the castle

199

returned to the family of Lancaster. When Henry Boling-broke landed at Ravenspur in 1399 he came to Pickering, where he gathered troops to march against Richard II, who was imprisoned here before his removal to Pontefract. The castle belonged to the Duchy of Lancaster until recent times. It was damaged by Roundheads during the Civil War, notably in the west wall where a breach was made by a battery on the other side of the moat.

The towers date from Edward II's reign and are known as the Mill, Diate Hill, Coleman and Rosamund's towers. The last is of three storeys and is mistakenly so called since 'Fair Rosamund', daughter of Lord Clifford and mistress of Henry II, died more than a century before the tower was built in 1323. The keep is shell type and stands on an artificial motte with the inner bailey wall running down from it. The solitary chapel of about 1226 has been restored, as has much of the curtain wall.

Department of the Environment. Open at normal times. Admission charge.

PONTEFRACT

One of the most famous English castles, Pontefract was first a Saxon stronghold on the route between Doncaster and York. The Norman castle was built by Ilbert de Lacy in 1086. Henry de Lacy, who lived here in the mid-thirteenth century, was made earl of Lincoln. After his two sons died – one fell from the battlements and the other was drowned in Denbigh – he bequeathed Pontefract to Edward I. The king bestowed the estate on his brother Edmund Crouch-back, whose son Thomas, Earl of Lancaster, led the rising that ended ignominiously at Boroughbridge. After being confined in Swillington tower, which he had constructed, he was beheaded on St Thomas's Hill. Like Pickering, the castle then passed through John of Gaunt to Henry Boling-broke. Richard II ended his days here after submitting to Henry at Flint and making the journey via Pickering.

Pontefract was strong enough to make an ideal prison. James I of Scotland was kept here as were the Duke of Orleans and other French prisoners after Agincourt. The castle remained in Yorkist hands through the Wars of the Roses. When Richard of Gloucester made his bid for the throne he put the protectors of his young nephews, Lord Grey and Sir Thomas Vaughan, in Pontefract dungeon, which they left only to be executed. In 1536 the Pilgrimage of Grace captured Pontefract from the Archbishop of York, who secretly supported the cause.

During the Civil War the garrison was attacked by Fairfax and in March 1645, after eight months siege, Sir Marmaduke Langdale's Northern Horse relieved it. Sir John Ramsden, the governor, finally surrendered in July. In 1648 the Royalists again captured Pontefract by driving a few carts carrying concealed soldiers into the bailey. The following year the castle was slighted.

Only Piper's Tower and the keep with its massive bastions remain today. The entrance is at the end of Micklegate and the walls contain a sports ground and garden.
Pontefract Borough Council. Open 8–dusk weekdays, 10–dusk weekends. Admission free. Museum.

RAVENSWORTH
According to Leland in the sixteenth century, Ravensworth consisted of 'two or three square towers and a fair stable with a conduit doming to the hall side'. It belonged to the Parrs. The gatehouse and an adjacent arch remain.

RICHMOND
The Count of Penhievre began the castle of Richmond in 1071. As a relative of the Duke of Brittany, he owed allegiance to both the king of France and the king of England. He was succeeded by his two brothers and then by his nephew Alan who married the daughter of the Duke of Brittany so that in 1146 the new Duke of Brittany, Conan, was the owner of Richmond. He is supposed to have built the keep, one of the finest in the north of England and in appearance somewhat similar to Portchester. Conan's daughter was betrothed to Geoffrey, son of Henry II, who took over the dukedom and the castle. Their son Arthur was murdered by agents of King John in 1203 and the castle, after a spell as a possession of the Earl of Leicester, passed to the Crown. After further changes of ownership, Richard II gave the castle to his queen, Anne of Bohemia, and Henry Bolingbroke gave it to the Nevilles. From 1453 to 1456 it went to Henry VI's half-brother, Edmund Tudor, whose son became Henry VII. The earls of Lennox became dukes of Richmond in 1601 and the castle remained their property until it passed to the Ministry of Works.

Richmond covers a large area and Scolland's Hall in the south corner is one of the earliest surviving Norman halls, with an outside stair leading to the first floor. The keep, once the entrance to the castle, dates from 1150. Most of the remains are eleventh- or twelfth-century. Richmond was in ruins by the sixteenth century.

Department of the Environment. Open at normal times. Admission charge.

RIPLEY

Ripley Castle is on the road from Ripon to Harrogate, and dates mostly from the sixteenth century although the gatehouse is believed to have been built in 1450. It was once a tower house. The Ingilbys have lived here for 600 years. According to tradition Thomas de Ingilby saved Edward III from a wild boar and was granted free hunting in Knaresborough Forest and later the right to hold a market in Ripley, where he settled. The family raised a troop of horse and fought at Marston Moor, Jane Ingilby accompanying them dressed as a trooper. On their return they discovered Cromwell had spent a night at Ripley, sitting with Lady Ingilby, who had a pair of pistols in her apron. The castle was rebuilt in 1780 and the village was replanned by Sir William Amcotts in 1827, modelled on a village in Alsace.

Major Sir J. Ingilby. Open Sundays and Bank Holidays May–September 2–6. Admission charge. Fine gardens, guided tour.

SANDAL MAGNA

The ruins of Sandal Castle, just outside Wakefield, are on the hill near the church. The original building dates from c. 1157 but the stone structure was not built until c. 1320 by Earl Warenne. During the Wars of the Roses, Richard, Duke of York, owned Sandal and he was killed when he left its safety during the battle of Wakefield in 1460. The Earl of Wiltshire captured Sandal and over 2,000 Yorkists were killed. It was the most overwhelming Lancastrian victory of the war. Richard III came here from time to time and later it belonged to the Saviles of Thornhill. During the Civil War it was held for the king by Colonel Bonivant and surrendered in October 1645. It was slighted the following year. A print of 1753 shows the castle in Elizabethan times with a north-facing keep with its two high towers and twin-towered gate-house abutting the curtain wall. In the middle is a barbican tower with a large dungeon underneath. There are stone-built outbuildings round the curtain wall and the draw-bridge, on an angle facing north, is the only entrance. One turret has a strange fleur-de-lis emblem on top and the west tower has a large chimney. Much recent excavation work has been carried out by the Wakefield Historical Society and their excellent booklets provide a fascinating picture of the castle's construction.

Wakefield Corporation. Open to the public at all times.

SCARBOROUGH

One of the great castles of Yorkshire and perhaps the most impregnable, Scarborough stands high on the cliffs north of the town. Once a Roman signal station and before that the site of a Bronze Age dwelling, the castle was built by William Le Gros, Lord of Holderness, in about 1136. It had a moat protecting the curtain on the harbour side and an extended barbican covering the main entrance. In 1138 William led the English forces at the battle of the Standard against the Scots. After William's death in 1179 at Bytham, Lincolnshire, Henry II took over Scarborough and built the keep, which, with its external steps, is reminiscent of Hedingham in Essex. Once this was 100 feet high but half of it was demolished in 1649.

In 1312 Piers Gaveston, favourite of Edward II, was besieged here and surrendered to the Earl of Pembroke. In 1536 during the Pilgrimage of Grace the castle resisted the cannon of Sir Robert Aske for three weeks. In 1553 Thomas Stafford captured the castle for three days by a trick. He took thirty friends disguised as peasants in to the bailey. They seized the guards at the main gate and let in armed retainers. The Earl of Westmorland recaptured it for Queen Mary; Stafford and four of his associates were executed.

During the Civil War the port at Scarborough was vital to the Royalist cause and Sir Hugh Cholmley held the castle for the king against Meldrum's troops. Cannon were placed in St Mary's church but the Royalists destroyed the chancel with accurate gunfire from the ramparts. Meldrum was mortally wounded and Matthew Boynton took command. Cholmley surrendered on 22nd July 1645, the garrison marching out in good order. In 1648 the garrison again declared for the king, and the leader of the revolt, another Boynton, (no relation to Matthew) held out until December before surrendering. He escaped to play a noble part in the Preston campaign, finally being killed at Wigan in August 1648.

In the eighteenth century the castle was used as an ammunition dump and a new barracks was built in the bailey. In 1914 the German battleships *Derfflinger* and *Van der Tann* fired salvoes into the town and castle, some of which demolished the barracks.
Department of the Environment. Admission charge.

SCARGILL
At Castle Farm, near Barningham in the North Riding, is this fifteenth-century gatehouse with a blocked entrance.

SELBY
Henry de Lacy had a castle here in 1143.

SHEFFIELD
A twelfth-century castle with a tower stood on Castle Hill market place. It belonged to the Talbots, earls of Shrewsbury. Mary, Queen of Scots, was a prisoner here for 14 years, guarded by the sixth earl. During the Civil War it was garrisoned for the king. Major-General Crawford finally captured it with the use of a culverin and it was then razed on orders from London.

SHERIFF HUTTON
This is one of the most spectacular ruins in Yorkshire. The original castle was built by Bertram de Bulmer about 1140 and was a keep and bailey with a large earth wall. In 1379 Lord Neville of Raby built a large four-towered castle, similar to Bolton. Each tower had four storeys. Elizabeth of York, wife of Henry VII, lived here for a time and it later belonged to Henry Fitzroy, illegitimate son of Henry VIII. By the seventeenth century it was in ruins and Charles I gave orders for it to be partially demolished. The gatehouse has a frieze with four shields and there are remains of the moat, which was double on the south side.

SIGSTON
Only earthworks remain of John de Sigston's castle. It passed to the Pygots and was a complete ruin by the early sixteenth century.

SKELTON
Near Saltburn, the present Skelton Castle dates from the late eighteenth century. It stands on the site of the de Bruce's castle.

SKIPSEA

On Albermarle Hill, not far from Bridlington in the East Riding, Drugo, the Lord of Holderness, built a castle in 1086. Earthworks are still visible.

SKIPTON

Originally built towards the end of William the Conqueror's reign by Robert de Romille, Skipton passed to his daughter and her husband William de Meschines and then to the earls of Albermarle. In 1269 it became Plantagenet property and Edward II gave it to his favourite, Piers Gaveston. After his death it was bestowed on the Cliffords, who have owned it until recent times.

The tenth Lord Clifford built much of the existing castle. The eleventh lord was made Earl of Cumberland by Henry VIII and was besieged here by the rebels of the Pilgrimage of Grace. He built the eastern part of the castle, now the private wing. Skipton was besieged in 1642 and Sir John Mallory did not surrender until 1645. Later it was repaired by the Lady Anne Clifford.

Skipton is remarkably well preserved. There are six round towers dating from the fourteenth century and a conduit court which leads to the great hall, where pictures from the British Museum were stored during the last war. It is air conditioned for this reason. The long gallery leads down to the octagonal tower and was built by the Earl of Cumberland when his son married the daughter of the Duke of Suffolk, niece of Henry VIII. Remains of the chapel were recently discovered when a partition wall was removed.

Open every weekday 10–6 and Sundays 2–6, except Good Friday and Christmas Day. Conducted tours on the hour from 10 weekdays and 2 Sundays. Admission charge. Self-guided tour sheets in French, German and English.

SLINGSBY

The impressive ruin that stands nine miles from Malton is of the uncompleted seventeenth-century house of Sir Charles Cavendish. It stands on the site of Ralph de Hasting's castle, crenellated in 1338. Not open to the public, the ruin is clearly visible from the road to the church.

SNAPE

Near Great Tanfield in the North Riding, Snape was built by the Nevilles. Catherine Parr lived here. It was acquired

by the Cecils in 1587 and rebuilt. The south wing is inhabited and the chapel is open at all times.
Gardens open last Sunday in July. Admission charge. No car park. Entrance to chapel through farmyard.

SPOFFORTH

Near Wetherby, Spofforth Castle can only just be seen from the road and only a third of it remains today. It was a thirteenth-century fortified manor of the Percy family, whose main residences were at Wressle and Topcliffe. In 1408 Henry Percy, first Earl of Northumberland, was killed at Bramham Moor in a rebellion against Henry IV. Henry Hotspur, his son, who was born at the castle, had been killed at Shrewsbury in 1403 and the third earl was killed with his brother fighting for the Lancastrians at Towton in 1461.

The castle is rectangular and today consists of a great hall and an undercroft. There is a particularly fine two-light west window that once belonged to the solar.
Department of the Environment. Open normal times. Admission free.

TANFIELD

Nothing remains of John Marmion's castle on the Ure near Ripon.

THIRSK

Roger de Mowbray had a castle here but apart from a street called Castlegate there is no trace of it today.

TICKHILL

Once a very important castle commanding the road from Lincoln to York, only the curtain wall, moat and a gatehouse stand today. Built by Roger de Busli it was acquired by Henry I and remained in royal hands. King John's retainers held it against Richard I, but on the latter's sudden return they were hanged outside its walls. The Count d'Eu, owner of Hastings castle, held it for some time, but in 1254 it formed part of the dowry of Eleanor of Castile, wife of Edward I. In 1322 Piers Gaveston was besieged here by Thomas, Earl of Lancaster. Charles I garrisoned it with eighty men and thirty horses, but it was finally captured in 1644 by Colonel Lilburn, slighted and never fully repaired.

TOPCLIFFE

On the river Swale in the North Riding was a motte and bailey castle known as Maiden's Bower. Built about 1174, it was the original home of the Percys. The Rising of the North was planned here and Charles I was a prisoner here while the Scots and Parliamentarians were negotiating his future. Nothing remains today.

UPSALL
Near Thirsk, Upsall is a Victorian house on the site of a four-towered quadrangular castle built by the Scropes in the thirteenth century. It had a park of 600 acres.

WEST AYTON
This ruined fourteenth-century pele tower still has two staircases and some tunnel vaulting.

WEST TANFIELD
The Marmion gatehouse by the church is all that remains of the fourteenth-century castle of Sir John Marmion, whose effigy can be seen in the church.

WHELDRAKE
Licenced in 1199, Wheldrake in the East Riding was once a Norman stronghold of the Percys.

WHORLTON
Isolated in the Cleveland Hills, Whorlton was a large castle covering two acres. It has long since been demolished but the gatehouse remains virtually intact. It was built by Robert de Meynell and passed to the Darcy family in the fourteenth century when the gatehouse was built. The last Darcy died in 1419 leaving a daughter who married Sir James Strangeways of Harlsey castle. It became Crown property for a time, Henry VIII granting it to the Earl of Lennox, father of the Earl of Darnley. Darnley's betrothal to Mary, Queen of Scots, is supposed to have taken place in the castle. The gate carries the coats of arms of the Darcy, de Meynell and Grey families.

WILTON
The old castle of the Bulmers once stood where the nineteenth-century building now stands.

WRESSLE
Remotely situated on the river Derwent, stands the ruin of Wressle. Founded by the Percy family, it was built about the time of Richard II and was considerably improved during

Henry VIII's reign. The Earl of Northumberland lived here in almost regal state. In 1538 Leland describes it as 'of very fair and great squared stone, both within and without, whereof (as some hold opinion) much was brought out of France. In the castle be only five towers, one at each corner . . . the gatehouse is the fifth'. It had a three-sided moat with the entrance on the dry side and in one of the towers 'a study called Paradise where was a closet in the middle of eight squares latticed about; and on the top of each square was a desk lodged to set books on'. There is a curious metal crucifix over the basement, strangely positioned as the chapel was in one of the towers. Wressle was damaged during the Civil War but it was a fire in 1796 which reduced it to ruin.

Farm property is open to the public on permission from the farmhouse. The ruin is unsafe and should be inspected with caution.

YA HORTH

A motte and bailey castle on the river Wiske, Ya Horth was abandoned in 1198.

YORK

York originally had two mottes. One is now Bail Hill and the other across the river is all that really remains of the castle – the remarkable Clifford's Tower. In 1190 the Jews of York were massacred on the hill. The wooden tower was burned, but replaced at once with another timber tower; the rebuilding in stone began in 1245 and was substantially complete in 1272. It has a quatrefoil plan consisting of four intersected towers each with a radius of 22 feet. The arms of the Clifford family, below Royal arms, are over the entrance. The tower possibly derives its name from the hanging in chains from its summit of Roger de Clifford after the Royalists had defeated the rebels at Boroughbridge in 1322. In 1684 it was blown up accidentally and many of the soldiers inside were killed. In 1825 it was repaired and a gaol was built in the bailey where the castle museum stands today.

Department of the Environment. Open normal times. Admission charge. Museum opposite (open 9.30–dusk) contains models, costumes, a street scene of old York and a model of Marston Moor battlefield. Closed Good Friday, Christmas Day and Boxing Day.

CASTLES OF WALES

ANGLESEY

BEAUMARIS

The finest preserved concentric castle in Britain, Beaumaris is on the Anglesey coast overlooking Lavan sands and the north-east end of the Menai Strait. When Caernarvon was captured by the Welsh in 1294 during the Welsh uprising Edward I decided to protect the harbour and ferry at the other end of the strait and began to build a new castle in 1295. It was completed in 1298 at a cost of about £1,400,000 in present-day currency. The garrison consisted of 10 men-at-arms, 20 bowmen and 100 foot soldiers. The upper storeys of the two gatehouses, the Great Hall and other internal buildings were never completed. Some further building of the curtain wall was carried out in 1306 and a few years later the north gate was strengthened.

The extensive dock is at the southern side of the curtain and is protected by a bastion called the Gunners Walk in which the castle watermill was situated. There was a drawbridge connecting the dock to the castle and a 40-ton ship could moor at the gate. There appears to be no well in the castle so there may well have been some system of piping water in from a stream, which would have been difficult with a sea moat round the outer ward, or of conserving rainwater.

One of the constables of Beaumaris was Henry Hotspur, who met his death at the battle of Shrewsbury in 1403. During the Civil War the Royalist commander, Colonel Bulkeley, surrendered on 14th June 1646 and the castle somehow escaped slighting. During the 1648 campaign Bulkeley raised a force in Beaumaris to aid the Scots but after Preston he had little hope of success. In September a Parliamentary force of about 1500 men, commanded by General Mytton, crossed the strait. Bulkeley occupied a position near the almshouses on the Beaumaris–Pentraeth road. A scrappy, confused battle took place here on 1st October in which Mytton suffered about 40 casualties and the Royalists 30 with about 300 men captured. Bulkeley and his second in command, Colonel Whiteley, shut themselves up in the castle but Mytton said he would kill the prisoners if the two did not surrender. For a short time Bulkeley was

209

imprisoned but he was allowed to ransom himself and eventually escaped to the Continent.
Department of the Environment. Open normal times. Admission charge.

BON-Y-DOM
Also known as the castle of king Olaf it is a ringwork in the southern corner of the island.

CASTELL CRWM
A ringwork at Llanrhwdrys looking out to the Skerries.

CASTELL LLEINIOG
The original castle here was built in about 1088 by the Earl of Chester and is known as 'Lady Cheadle's Fort'. Lleiniog was used by the Royalists in 1648 for storing ammunition. Only a small portion of it remains, in a field behind a new house called Penrhyn between Beaumaris and Renmon.

BRECONSHIRE

BLAENLLYNFI
A few stones stand of this Norman castle at Bwlch that once belonged to the de Braose family.

BRECON
Brecon Castle stands high above the bridge over the Usk. The castle dates from 1090 when Bernard de Neufmarché built a motte and bailey with stones taken from the Roman camp of Gaer. Remains of these are in the Deanery garden. Brecon successfully withstood two sieges by Llywelyn the Great in 1216 and 1233. It was occupied by Henry IV and defended by 100 men-at-arms and 300 archers who received one shilling (5p) and 6d (2½p) per day respectively. During the troubled reign of Richard III the Duke of Buckingham plotted with Bishop Morton of Ely, who was his gaoler, and collecting a small army marched to the Severn where the rains had flooded the roads so much that his dispirited army deserted. Unable to cross the river, he surrendered to Richard's soldiers and was executed for treason. His son was equally unfortunate and was beheaded on a trumped-up charge of treason by Henry VIII in 1521.

Charles I came to Brecon after Naseby. By then parts of the castle had been dismantled by townsfolk, so that it could not be fortified. The main part of the castle has been attached to the Castle Hotel and can be seen from the garden.

Postcards and permission to see the outside of the castle should be obtained from the Castle Hotel. The interior is not open. Bishop Moreton's Ely Tower is opposite.

BRONLLYS

Between Brecon and Hay, on the banks of the Lynfi, Bronllys Tower is 80 feet high and has two passages inside the wall. It is of early Norman date. Used as a base by William Rufus, it later passed to the Bohuns and in the reign of Henry VII to the Staffords.

Department of the Environment. Open at all times October to April. Key obtainable from Bronllys House.

BUILTH

Bernard de Neufmarché's castle has vanished and its successor, completed by Edward I in 1282 is said to have been the most perfect concentric castle in Wales. At a ford over the Irfon Llywelyn the Last was killed in 1282 after he had failed to persuade John Giffard, constable of the castle, to join his side. The man who killed him, Adam de Francton, did not recognise him and only realised when he returned later to the spot, which is now marked by an obelisk. The castle was destroyed during Elizabeth I's reign to build the White House nearby.

CRICKHOWELL

A ruin is all that remains of Alisby's castle destroyed in 1403 by Owain Glyndwr. The archers from Crickhowell were famous in Edward I's army.

HAY-ON-WYE

Hay is situated on the border with England. The word 'Hay' is from the French *haie*, meaning an enclosure. The first castle was a motte and bailey near the church. The Norman castle was constructed by Phillip Walwyn and afterwards passed to William Revell, who presented land to form the parish in 1130. The next owners were the de Braose family and William de Braose rebelled against King John. His wife Maud de Valerie refused to give up her sons as

211

hostages to the king and accused him of murdering his nephew Arthur. For this she was thrown into the dungeons of Corfe Castle where she died.

During Owain Glyndwr's rebellion the castle and town were destroyed and only the gateway and one tower remain. In Elizabethan times a mansion was built next door.

Richard Booth Esq. Not open to the public.

LLANGOED
Near Erwood the twentieth-century castle of Llangoed stands on the site of an earlier castle. A porch dating from 1632 was discovered when repairs were carried out.

PENCELLEY
Near Crickhowell a few stones remain of this Norman castle.

TRETOWER
Tretower Castle stands between Abergavenny and Brecon where the Rhiangoll flows into the Usk. After the conquest Bernard de Neufmarché's Norman soldiers built a wooden stockade which was replaced by stone in the mid-twelfth century and a hall and solar were built beneath the motte. In the thirteenth century John Picard demolished these two buildings and more of the inner court to build his great cylindrical tower, which is virtually intact today. There was a wooden bridge from the parapet to the curtain and the old entrances were blocked so that a few men could defend the castle. It was successfully held against Owain Glyndwr by Sir James Berkeley.

The castle was not very comfortable and Sir Roger Vaughan, who was granted Tretower by his half-brother William Pembroke, built Tretower Court on the site of an earlier house probably destroyed during Glyndwr's rising, and in 1480 it was enlarged by Sir Thomas Vaughan. In the seventeenth century Henry Vaughan the poet lived here and about the same time a young member of the family was killed by a snake. He is commemorated by a stained glass window in one of the upper rooms.

The court has recently been thoroughly restored and is one of the finest manor houses of its type in Britain.

Department of the Environment. Court and castle open normal times. Admission charge.

CAERNARVONSHIRE

BELAN FORT

At Llanwnda, on the south tip of the Menai Strait, this fort was built in 1776 and strengthened in 1826. It was manned by the Royal Newborough Volunteers.

CAERNARVON

The Romans first built a fort called Segontium or Y Gaer yn Arfor, which was the original settlement on the Beddgelert road on the Seiont river. The first castle on the present site was built about 1090 by Earl Hugh of Avranches and consisted of a large motte with timber walls. The bailey was probably what is now Castle Square.

In 1282 Llywelyn ap Gruffydd (the Last) was killed attacking Builth Castle and Edward I captured Dolwyddelan Castle, ensuring his control of North Wales. In the summer of 1283 work started on the present castle, which encircles Hugh's motte. Up to 1292 when the work ceased – although the castle appears never to have been finished – a total of nearly £1¼ million (today's value) had been spent on the massive undertaking which included the town walls. Since that date only the additional work on the north side and the heightening of the Eagle Tower and other turrets has been carried out, apart of course, from various internal alterations.

In April 1284 Edward I's second son was born at Caernarvon and in 1301, after his elder brother had died, young Edward was formally presented to the Welsh people as their Prince of Wales. Tradition states that this event took place at Caernarvon but it is more likely that it was at the older castle of Rhuddlan. In 1294 Madoc ap Llywelyn's revolt destroyed the town walls and the wooden buildings of the castle were burnt. The following year the damage was repaired and the town-side castle walls were built up to their present height. It was at this time that the multiple arrow loops were put in by the Granary Tower so that three men could shoot through each slit in different directions at the same time. In 1304 there was another fire and damage had to be repaired so that the total amount spent on construction finally came to about £2½ million.

After the accession of Henry VII there was no need to garrison Caernarvon and the castle gradually fell into decay. Roofs fell in and were not repaired and the glass was not replaced in the windows. In 1660 orders were given for the complete demolition of the castle. The work was never started, perhaps due to lack of finance, and in the nineteenth century prosperity came to the port with the increase in the slate trade. Sir Llewelyn Turner, Deputy Constable, repaired much of the stonework, rebuilt the well tower top and, using sandstone, added a great deal of character to the castle.

Apart from the multi-angular towers, the passages inside the walls and the visual splendour of the castle, the most interesting item for visitors is the Royal Welsh Fusiliers' Museum in the Queen's Tower. Here one can see on three floors, four Victoria Crosses, numerous flags, the keys of Corunna, medals of Waterloo veterans, First and Second World War relics and the silver cigarette case of Major Compton-Smith D.S.O., which he presented to the regiment on the night before he was shot by the Sinn Feiners when captured in Ireland in 1920.

Caernarvon has now been the scene of two royal investitures – Prince Edward, later the Duke of Windsor, in 1911, and Prince Charles in 1969. Perhaps before there is a third investiture, the work started by Edward I will finally be completed.

Department of the Environment. Open normal hours. Admission charge. Museum extra.

CONWAY

Although the mouth of the Afon Conway was a natural position for a castle, the earliest castle in the area was at Deganwy overlooking the estuary. Edward I, having captured Dolwyddelan, moved to Conway in 1283 and James of St George was given the task of building the great castle at the river mouth. Much of the material from ruined Deganwy was used in its making. By 1287 it was complete having cost, by today's standards, about £2 million. Within two years it was fit for a garrison and in 1294 during Prince Madoc's rising Edward was besieged here and had to be rescued by his fleet.

A hundred years later Richard II received the Duke of Northumberland here as an emissary from Henry Bolingbroke. Richard set out for Flint and for his downfall. During the Wars of the Roses Conway held out for the Yorkists and a Lancastrian, Rhys ap Gruffydd Goch, was supposed to have been killed at a range of half a mile by an arrow shot by the Yorkist marksman, Llewelyn of Nannau.

By 1627 the castle had fallen into decay and was sold for £100 to Viscount Conway. In the Civil War Bishop John Williams refortified it for the King. Conway town walls were strengthened. Sir John Owen, who did not trust the bishop, took over the command of the castle. Major-General Mytton attacked and captured the town in August 1646. He then turned his artillery on the castle to little effect and Owen held out until November when his men marched out on favourable terms, secured for the most part by the bishop. After the Restoration it fell into disrepair again and has been roofless since Lord Conway sold the roof lead in 1665.

During the nineteenth century the railway company was prevailed upon to repair the stonework that suffered from the constant shaking by freight trains and John Parker of Oxford restored the floors of the high tower at his own expense, so that 'visitors could come and sit and sketch'. In 1865 Sir Richard Bulkeley, the last Constable appointed by the Queen, died and the castle passed to the local corporation. In 1953 it was taken over by the Ministry and the Telford Bridge, built in 1826, was acquired by the National Trust in 1966.

Department of the Environment. Open normal times. Admission charge. National Trust Information centre in Toll House.

CRICCIETH

Criccieth is a small seaside resort on the A497 to Pwllheli. The castle stands high above the bay and was probably built by Llywelyn ap Iowerth who imprisoned his half-brother Gruffydd here in 1239. The inner ward with its two drum towers dates from 1230. The outer ward with its rectangular towers dates from about 1290 when Edward I strengthened it, making the inner gatehouse higher, and refaced the Cistern Tower which is common to both inner and outer wards.

In 1284 Edward I appointed William de Leyburn as constable with a garrison of 30 men. In 1343 it belonged to the Black Prince. The constable at this time was Sir Hywel ap Gruffydd, a redoubtable warrior nicknamed 'Howell of the Battleaxe', who was knighted on the field of Poitiers. There are traces of fire, particularly on the Leyburn Tower, which probably date from the castle's destruction by Owain Glyndwr in 1404. In spite of this the castle was inhabited

215

up to the beginning of the seventeenth century and there was, even then, a tradition that the meat was carved with Sir Hywel's battleaxe and, at royal expense, distributed after the meal to the poor. There was a special guard of eight yeomen who received 8d a day for guarding the kitchen during this ceremony.

Department of the Environment. Open normal times. Admission charge.

DEGANWY

This is one of the oldest castle sites in Wales. To reach it take A496 at the roundabout before Conway and turn right up a steep hill to York Road. There is a footpath leading towards the hill and Deganwy Castle is on the summit. Mentioned as the home of Maelgwyn Gwynnedd in the sixth century, the castle was built by Hugh Lupus, Earl of Chester. In 1088 Robert, Earl of Chester, surprised by Gruffydd ap Cynan's invasion force, left his castle with one man. The Welsh 'cut off his head fastening it to the mast, and sailed off in savage triumph'. Llywelyn ap Gruffydd finally destroyed Deganwy in 1263 to prevent it falling into Edward's hands.

DOLBADARN

On A4086 between the two small lakes, Llyn Padarn and Llyn Peris, Dolbadarn Castle stands 80 feet above on a small rock. There are remains of a curtain wall that enclosed an area of about 12,000 square feet. The road once ran very close to the castle to avoid a swamp. Originally Dolbadarn was a stronghold of Arfon, an area of North Wales built by the Welsh to guard the valley.

The circular tower, well preserved today, dates from the thirteenth century and may have been built by Llywelyn Fawr (the Great). Traditionally his grandson Llywelyn ap Gruffydd held his brother prisoner here for nearly twenty years. On Llywelyn's death at Builth in 1282 Dolbadarn passed into Edward I's hands and henceforward ceased to be of importance. In 1284 parts of it were dismantled and the timber was used for the construction of Caernarvon. During Owain Glyndwr's rising Dolbardarn was the prison of Lord Grey of Ruthin but it is unlikely that it was used for warfare after this time.

The last owner, Sir Michael Duff, presented it to the Ministry of Works in 1941 and a great deal of repointing,

26. *The gateway of Newark Castle, Nottinghamshire, is the largest of any castle in England.*

27. *William Lovell of Minster Lovell Castle, Oxfordshire, was one of the few Yorkist leaders to escape alive.*

28. *Stokesay in Shropshire is the best preserved fortified manor house in England.*

29. *Whittington Castle, Shropshire, was defended by five towers and a series of flooded ditches and a bog.*

30. *At Nunney Castle, Somerset, is seen the unique influence of French castles on English castle building.*

31. *The shell-keep of Tamworth Castle, Staffordshire, was built by the Marmions, Royal Champions of England in Norman times.*

32. *Mary Queen of Scots was imprisoned at Tutbury, Staffordshire, and was allowed a retinue of forty-seven people and ten horses – plus a guard of thirty soldiers.*

33. *Framlingham, the most important castle in Suffolk, was rebuilt between 1190 and 1210 in the style of Windsor and Dover castles, relying upon wall-towers for defence.*

34. *Orford Castle, Suffolk, was built by Henry I from 1166-1172, with a keep which is polygonal on the outside and circular inside.*

35. *The south front and gatehouse of Wingfield Castle, Suffolk, are original and date from the building of 1384 by Michael de la Pole.*

36. *Arundel Castle, Sussex, was a ruin for 150 years until restoration, at a total cost of £600,000, was begun in 1716 by the tenth duke. The work was finished by the fifteenth duke in 1903.*

37. *Lewes Castle, Sussex, is remarkable for its two mounds, the northern one being the present Black Mount. The fine barbican was erected in the fourteenth century.*

38. *Bodiam Castle, Sussex, was built in 1385 to protect the river Rother from French raiders. It is now the National Trust's finest ruined castle.*

39. *Queen Elizabeth visited the lake fortress at Kenilworth, Warwickshire, in 1575 for seventeen days. The entertainment cost to the earl of Leicester amounted to £1,000 a day.*

clearing and repair work has been carried out since this date.

Department of the Environment. Open normal hours April–September; June–September, Sundays 11–7. Admission charge.

DOLWYDDELAN

On A496 between Betws-y-Coed and Blaenau Ffestiniog, the tall tower of Dolwyddelan Castle stands out overlooking the road. It is famous as the presumed birthplace and early home of Llywelyn the Great. When Owain Gwynnedd died his sons divided up North Wales and Llywelyn's father Iowerth, who died in about 1173, when his son was born, ruled over Nant Conway with Dolwyddelan tower as his headquarters.

In 1283 the English captured Dolwyddelan on their successful campaign in North Wales and it was repaired. In the fifteenth century it belonged to Meredydd ap Ievan, a descendant of Llywelyn, and on his death it fell into decay. The roof and battlements were added in the nineteenth century and the Ministry of Works has cared for it since 1930.

The castle originally had two towers and a stone curtain with a ditch on the east and another to the west. The old road passed under the west tower at one time. The keep is constructed in the English style with the entrance on the first floor up a steep staircase interrupted by a drawbridge pit. The basement was entered by a ladder and the main living quarters must have been the one room, now much restored, with its window seats and chimney. At one time there was a gabled roof There are few castles in Wales so well looked after as Dolwyddelan.

Department of the Environment. Open normal hours except March–October Sundays 9.30–4. Admission charge.

GWYDIR

On A496 between Betws-y-Coed and Conway, Gwydir stands on a fortified site dating from A.D. 600. The original building was a fourteenth-century watch-tower built by Hywell Coetmor. Meredydd ap Ievan built on to this in about 1500 and his son, John Wynn ap Meredydd, enlarged the fortified manor. A secret priest-hole in one of the rooms was probably put in during the seventeenth century, for the Wynns were notable Catholics. It remained in the hands of the Wynn family until the death of Sir Richard Wynn in 1674 when it passed by marriage to the Bertie family. In 1899 the Duke and Duchess of York (later George V and Queen Mary) stayed here and in the Statesman's Gardens outside are trees planted to commemorate the visits of the Duke of Norfolk, Lord Ganford and other friends of Lord Carrington, the nineteenth-century owner.

In 1924 Gwydir was severely burnt and remained a ruin. Twenty years later it was bought by Arthur Clegg who rebuilt it, stone by stone, with very little outside assistance. His son, Richard Clegg, owns the house today and it is still in process of restoration.

There are some original hammer beams in the music room, which was the only room not destroyed in 1924, and other beams were purchased by Mr Clegg from Aberconway Abbey. Upstairs the Wynn four-poster bed dates from 1570 and has carvings representing various biblical scenes.

Open daily Easter–October 10–dusk. Guided tours. Admission to chapel (with famous painted roof) extra.

LLYS EURYN

At Rhos-on-Sea off Tan-y-Bryn Road are the remains of a fifteenth-century manor which replaced Ednyfed's castle constructed in the thirteenth century.

PENRHYN

On the main A55 between Conway and Bangor, just by the junction with A5, Penrhyn was built in 1827 of Mona marble. Its keep was modelled on Castle Hedingham. It contains the Elizabethan 'Hirlas Horn' that belonged to the sailor Piers Gruffydd.

National Trust. Open June–September weekdays 11–5, Sundays (July and August only) 2–6; April, May and October Mondays, Wednesdays and Thursdays only 2–5. Admission charge.

SEGONTIUM

At Caernarvon, the Roman fort of Segontium on the Beddgelert road is worth seeing for its museum.

Department of the Environment. Open normal hours. Admission charge.

CARDIGANSHIRE

ABEREIRON
Lord Rhys built a motte at the head of the estuary in about 1156. It is also known as Castell Gadwgan.

ABERHEIDOL
Near Aberystwyth Gilbert Fitzrichard had a castle which was destroyed by the Welsh in 1136 and 1143.

ABERYSTWYTH
Near St Michael's church, the ruins of Aberystwyth Castle overlook the sea and have been formed into a small park. The castle was built by Edmund Crouchback, brother of Edward I, and was concentric in plan, the outer walls measuring 160 yards from north to south and 80 yards from east to west. It fell to Owain Glyndwr in 1404 and was recaptured by Prince Henry in 1408.

During the Civil War it was held by the Royalists until attacked and captured by Parliamentary forces in 1646. The Governor was Colonel Roger Whitley who was second in command of the Royalists in Anglesey. Although captured in Beaumaris, he lived to see not only the Restoration but the accession of William III when he became a Whig and was made Mayor of Chester.

Aberystwyth Corporation. Open at all times. Admission free.

BLAENPORTH
This was a Norman motte and bailey castle, surrounded by streams and which was captured in 1215. The site is on the main Cardigan–Aberystwyth road near Aberporth aerodrome.

CAERWEDROS
Near New Quay, this castle was captured and destroyed by Owain and Cadwallader in 1136.

CARDIGAN
The original site was at Old Castle Farm nearer the sea. Lord Rhys sold his castle here to King John in 1199 and it was abandoned when Gilbert de Clare's castle was constructed. At one time Cardigan was one of the most important castles in this part of Wales.

CASTELL GWALTER
This was a small motte and bailey castle near Llandre which was destroyed in 1136.

CASTELL HOWELL
Also known as Duke Humphrey's Castle, it is near Pontshaen between Lampeter and Newcastle Emlyn. It was destroyed in 1136 and rebuilt seventeen years later.

CASTELL MEURIG
The Welsh built a motte and bailey castle at Ystrad Meurig, a few remains of which are still visible.

DINIERTH
There are some signs of the masonry of this motte and bailey castle near Aberystwyth. It was destroyed in 1208.

LAMPETER
In the grounds of the college King Stephen had a motte, destroyed in 1136. It is also known as the castle of Mabwynion.

LLANIO
At Llanddewi Beefi is the site of Richard de la Mare's castle known as Tomen Llanio.

YSGUBOR Y COED
Eighteenth-century Glendyfi Castle stands on the site of Rhys ap Dafydd's castle on the Dovey.

YSTRAD PEITHYLL
This small motte and bailey castle near Strata Florida was destroyed in 1116.

CARMARTHENSHIRE

CARMARTHEN
Little remains of the Norman castle which stood where the county offices are today. It was built about 1094, strengthened in 1145 and 1150 and was captured by Llywelyn in 1215. It later became a royal fortress and in 1275 consisted of 'a five-towered donjon, the great tower, hall, chapel, stable and kitchen, the castle gate and wall all in a great state of dilapidation and the whole value of the lordship under £50

per annum'. Captured by Owain Glyndwr in 1403 it was held by him for over two years. During the Civil War the town was fortified by the Royalists and captured and destroyed by the Parliamentarians.

CARREG CENNEN

The spectacular castle of the Cennen valley, some seven miles south-east of Llandeilo, was built in the thirteenth century on the site of a Roman fort. In 1254 it was taken by Rhys Fychan, one of the sons of Lord Rhys. In 1282 Lord Rhys's wife took the castle from her son and delivered it to the English, but it was recaptured by Gruffydd and Llywelyn, sons of Rhys Fychan. They could not hold it for long, however, and in 1283 it passed to John Giffard, owner of Llandovery Castle.

In 1323 Edward II granted it to his favourite Hugh Despencer after Giffard had been executed for treason. It changed ownership on Hugh's downfall and eventually passed in 1362 to John of Gaunt and the Duchy of Lancaster. In 1403, when the defences must have been complete, it held out against Owain Glyndwr under its constable John Skydmore. During the Wars of the Roses it was held by Gruffydd ap Nicholas, whose sons fought for the Lancastrian army at Mortimer's Cross in 1461. The following year a Yorkist force commanded by Sir Richard Herbert of Raglan and Sir Roger Vaughan of Tretower captured Carreg Cennen and, because it had become the headquarters of thieves, it was demolished by the Sheriff of Carmarthenshire for £28 5s 6d. In the nineteenth century the ruins were restored by the Earl of Cawdor.

The approaches to the castle are unusually complicated. There were two gates with drawbridges over deep pits and a square prison tower commanding the final approach. There is a mysterious cave in the south-east corner of the Inner Ward which is approached by a long narrow passage and may have once led out to the Outer Ward. Carreg Cennen is supposed to have been the home of Urien, one of King Arthur's knights.

Department of the Environment. Open normal times. Admission charge.

DRYSLLWYN

A few miles from Dynevor and standing on top of a steep hill it belonged to Lord Rhys ap Meredudd who rebelled against the English in 1287 and captured Swansea. The Earl

of Cornwall attacked him at Drysllwyn with 11,000 men and undermined the castle. William de Montchensh and about 150 Staffordshire men were killed when the mine caved in and part of the castle collapsed. Eventually captured at York, Rhys was tried and executed, his castle going to Robert of Tibetot.
Open at all times. The castle can be reached up a farm track off B4297.

DYNEVOR

Near Llandeilo, modern Dynevor Castle was built in 1856. The old castle in the grounds is thirteenth-century. It has a long history, dating from 876 when it was held by Rhodri Mawr against the Danes. In Norman times it held out against the conquest under its constable, Rhys ap Tewdwr, but was eventually captured and rebuilt. In 1257 it was besieged by the English and Llywelyn raised the siege. In Tudor times it was granted to Sir Rhys ap Thomas and Henry VIII seized it, executing Sir Rhys on a trumped-up charge of treason. In the eighteenth century it was damaged by fire and today only the round keep and a square tower with a moat carved out of the rock are visible over the river Towy.
Open to the public only with written permission from the owner.

KIDWELLY

Kidwelly lies on A484 between Carmarthen and Llanelli. The castle and town stand at the head of the wide estuary of the river Gwendraeth overlooking a flat expanse of marsh. The first castle was erected by Roger, bishop of Salisbury, in 1115. In 1136 a battle was fought between Gwenllian, wife of Gruffydd ap Rhys, and Maurice de Londres, constable of the castle. The Welsh were defeated and Gwenllian and her son killed.

Lord Rhys's son Meredith had his revenge in 1215 when he captured and burnt the castle. Llywelyn forced him to restore it to the English and it passed to Hawise, daughter of the last of the de Londres male line. She married Walter de Braose and, on his death in 1244, Patrick de Chaworth. In 1257 the Welsh failed to capture the castle and on Patrick's death in 1258 his sons Payn and Patrick succeeded. Hawise died in 1274 and her sons not long after. Patrick left a daughter, Matilda, who married Edmund Crouchback, Earl of Lancaster, brother of Edward I. Edmund's son Thomas took a leading part in the revolt against Edward II and was executed after his defeat at the battle of Borough-bridge in 1322. Kidwelly passed into Crown hands on the accession of Henry IV.

Kidwelly was once a fortified town and a fourteenth-century gateway remains in Bailey Street. The river protected the eastern flank and a deep ditch the western flank. There is a small motte in front of the main gatehouse which might be the motte of the original castle. The inner ward dates from the thirteenth century and the hall, chapel and living quarters were possibly constructed during the minority of Matilda de Chaworth. The gatehouse was only completed about 1400, and in 1402 the Welsh, aided by a French force, damaged the roof so that a large sum had to be spent on repairs. Lead was brought from Bristol and finally a new hall was constructed in the outer ward.

During the fifteenth century it belonged to the Tudors and in the sixteenth to the Earls of Cawdor, one of whom presented it to the Ministry of Works in 1927.

Department of the Environment. Open normal times. Admission charge.

LAUGHARNE

Between Llanstephan and Pendine, the keep and Henry II tower still remain of the thirteenth-century castle. At the beginning of the fourteenth century it was held by Sir Guy de Brian. Sir John Perrot rebuilt it as his home during the sixteenth century and it was captured by Parliament during the Civil War.

Open at all reasonable times. Apply to Castle House by the Town Hall. Admission charge.

LLANDOVERY

On A40 between Brecon and Llandeilo, Llandovery Castle is a motte with a ruined shell-keep standing in the car park. The first record of the castle is in 1116 when it was attacked by the Welsh. It was held by Richard de Pons. In 1208 it was captured by Rhys Fychan but he did not hold it for long. The English strengthened it and once more the Welsh under Rhys ap Meredudd captured it. Edward I made peace with Rhys, who was traditionally an enemy of Llywelyn and thereafter Llandovery remained in English hands. It was garrisoned by English troops under John Gifford and appears to have played no further part until its ultimate destruction by Cromwell.

The ruins are open at all times.

LLANEGWAD

To the east of Carmarthen a few traces of a thirteenth-century castle stand on a motte. An alternative site at Allt y Ferin stands nearby.

LLANSTEPHAN

Opposite Kidwelly on the Towy estuary, Llanstephan Castle was built on an Iron Age site, probably by Gilbert de Clare. It was captured by the Welsh princes in 1146. Young Prince Maredudd flung down the Norman scaling ladders when an attempt was made to recapture it. Henry II took it and gave it to William de Camville, who strengthened it in 1192. His family held it for 200 years in spite of frequent successful Welsh attacks. Another William de Camville died in 1338 and the castle went to his daughter and her husband, Robert de Penrees. In 1403 it was captured from Sir John Penrees by Owain Glyndwr and held for three months. In 1443 it passed to the crown. Henry VII presented it to his uncle Jasper Tudor in 1495. In the eighteenth century it reverted to private hands.

Department of the Environment. Open at all reasonable times. Admission free.

NEWCASTLE EMLYN

One solitary arch stands in a field on a bend in the river Teifi. Originally built by Prince Maredudd, of Llanstephan fame, it was captured by Edward I in 1288 when siege engines had pounded the walls. During the Glyndwr revolt it was captured and destroyed. Dafydd ap Gwilym, the Welsh poet, was brought up here when his uncle Llywelyn became constable in 1343. During the Civil War it held out for the king for some time but was completely slighted.

PENCADER

A motte and bailey castle stood at the junction of two streams, probably built about 1145.

ST CLEARS

A mound by the river marks the site of Lord Rhys's castle which was probably destroyed at the same time as Carmarthen Castle (c. 1215).

DENBIGHSHIRE

CASTELL CAWR

A short distance south of Abergele is a British camp on a low wooded hill once occupied by the Romans. Abergele is also the site of a battle between Harold Godwinson and Gruffydd ap Llywelyn in which the English were defeated.

CHIRK

On A5 between Shrewsbury and Llangollen, Chirk Castle stands on the Welsh border in the middle of a large estate. During the war between Llywelyn the Last and Edward I Roger Mortimer played a notable part. As a reward he was granted the lands of Chirk where there was a castle near the church. He built a new castle between 1274 and 1310 probably incorporating some of the old castle material at Chirk. There were two other castles on the same land, Castel y Waun and Dinas Bran, both at Llangollen, which had been built by Gruffydd ap Madoc. This was rectangular in plan with a circular tower in each corner and parapets wide enough for two men to walk abreast.

Chirk passed from the Mortimers to the Arundels and the Mowbrays. In 1397 Mowbray was executed for treason and the estate passed to the Beauchamps. Edward IV presented it to Lord Stanley, famous for his late intervention at Bosworth. He was executed in 1495 for supporting Perkin Warbeck, so Chirk passed to the King. Henry VIII gave it to Thomas Seymour and Elizabeth I granted it to her favourite, the Earl of Leicester. It seemed never to have remained for long in one family until it was sold to Sir Thomas Myddelton in 1595 and it remains the home of the Myddelton family today.

His son, another Sir Thomas, was M.P. for Denbighshire and during the Civil War was made Major-General of the Parliamentary forces in North Wales. During his absence Colonel Ellis captured Chirk for the Royalists and Colonel Watts was made governor. For three days in 1644 Myddelton besieged Chirk, but as it was his own home he did not want to use artillery. With planks and tables he tried to get in through a drain but Watts rained stones down on him and killed his engineer. In 1646 Sir John Watts (he had been knighted by Charles I), realising that the war was over surrendered Chirk and the garrison 'stole all privately away'.

In 1659 Myddelton, restored to his lands, supported the

cause of Charles II. He was a year too early and General Lambert attacked Chirk with cannon doing a fair amount of damage. At the Restoration he was awarded the large sum of £30,000 for its repair. During the next few years the long gallery was constructed and many of the present treasures were purchased for the castle. The dining room decoration dates from the eighteenth century and much work was done by Pugin in the nineteenth century, but Chirk still remains unspoilt as one of the few inhabited castles in Wales.

Lt. Col. R. Myddelton. Open Easter Saturday–September Tuesdays, Thursdays, Saturdays and Sundays 2–5, Sundays in April; Bank Holidays 11–5. Admission charge.

DENBIGH

One of the most ruinous and yet most interesting of all the Welsh castles, Denbigh stands high up in the centre of the county town. Dafydd ap Gruffydd, Llywelyn's brother, lived here for a time. The castle, built by Hugh de Lacy, Earl of Lincoln, in 1282 was probably built on the site of Dafydd's fortified house. The Welsh captured Denbigh in the revolt of 1292 but de Lacy recaptured it, dying before it was completed in 1311. The castle passed to Thomas, Earl of Lancaster, de Lacy's son-in-law, who was executed in 1322 at Pontefract, after his defeat at Boroughbridge. Edward II granted it to his favourite Hugh Despenser but after he was hanged at Bristol the property passed to Roger Mortimer who suffered the same fate at Tyburn in 1330.

After this the castle passed through several hands until it became the headquarters of Henry Percy (Hotspur) in 1399. It is possible that Owain Glyndwr visited Percy at this time but this did not prevent the town being burnt during the rising by Glyndwr. During the Wars of the Roses it changed hands more than once. Jasper Tudor burnt it in 1468 when it was held by the Yorkists and henceforth the town was constructed outside the old city walls – the gate on the north-west side still stands – with the exception of Leicester's Chapel which lies below the castle and appears never to have been completed.

Robert Dudley, Earl of Leicester, owned Denbigh from 1563 to 1588 when it reverted to the crown. During the Civil War it was garrisoned for the King by Colonel Salesbury and Charles came here after his defeat at Rowton Heath. The castle was besieged from April to 26th October, 1646, when, on the command of the King, Salesbury surrendered to General Mytton. The Royalists marched out 'with flying colours, drums beating, matches lit at both ends, bullets in the mouth and every soldier with 12 charges of powder'. The castle was destroyed just before the Restoration so today only a portion of the gatehouse with its three towers, some ruinous walls and bases of other towers remain.

Inside the gatehouse to the right is a small museum. There is a model of Sir Henry Morton Stanley's birthplace in the town. It was he who as a journalist for the *New York Herald* found David Livingstone. The museum has Roman pottery, coins, swords and cannonballs with other relics of the siege. *Department of the Environment. Open normal times. Admission charge. Extra charge for admission to town walls and Leicester's Chapel.*

DINAS BRAN

One of the most spectacular castles in Wales, Dinas Bran looks down from its heights above Llangollen. Once the home of Madoc ap Gruffydd Maelor, founder of Vale Crucis Abbey, in 1390 it was the home of Myfanwy Fechan. By 1578 it was already being described as a ruin. To reach it take the road over the river from the A5 and carry on over the canal past the Catholic church.
Ruins open at all times.

GWRYCH

A modern spectacular castle on A55 at Abergele built in 1815 by a Mr Hesketh on the site of an old fort with eighteen towers, the main one being 93 feet high.
Open every day between Easter and October. Admission charge.

HOLT

Between Nantwich and Wrexham on A534 Holt is on the Welsh side of the river Dee, Farndon is on the other side. The bridge was once fortified like Monmouth bridge and traces of a fort can be seen on the Farndon side. Holt Castle is remarkably difficult to find. It lies below a riding school on the bank of the Dee and to reach it you have to take a footpath opposite the Free Presbyterian Church. Little remains but one tower on a raised bank.

The original castle was built by John de Warenne, Earl of Surrey, at the end of the thirteenth century on the site of Bovium, a Roman fort used for supplying Chester. Later it was called Castle Lyons and a print in the British Museum shows it in 1670 as a five-towered almost triangular castle with a double drawbridge and moat looping round to the river. There is a small squat gatehouse and four of the towers have cylindrical chimneys. The tower nearest the river is rectangular and the others are round.

During the Civil War Holt was often the centre of events. The Roundheads pushed back the Royalists from the bridge when they captured Wrexham but failed to take the castle. Langdale used it as his headquarters before the battle of Rowton Heath in September 1644. Finally Mytton tried to capture it from its stout defender, Sir Richard Lloyd. 'The siege of Holt hath been of late of great difficulty', wrote Mytton in 1645, and the little castle was the last in Wales, apart from Harlech, to hold out, Lloyd finally surrendered on very favourable terms on 13th January 1647. The castle was not destroyed by Parliament and it is possible it was dismantled to help repair the town and the bridge.

Ruins can be seen at all times but are unsafe to enter.

LLANFAIR RHYD CASTELL

This was a castle given to the monks of Aberconway by Llywelyn ap Iowerth in 1198. Nothing remains of it today.

RUTHIN

The first reference to Ruthin Castle, which is a large, mostly Victorian, hotel today, was in 1282 when it was taken by Reginald de Grey in the war against Llywelyn the Last and used as his headquarters. De Grey, one of Edward I's generals, had a force of about 400 infantry under his command until the death of Llywelyn in Builth at the end of 1282. In 1294 when Caernarvon was seized in another Welsh rising, de Grey raised 5,000 men and saved Flint, Rhuddlan and the land east of Ruthin from capture and destruction.

The castle was enlarged and mostly rebuilt by de Grey. Originally a small Welsh stronghold, it was turned into a large seven-towered rectangular castle, the north side being angled outwards where the main entrance gate was covered by the central and eastern towers. The third baron, another Reginald de Grey, quarrelled with Owain Glyndwr who attacked Ruthin in September 1400, burning the town but failing to capture the castle. Two years later de Grey was captured when outside his castle walls by Glyndwr's men who held him hostage in Snowdonia until Henry IV agreed to pay the large ransom of about £650,000. This payment ruined the de Greys and in 1508 the castle was sold to the Crown.

At the beginning of the Civil War Ruthin belonged to

Sir Thomas Myddelton, the owner of Chirk. Denbighshire was a Royalist county however and Ruthin was garrisoned for the King. Myddelton failed to capture it and later it held out for three months against General Mytton. Traditionally supplies were brought in through an underground passage from the Red Lion in Clwyd Street. The governor, Colonel Trevor, finally surrendered on favourable terms and in 1647 the inevitable slighting took place.

The present building was erected by the Myddelton-Wests in 1849 and was designed by Henry Clutton. The last descendant of the Myddeltons was Theresa, whose guardian was Admiral Cornwallis. She married Frederick West and they were known as Cornwallis-West. In the hotel today the portrait of Mary Cornwallis-West by Gordigiani is a pleasant reminder of the last links with the seventeenth-century owner.

Guide books and postcards available at the hotel. The castle is not open to visitors.

SYCHARTH
Near Llangedwyn just off B4396 a moated mound marks the site of this castle, once supposed to have been inhabited by Owain Glyndwr.

WREXHAM
A motte and bailey castle was built here on Offa's Dyke. It was mentioned in 1161–62.

FLINTSHIRE

BASINGWERK
Famous for its abbey, Basingwerk also had a castle of Henry II which was captured by the Welsh in 1166.

CAERGWRLE
Caergwrle Castle is a ruin on a rocky ridge near Hawarden and was originally a Roman station where a castle (sometimes known as Hope) was constructed by Powys Fadog. Edward I captured and rebuilt it and gave it to Daffydd who used it as a base to attack Hawarden.

DYSERTH
The castle here still has a few stones. It was finally destroyed by Llywelyn ap Gruffydd in 1261. The fifteenth-

century ruined manor house might have been the home of the constable at one time.

EWLOE

One of the surprising castles of North Wales, Ewloe is easy to miss. It lies a few miles out of Hawarden on A55 to Holywell and is not visible from the road. It was built about 1146 when Mold Castle was captured by Owain Gwynnedd. Near here Owain won a battle against Henry II. It appears to have been placed in a dip so that it would not be seen and it must have fallen into disrepair for it was mostly rebuilt about 1257 by Llywelyn ap Gruffydd.

The Welsh Tower with its south external staircase dates from about 1200 and the lower ward and west tower were probably built by Llywelyn. In 1277 the building of Flint Castle and the conquest of the area by Edward I lessened the importance of Ewloe. The castle has a well in the lower ward but there is no trace of a chapel which could have been in the south-east tower which no longer remains. In 1922 the ruins were covered in ivy and the Ministry cleaned out fallen stones and earth, building up the floor of the north side and making the approach to the ruin easier.

Department of the Environment. Open April, weekdays 9.30–5.30, Sundays 2–5.30, May–September, weekdays 9.30–7, Sundays 2–7. No car park. Castle is five minutes walk from lay-by.

FLINT

The first of Edward I's great castles stands on the Dee estuary in the middle of an industrial centre. It was originally supplied from the sea and had a moat round the outer bailey. The great tower was unusually placed outside the main curtain and is connected by a separate drawbridge. Inside the keep has a circular gallery with three doors and steps down to the central chamber. The tower was fitted with a wooden brattice so archers could command the drawbridge. Flint was not completed until 1280 and was besieged in 1282 by Llywelyn, whose death that year ended the war.

In August 1399 Richard II was at Flint when Henry Bolingbroke forced him to abdicate. During the Civil War Flint changed hands on more than one occasion. It was garrisoned by Roger Mostyn, a young Royalist Colonel and in 1646 it was closely besieged by Brereton's Parliamentary army, fresh from the capture of Caernarvon. Mostyn let his cavalry escape and resisted until his provisions ran out when he surrendered on honourable terms. In 1652 the castle was slighted.

Department of the Environment. Open normal times. Admission charge.

HAWARDEN

On A55 from Chester to Conway and Bangor, Hawarden Castle stands close to Offa's Dyke. It dates from the reign of Henry III and was built by the Montalts to keep the Welsh at bay. During the Baron's War Simon de Montfort's son Henry met Llewelyn here and granted him the castle. The English failed to keep their word, and in 1265 the Welsh prince and his army destroyed it. Montalt was captured and forced to swear not to fortify the castle again. He was released in 1267 and promptly rebuilt Hawarden. Once again in 1282 the Welsh attacked and captured it, Roger Clifford, the constable, being taken prisoner in his bed. It was rebuilt by Edward I.

During the Civil War Hawarden remained, for the most part, in Royalist hands. The Parliamentarians captured it briefly in 1643 but were flung out by an Irish force commanded by Sir Michael Ernley and Captain Sandford. Sir William Neale then garrisoned the castle until 16th March, 1646, when he surrendered after obtaining permission from the King whom he had sheltered after the Battle of Rowton Heath in September 1645.

Apart from the keep and a few walls standing on the site of earlier earthworks, there are few remains of the old castle. The new building to the east, originally Broadlane Hall, was constructed in 1752 and gothicised early in the nineteenth century. It became famous as the home of Mr Gladstone and the family are still there.

Hawarden R.D.C. Open to the public Easter–October, Wednesdays, Saturdays and Sundays 2–6. Entrance by Leopold Gate. Gardens open 2–6, two days, mid-month April, May and June. Park open at all reasonable times through the Garden Centre.

LLYS EDWIN

At Celyn Farm a moated island castle of an early fortified settlement was excavated in 1931.

231

MOLD

The original name for this town was Monte and the site of the castle is now a recreation ground on Bailey Hill. It was built by Robert de Monte Alto and captured by Owain Gwynnedd in about 1146.

PRESTATYN

The English strengthened a Welsh castle here which was destroyed by Owain Gwynnedd in 1167.

RHUDDLAN

Rhuddlan has long been a site of importance as it commands the ford over the river Clwyd, thus protecting the road from Chester to Conway. In 795 the Saxon Offa defeated Caradog of Wales here. Gruffydd ap Llywelyn was based here when King Harold defeated him in 1063 and destroyed his camp. The first castle was a Norman motte and bailey built about 1073 by Robert of Rhuddlan, the deputy of Hugh, Earl of Chester. There was an important mint here from 1066 to 1072 and silver was mined in the vicinity for the next 200 years until Llewelyn posed a major threat. The castle was alternately in the possession of the Welsh or the English.

Edward I chose Rhuddlan as his base for the conquest of Wales, starting to build here after Flint and continuing after the surrender of Llywelyn in 1282. A new site was chosen and under the capable control of James of St George, Rhuddlan was constructed so that it could be supplied from the sea. A dyke was built and the river diverted. Men were brought in from all over England to dig the ditch and moat and some kind of swing-bridge was constructed so that ships of up to 40 tons could sail right up to the castle. The castle originally had three gates, the Turret Gate at the south-east, the River Gate on the west, and the Town Gate, which had a complicated turning bridge and stood at the end of the moat. It appears the bridge never spanned the moat as there is a pit where the bridge must have been. It is possible that the turning bridge was abandoned at an early date in favour of a drawbridge for greater security. Edward used the castle as a base for his wars in 1277 and 1282 and in 1284 he promised to present the Welsh people with a 'Prince born in Wales, who could speak no English and whose life and conversation nobody could stain.' Young Edward, later Edward II, who was born at Caernarvon, was the first Prince of Wales but history has never quite determined where the ceremony took place.

Rhuddlan was drastically slighted during the Civil War after Colonel Mytton had captured the castle for Parliament. The towers give the impression of being fired on from close range as only their base portions are substantially damaged.

Rhuddlan must have been a fairly simple castle to capture as it has, unlike the other Edwardian castles, two main entrances to the diamond-shaped inner ward and the moat is so narrow it would have been simple to cross with planks and ropes.

Department of the Environment. Open normal times. Admission charge.

GLAMORGANSHIRE

BARLAND
Near Bishopston, this was a Norman ringwork.

CADWALLON
A motte and bailey castle stood here. It was in royal hands in 1196–97.

CAERPHILLY
The largest castle in Wales and one of the largest in the British Isles, Caerphilly lies seven miles north of Cardiff on A469. Once a Roman fort, the first castle was probably built within the fort. The Welsh controlled the area until 1266 when Earl Gilbert of Gloucester who had helped Henry III overthrow Simon de Montfort, attacked Gruffydd ap Rhys and confiscated his land. To secure his conquests he started a vast building programme but before a year was out Llywelyn attacked and destroyed what had been built. By 1272 Gilbert had built a fortress surrounded by a lake. It had two entrances, a large western hornwork and a central inner ward similar to Harlech, but covering a larger area. The main entrance on the east or town side has two platforms on each side behind an outer moat with a water gate – the whole making a fortress that must have been practically impregnable.

In 1326–7, during the reign of Edward II the castle was besieged by Queen Isabella. After the king had been captured, terms were agreed and the garrison marched out. Edward IV granted the castle to the Earl of Pembroke. During the Civil War a large earthwork was built in the north-west corner. There was no siege and the slighting that took place in 1646 was believed to be a Royalist precaution to prevent a resident garrison from being inflicted on the town. The towers were blown up by gunpowder and one of them has been leaning precariously ever since.

The Marquess of Bute did some restoration in the 1930s and the main entrance bridge was repaired in 1958.

The great hall is in the process of being restored. It measures 70 feet by 35 feet and has roof arches supported by columns, tall decorated windows, now completely re-dressed with white stone, and ballflower ornamentation.

Department of the Environment. Open normal times. Admission charge.

CANDLESTON

A few miles south of Bridgend just off A4106 are the remains of the fifteenth-century home of the Cantelupes. Nearby on Merthyr Mawr Warren a tumulus containing six Iron Age burial places was discovered and there is a model of it in the Swansea Royal Institution. The castle was inhabited in the nineteenth century but the encroaching sand forced the residents to leave.

Open to the public at all times.

CARDIFF

Originally a Roman fort, Cardiff Castle was built to defend the Taff estuary. In 1090 the Normans used the same site for their motte and surrounding moat built by Robert Fitzhamon. The Welsh leader Ivor Bach captured the Norman stronghold in 1158. The buildings that remain today on top of the motte are thirteenth century and were erected by Gilbert de Clare. He put a wall across to the main gatehouse, thus creating two baileys. Further building took place in Tudor times along the west wall and the outer curtain was built up to the probable Roman height.

The last of the de Clares was killed at Bannockburn and the castle was acquired by the Despencers, favourites of Edward II, and later by the Earls of Warwick. On the death of Richard Neville, 'Warwick the Kingmaker', at the battle of Barnet in 1471, it passed to Anne Neville who married the Duke of Gloucester, who became Richard III. In the seventeenth century it passed to the Earl of Pembroke and

234

then to Viscount Windsor, an ancestor of the Marquess of Bute who was responsible for the massive Victorian additions. His architect, William Burges, built the tall clock tower, the guest tower and the octagonal tower spire and completely redesigned the interior in the current medieval romantic style, similar to Castell Coch. In 1947 the castle was presented to the citizens of Cardiff.

Open weekdays. Conducted tours (with 101 steps to climb) May–September 10–12, 2–6.30, Sundays 2–5; in March, April and October open 10–12, 2–4 weekdays only. Closed November–February. City car parks. Admission charge.

CASTELL COCH

William Burges's nineteenth-century castle stands in a wood near Tongwynlais, about half a mile from the A470 Cardiff to Pontypridd road. The Marquess of Bute hired William Burges in 1872 to prepare plans for rebuilding a thirteenth-century ruin, once the home of the de Clares, that stood on a natural shelf overlooking the river Taff. Burges decided that the original building had been constructed in two periods, the first with red sandstone, the second with ashlar. Using the old base he built three circular towers with a roofed Elizabethan-style gallery forming the inner court. He used conical roofs on the theory that in medieval times they would have kept out arrows and the site was unsuitable for siege engines.

The Well Tower has a roof that fits inside the top of the tower so that the parapet could be manned. Burges fitted wooden slats in the embrasures, copying a design he had seen in the British Museum. The drawbridge has a counterweight and must be similar to the original. Inside the rooms are decorated in the same style as Cardiff perhaps with more startling effect because they are smaller. The Banqueting Hall has a tall fireplace with a statue of St Lucius, painted in gilt and in the Drawing Room are three figures representing the daughters of Zeus. The Lord's Room is small and the bed looks uncomfortable but the Lady's Room at the top of the keep has a Moorish appearance, a double dome and a remarkable Gothic bed, which must have been cold and nightmarish to sleep in. The enthusiast for Victoriana should not miss Castell Coch.

Department of the Environment. Open normal times. Adequate car park at the top of the drive. Admission charge.

COITY

Coity Castle is a few miles north of Bridgend. It has a circular inner ward surrounded by a moat and an outer ward first mentioned in 1090. The Norman keep once had four storeys. There is an unusual round tower on the south side wall of the inner ward. This defended the moat and the east gate tower on the north defended the other side.

Coity was the home of the Turbervilles for three centuries. Payn de Turberville attacked the castle when it was held by a Welsh ruler. According to tradition he was given the choice of fighting the Welsh defenders or of winning the hand of the ruler's fair daughter. Understandably he chose the latter and thereafter the lordship was held from the Earls of Glamorgan 'by the serjeantry of hunting for him'.

When the last of the Turbervilles died in Edward III's reign the castle passed through marriage to Sir Roger Berkerolles. When his son died the new owner, Sir William Gamage, held out in a long siege against Owain Glyndwr. Barbara, the last of the Gamage family, married Robert Sidney, brother of the famous Sir Philip, who was responsible for the Tudor apartments in the inner ward and the windows in the hall.

Department of the Environment. Open normal times. Adequate car park. Admission charge.

FONMON

About seven miles west of Barry, Fonmon Castle was built in Norman times and has been lived in ever since. It belonged to Colonel Jones, a friend of Oliver Cromwell and was largely rebuilt in the seventeenth century.

LANDIMORE

In North Gower overlooking the marshes are the remains of Landimore or Bovehill Castle which once belonged to Sir Hugh Ionys. In about 1450 he had lead pipes placed to bring water to the castle from Cefn Bryn, the highest point in Gower.

LLANDDEWI

Near Reynoldston is the sixteenth-century home of the Mansels built on the site of the thirteenth-century fortified manor of the Bishop of Gower.

LOUGHOR

Off the main Swansea–Llanelli road, Loughor Tower is all that remains of a Norman castle destroyed in 1151 by Rhys ap Gruffydd. Some of its masonry is of a later date.

Department of the Environment. Open at all times. Admission free.

MORLAIS

Near Merthyr Tydfil, Morlais Castle was never completed. A piece of curtain wall stands over the ward and two drum towers, one with a vaulted chamber, remain. It was built by Gilbert de Clare and is believed to be the cause of an argument between him and the Earl of Hereford. Clare's men stole Hereford's sheep and Edward intervened by fining them both, and thus reducing the power of two of his over-mighty subjects.

NEATH

The ruins of a twelfth and thirteenth-century castle are still visible here, first mentioned in 1129.

NEWCASTLE

On the west of the river Ogmore, near Bridgend, Newcastle has a Norman castle which consists of a small piece of curtain wall and a gateway. Like Coity it belonged to the Turbervilles, Gamages and Sidneys. In 1718 it was bought by Samuel Edwin of Llanfihangel and then it passed to the Dunraven estate.

The richly carved Norman gateway is unusual and was often thought to have been taken from a church. There is no evidence for this and the doorway has been dated at 1175 which might explain the name Newcastle. It is probable that it was built after Coity.

Department of the Environment. Open weekdays 10–dusk, Sundays 2–dusk. Admission free.

OGMORE

Near the mouth of the Ogmore river, the ruins are reached over stepping stones by the Pelican Inn. The keep was first mentioned in 1106 and had three storeys. The probable builder was Gwilim O'Lundein. A vaulted passage leads to another rectangular building opposite which is a fifteenth-century courthouse.

Open every day. Admission free. Key from nearby farmhouse.

DISCOVERING CASTLES

OLD BEAUPRE

Just off A48 near the village of St Hilary, down an un-
signposted lane near the church, is the ruin of the sixteenth-
century manor house of the Basset family. It was only
partially castellated, having an outer gatehouse and crenellated curtain walls, and fell into decay when Sir Richard
Basset lost his money as a Royalist in the Civil War.

*Department of the Environment. Open at all times during
the week. Closed on Sundays. Admission free.*

ORCHARD CASTLE

The ruins of the Berkerolle's castle look over the river
Thaw near Barry and St Athan's church contains the
fourteenth-century monuments of the family.

OXWICH

Built by the Mansels in the sixteenth century, Oxwich is
a fortified manor at the top of a winding lane a mile from
Oxwich beach. The building is partly used as a farm and
is in need of restoration. Sir Rice Mansel built his house in
1541 on the site of a Norman fort. In 1557 a ship was
wrecked at Oxwich and Sir George Herbert of Swansea
claimed the contents. Sir Rice and his son Edward had
however already helped themselves to most of the spoils
and when Herbert's men protested a fight ensued in which
a stone hit and killed Anne Mansel in her own doorway,
which still carries the family coat of arms.

Oxwich is not open to the public.

OYSTERMOUTH

Between Swansea and Mumbles there is a small thirteenth-
century castle which stands high up in a park a few minutes
walk inland from the beach. The original castle at Oyster-
mouth was built in 1100 and destroyed in 1215 and was
abandoned by the owner, William de Londres. It was rebuilt
by William de Braose but was burnt again by the Welsh.
Edward I stayed here in 1284 and three years later the
Welsh attacked it again. The gatehouse and curtain walls
were added and the rectangular keep strengthened. Today
it presents a compact and remarkably complete structure,
unique amongst Welsh castles.

*Swansea Borough Council. Open every day 12–9, summer
only. Admission charge.*

PENARD
This is a thirteenth-century ruin overlooking Three Cliffs Bay. It consists of a curtain wall and a piece of the great hall. The castle was excavated in 1961 and four chambers were revealed, the hall, private rest room and two store-rooms. The ruins were reburied and the sand has encroached on the remaining stones.
Penard Cliff belongs to the National Trust.

PENMAER
Between Oxwich and Bishopston, Penmaer had an oval-shaped ringwork with a rectangular gatehouse that was destroyed by fire.

PENMARK
About a mile north of Fonmon are the ruins of Penmark, an early thirteenth-century castle of the Umfravilles. It has two wards, the outer merging with the inner on the north side where there is a steep bank.

PENRICE
Near Oxwich, Penrice stands in the middle of a private park. It is diamond-shaped with a circular keep and dates from about 1275 but the original ringwork it stands on dates from about 1099. The stone pigeon house dates from 1500 and is on the opposite side of the curtain wall from the gatehouse. The Maunsells or Mansels who lived here and later built the large mansion with its park by Capability Brown were Lancastrians and Royalists. The portrait of Admiral Sir Robert Mansel painted in 1615 is in modern Penrice Castle which is the home of Mr Methuen Campbell. The park, once famous for its fairs, is now the setting for the annual Gower Agricultural Show.

RUPERRA
A quadrangular building ten miles north of Cardiff with round towers at each angle is said to have been built by Inigo Jones. It is a ruin today and is not open to the public.

ST DONATS
Near Llantwit Major, St Donats Castle was built in the fifteenth and sixteenth centuries on the site of the Stradling family castle.
Atlantic College. Open Sundays in July and August, 2–6. Admission charge.

ST FAGANS

The castle here was built by the Normans and changed hands many times, once being sold by the Herberts to raise money for Sir Walter Raleigh's expedition to Guiana. There was a battle here in 1648 when General Horton defeated the Royalists. The present ruins are sixteenth century and the site is now the Welsh Folk Museum.

Open to public October–March, Tuesdays and Saturdays 11–5; April–September 11–7; Sundays all year 2.30–dusk; closed Mondays except Bank Holidays. Admission charge.

SCURLAGE

Next to a caravan site and a new housing estate on the south Gower road there are the ruins of Sir Herbert Scurlage's castle which are now part of a farm. One of the Scurlages married a Mansel in about 1350 and later members of the family turned to smuggling as an extra source of income.

SWANSEA

The early twelfth-century castle has vanished and the present remains are of Bishop Gower's fortified manor house built c. 1340 and destroyed by Owain Glyndwr.

WEOBLEY

On the north coast of Gower near Landimore, Weobley is a fortified manor house dating from the thirteenth and four-teenth centuries. It stands on a grassy hill overlooking Llanrhidian sands and was originally built about 1300 by the de la Bere family. It passed to Sir Rhys ap Thomas, the Herberts and the Mansels. It was damaged in 1409 by Owain Glyndwr and in Henry VIII's reign it belonged to Lady Catherine Edgecumbe. The last owner was Miss Talbot of Penrice who gave it to the Ministry of Works in 1911. The hall still possessed a roof at this time as it had been used as a farmhouse, but today only the forebuilding is roofed over.

Department of the Environment. Open weekdays 10–7 and Sundays 1–7 April–September; weekdays 10–4 and Sundays 1–4 October–March. Admission charge.

MERIONETHSHIRE

BALA

There was a castle destroyed c. 1202 on a motte and bailey site near the lake.

CASTELL GARNDOCHAN
There are a few remains by the river Lliw just off the A494 at Llanuwchllyn.

CASTELL Y BERE
Tucked away at the top of the Dysynni valley about eight miles from Towyn, Castell y Bere gives the impression of once being an island fortress now surrounded by land. Nearby is Bird Rock, the only inland nesting ground for cormorants in this area. The ruin consists of a few stones dating from the thirteenth century arranged in two parts, the south section having a postern gate protected by a drum tower. It was a stronghold of Llywelyn the Great and later of his brother Dafydd. Eventually captured by the Earl of Pembroke it fell into decay.
Department of the Environment. Open at all times. Admission free.

CASTELL Y GAER
This was a hill fort near Llangelynin. To reach it take the turning by Llwyngwril church.

CROGEN
There is a reference to a motte and bailey castle here in 1202.

HARLECH
Harlech is unquestionably Edward I's most magnificently situated castle. It stands on a rock overlooking the sea with its enormous gatehouse on the town side compactly set in the east wall and guarded by the four huge circular corner towers and the high curtain. It was built by Edward I between 1283 and 1289, coming under siege in 1294 when Madoc ap Llywelyn unsuccessfully attacked. Owain Glyndwr next attacked it in 1401 and for four years it was an English outpost in hostile country. Finally worn out by disease and desertion the garrison were bribed to surrender by Glyndwr. For four years the Welsh leader used it as his home. In 1408 after a short siege it was captured by the Talbots' army of a thousand men equipped with siege engines that fired huge cannonballs, one of which was 22 inches in diameter.

During the Wars of the Roses, Harlech held out for the Lancastrians until 14th Agust 1468 when Daffydd ap Ieuan and his 'Men of Harlech' were confronted by the Earl of Pembroke, his brother, Sir Richard Herbert and their

'Saxons', and the castle fell. During the Civil War it was held for the King, finally surrendering to Colonel Mytton in 1647. Unlike Rhuddlan and Pembroke it was never slighted and Cromwell used it as a gaol for the Scots captured at Dunbar.
Department of the Environment. Open normal times. Admission charge.

PORTMEIRION

Famous for its Italian-style architecture, Portmeirion once had a castle that was built by Gruffydd ap Cynan. It was demolished by Sir William Fothergill Cooke and a hotel was built on the site.
Village open to public. Admission charge.

TOMEN-Y-MUR

Near Trawsfynydd, well-known for its nuclear power station, is the Roman site of Tomen-y-Mur. The Normans built a motte and bailey castle inside in about 1090.

MONMOUTHSHIRE

ABERGAVENNY

Founded by Hamelin of Ballon between 1087 and 1100 Abergavenny Castle was originally a timber structure on a mound surrounded by a stockade. The timber was later replaced by stone and a ditch was added on the north face towards the walled town. In Henry II's reign it passed to the de Braose family. William de Braose's uncle had been killed by Sitsyllt, Welsh leader of the Dyfnwal tribe, and in 1175 de Braose invited Sitsyllt and his warriors to a great feast. During the meal the Welsh were all put to death and William then took his murderous band to Sitsyllt's Castle Arnold nearby where they murdered the leader's wife and son.

In 1182 the other sons of Sitsyllt invaded the castle by filling the moat with brushwood, and killed with their arrows all those who did not reach the square keep. De Braose, who was absent, eventually lost favour with King John. He went to France and died there a beggar in 1213. Reginald de Braose, William's son, regained the castle but sided with Llewelyn the Great in his rebellion and disagreed with his son, another William, who was a supporter of Henry III. The castle then passed to the de Cantelupe family and eventually to the Crown. In Edward III's reign it was held by Lawrence

242

de Hastings who was created Earl of Pembroke and fought in the French wars. The last Lord Hastings's widow married William de Beauchamp, who lived here during Glyndwr's rising. His constable was killed in 1402 by an angry mob who rescued three townsmen from the gallows and imprisoned Lady Beauchamp in the keep. Later the castle passed to the Nevilles and during the Civil War Charles I came here to try and raise more troops. He ordered the castle to be destroyed to prevent it from falling to the Scots in 1645.

The gatehouse of the castle dates from the fifteenth century and the keep from the nineteenth. It houses a very interesting small museum with, amongst other things, a photograph of the Bleriot monoplane in which a Mr Radley flew in the nearby park on 17th May, 1910.

Open every day 9–dusk. Museum open April–May, Tuesdays, Thursdays, weekends, 2.30–5, June–September, daily 2.30–5. Admission charge. Car park near St Mary's church (which has some outstanding monuments).

CAERLEON

Famous for its Roman amphitheatre, Caerleon Castle had a Norman keep and is one of those associated by legend with King Arthur. Today the site is marked by a garden outside the east wall of the Roman fort. The Roman amphitheatre, barracks and the museum should not be missed.

CAERWENT

A motte, referred to in 1150, was built here over the south-east part of the Roman site.

CALDICOT

The impressive castle at Caldicot, which is a few miles west of Chepstow, between Caerwent and the Severn, was originally a motte and bailey castle built by Walter Fitzroger and his son Milo during the reign of Henry I. Milo's sons all died accidental deaths and Roger, who succeeded, became a monk. His son Walter, the Sheriff of Gloucester, also became a monk. Milo's daughter Margaret thus inherited Caldicot and it came to her husband Humphrey de Bohun. The de Bohuns added the stone keep and the curtain walls. Humphrey, the fifth Earl of Hereford, was godfather to Prince Edward, son of Henry III, and this is the reason why he was pardoned after his capture at Evesham in 1265 when fighting for Simon de Montfort. The seventh earl refused to go on a military expedition to Flanders in 1297 and although

243

the king threatened to execute him, he lived to become a champion of the baronial cause. The eighth earl, whose coat of arms is above the massive castle gateway, married Elizabeth, daughter of Edward I. He was captured at Bannockburn, and was exchanged only to die in 1322 at Boroughbridge. The ninth earl was also prominent in the wars of the time and with his son fought against the French at Crecy. Finally the tenth earl died young leaving two daughters, Eleanor and Maria. The former married Thomas Woodstock, brother of John of Gaunt and the Black Prince. He added the Woodstock tower and the main gatehouse in about 1385 but he opposed Richard II's marriage to Isabelle de Valois and was 'by the direction of the Earl Marshal, smothered between two feather beds'.

During the Wars of the Roses Caldicot was held by the Staffords who were Yorkists. On the accession of Edward IV Caldicot was granted to William Herbert, Earl of Pembroke. He was killed after the battle of Edgecote and once more it was in the hands of the Crown. Henry VII restored it to the Staffords until Edward Stafford's execution for treason in 1521 when it became part of the Duchy of Lancaster. During the Civil War it was too decayed to be of much use as a stronghold and it was not until John R. Cobb purchased it in 1885 that it was repaired. His son G. Wheatley Cobb was the owner of Nelson's frigate *Foudroyant* and in the castle there are relics of the ship including the figurehead. Other exhibits at the castle are eighteenth-century costumes and old agricultural instruments. Today the nineteenth-century banqueting hall can be leased for medieval banquests and the menus are printed with the Code of Behaviour which stipulates: 'Burnish no bones with thy teeth, for that is unseemly' and 'Fill not thy mouth too full lest thou perhaps of force must speak'.

Chepstow Rural District Council. Open Easter–October, Mondays, Fridays 1–5, weekends, Bank Holidays, 2.30–7. Admission charge.

CHEPSTOW

Chepstow Castle is unusually placed. It is at the bottom of the hill by the river and not at the summit where it would have commanded the area. The first building was done by William Fitz Osbern, Earl of Hereford, shortly after the Norman conquest. His great tower still stands – one of the finest remaining Norman keeps, altered and added to in height over the centuries. In 1075, Roger, son of William Fitz Osbern, was disgraced for joining the Earl's Rising and it passed to the Crown. In 1115 the castle was granted to Walter Fitz Richard. In 1189 it passed by marriage to William Marshal. This great soldier and his four sons built most of the present castle, putting a curtain wall between the middle and lower baileys with circular towers at each end in which there are very early cross-shaped arrow slits. An unusual enclosure called the Barbican was added at the south-west corner and at the other end a strongly built outer bailey and main gatehouse were built.

Chepstow passed to the Bigods in 1248. Roger Bigod, Earl of Norfolk, built Marten's Tower in the outer bailey and his son added the western gatehouse in about 1272. The property passed to the Crown after Roger's death and thereafter was held by various constables including the Despencers and Thomas Mowbray, another Duke of Norfolk.

In 1468 William Herbert, Earl of Pembroke, owned Chepstow. It passed, on his grand-daughter's marriage, to Charles, Earl of Worcester, whose family owned it until the twentieth century. A few windows and fireplaces were added at this time. During the Civil War the fifth Earl and first Marquess of Worcester held Chepstow for the King. In October 1645 it surrendered after a brief siege in spite of being held by a garrison of 64 men and seventeen guns. In 1648 Sir Nicholas Kemeys, who owned land in the area, supported Major General Laugharne and the valiant defenders of Pembroke. Cromwell sent Colonel Ewer from Gloucester to batter down the walls with his heavy siege train. A breach was made near Marten's tower and many of the defenders escaped. Sir Nicholas failed to escape by boat and was caught and killed by Ewer's men.

The usual slighting did not take place and a permanent garrison remained at Chepstow until 1690 – the towers being used as a prison for Henry Marten, who was there for twenty years so that his prison is now called Marten's tower, and Jeremy Taylor the Royalist bishop, who was imprisoned there during the Commonwealth. The garrison was removed in 1690 and the building fell into decay until 1953 when it was taken over by the Ministry of Works from the last owner, Mr D. R. Lysaght.

Department of the Environment. Open normal times. Admission charge. Large car park.

DINGESTOW

A motte and bailey was constructed at this point on the river Trothy c. 1182.

GROSMONT

Grosmont, one of the three trilateral Gwent castles of the Welsh border, is built on a hill and can be reached by B4347 from Skenfrith and Monmouth. The original castle was built of wood and at the time of the Norman Conquest belonged to one of the three sons of Prince Gwaethfoed. In the early thirteenth century the large two-storey hall was built and in about 1220 Hubert de Burgh added the gate-house and towers, probably deepening the moat. Finally in 1330 an additional range of buildings outside the north curtain wall was built including the tall surviving chimney. De Burgh's towers were destroyed by the Welsh who attacked Grosmont at night in November 1233 and captured many of Henry III's supporters who had camped outside the moat, others escaping in their nightshirts. In 1405 Owain Glyndwr besieged the castle and burnt the village. Young Harry of Monmouth came to the rescue and defeated the besiegers capturing one who, as he wrote to his father, was lately a 'great chieftain among them whom I would have sent up but that he is not yet able to ride at his ease'.

In Grosmont church is the effigy of a knight supposed to have been a descendant of Edmund Crouchback.

Department of the Environment. Open at all times. Guide book obtainable from the post office. Admission free.

LLANGIBBY

The de Clare castle here was a Roundhead stronghold in the Civil War until its owner, Trevor Williams, became a Royalist and was forced to flee to France. It is known as Tregraeg Castle.

LLANVAIR

Two miles north-west of Caerwent are two towers and a piece of curtain wall 'bosom'd high in tufted trees', which are all that remains of what was once a large thirteenth-century castle.

MONMOUTH

The scanty ruins of Monmouth Castle, birthplace of Henry V, stand next to the impressive Great Castle House.
Open to the public, Monday–Friday, May–September 1–5. Admission free.

NEWPORT

The original castle here was Norman. Its successor was sacked by Glyndwr. The present ruin by the river is mostly fifteenth-century and was used as the Castle Brewery for many years.

PENCOED

Near Newport, the ruined fifteenth-century fortified home of the Morgans has a gatehouse and one tower standing next to the newer mansion.

PENHOW

Part farm and part castle, Penhow stands on a hillock by the main A48 road between Caerwent and Newport. It was once the home of the Seymours.

RAGLAN

Raglan is about halfway between Abergavenny and Monmouth on the A40. The castle entrance is where the Usk road joins the A40. The present building, which is not so decayed as to be classed as a complete ruin, dates from the fifteenth century but is believed to stand on the site of a twelfth-century fortress. The first owners of the land were the Bloets but it passed through the female line to Sir James Berkeley. His wife, Elizabeth, married again after he died in 1405, and her husband William ap Thomas was responsible for building Raglan.

Thomas was knighted in 1426 and became Steward of Usk. He had a large retinue and to safeguard his new castle from gunpowder he built the six-sided Great Tower with its surrounding moat, known as the Yellow Tower of Gwent from the colour of the stone. It is a remarkable piece of architecture and originally had an extra storey with battlements matching the other two towers of Raglan. On the ground floor the arrow loops are combined with gun-ports and there was a double drawbridge. Vertical grooves in the side of the tower were for the beams of the single and double drawbridges so that when closed they were flush with the tower. The only similar drawbridge to this is in Milan.

The next owner William Herbert, son of ap Thomas, was a prominent Yorkist and adviser to Edward IV. He was created Earl of Pembroke and constructed the main castle building round a courtyard known as Fountain Court. Herbert was executed after his defeat at Edgecote in 1469

247

and his son inherited Raglan. Through his daughter Elizabeth the castle passed to Sir Charles Somerset, Lord Chamberlain to both Henry VII and Henry VIII. His son William was a patron of Elizabethan drama and rebuilt the Pitched Stone Court. The hall was raised in height and an office building was erected next to the kitchen tower. A long gallery was built over the chapel and buttery so that by 1589 when Somerset, who was the third Earl of Worcester, died, he left behind a fortified Elizabethan manor. Edward, the fourth earl, was responsible for the niches in the wall round the Yellow Tower which once contained statues.

The fifth earl, created Marquess of Worcester, was reputed to be the richest man in England and much of his fortune went to supporting the Royalist cause in the Civil War. His son, Lord Herbert, constructed a water engine at Raglan which made 'a fearful and hideous noise' and was used to great effect to drive away local men who came in search of arms. Charles I stayed at Raglan on more than one occasion and in 1646 the castle was besieged by a strong force of Parliamentarians, led at the end by Fairfax, so that the Marquess, after a desperate fight, finally surrendered on 19th August. 'The house almost starved . . . had like to have eaten one another' was the report and the Parliamentarians called in the local people to help demolish the Marquess's home. For over 200 years the ruin decayed and, of the interior, one fireplace and some panelling were conveyed to Badminton House which was built by the third Marquess after the Restoration.

Department of the Environment. Open weekdays 9.30–dusk, Sundays 2–dusk. Admission charge.

SKENFRITH

Not far from Monmouth at the junction of B4347 and the B4521 stands Skenfrith Castle, another of the trilateral castles built beside the river Monnow to defend the Welsh border. Originally a motte in a rectangular enclosure protected by a bank and a ditch which measured about 700 feet by 400 feet and included the church, it was a village enclosure on which the tower was built.

In 1201 Skenfrith was granted to Hubert de Burgh by King John and he probably built the keep and held it with Grosmont and White Castle until 1232 except for a brief period early on when it was held by William de Braose. In 1232 the crown requisitioned the three castles keeping them until 1254 when Skenfrith passed to Henry III's son Prince

40. *The original castle at Warwick was built by William the Conqueror on Saxon foundations. After repairs in 1604 it became 'the most princely seat within the midland parts of this realm'.*

41. *Skipton Castle, Yorkshire, was besieged during the Civil War in 1642; Sir John Mallory refused to surrender until 1645.*

42. *The magnificent Caernarvon Castle was begun by Edward I after he had gained control over Wales. Work progressed for nine years but even today the massive building operations have not been completed.*

43. *Beaumaris, Anglesey, is the finest preserved concentric castle in Britain, built by Edward I during the Welsh uprising.*

44. *During the Wars of the Roses Conway Castle, Caernarvonshire, held out for the Yorkists. A Lancastrian is said to have been killed at a range of half a mile by a Yorkist marksman's arrow.*

45. *Rhuddlan, Flintshire, was of strategic importance from Saxon times and Edward I chose it as his base for the conquest of Wales. The castle was drastically slighted during the Civil War.*

46. *The largest castle in Wales, Caerphilly lies on the site of a Roman fort. The castle is defended by an extensive moat system.*

47. *Harlech, Merionethshire, is the most impressively situated of Edward I's castles, standing on a high rock overlooking the sea.*

48. *Charles I stayed at Raglan Castle, Monmouthshire, and while being besieged by Parliamentarians 'The house almost starved . . . had like to have eaten one another'.*

49. *Chepstow Castle, Monmouthshire, is placed at the bottom of a hill by the river and the first building dates from Norman times.*

50. *Carew Castle, Pembrokeshire, is one of the most interesting and compact ruins in Wales and is accompanied by an equally fascinating history.*

51. *Manorbier Castle, Pembrokeshire. In the twelfth century Manorbier was noted for 'its towers and ramparts' and 'a most excellent harbour for shipping.'*

52. *Roch Castle, Pembrokeshire was built by Adam de Rupe on a rock, apparently because of his fear of adders – one of which later killed him.*

Edward. In 1267 Edward gave all three to his younger brother Edmund Crouchback. Skenfrith remained part of the Duchy of Lancaster until passing to Mr Harold Sands who presented it to the National Trust in 1936.

The castle is primitive in design, consisting of a two-storey tower on the motte, originally possessing an outside staircase, and a quadrangular curtain wall with five circular towers. There are traces of a moat on the south and west sides and the river flows so close to the east side that the river gate has had to be blocked due to floods. Inside the church with its half-timbered tower is the monument to John Morgan, governor of the castle in the sixteenth century.

National Trust and Department of the Environment. Open at all times, admission free. Guide book obtainable from the post office.

USK

The best view of Usk Castle is from the church looking up at the hill. It stands on private property up a lane by the fire station. It has two towers and a square keep and dates largely from the fourteenth century. The castle was built by the de Clares c. 1100 and passed to the Mortimer family. It was destroyed by Owain Glyndwr, repaired and finally reduced to its present state in the Civil War.

The ruins are not open to the public.

WHITE CASTLE

Near Abergavenny off B4521 or B4233, White or Llantilio Castle is with Grosmont and Skenfrith one of the trilateral Norman castles built to secure Gwent. The first known owner was Payn Fitz John, a soldier of Henry I's army. The first structure on this remote hill was probably a wooden tower which was replaced before the beginning of the thirteenth century by a rectangular stone keep surrounded by a curtain enceinte. The owner was then William de Braose and later his son, who gained control over the castle during the troubled last years of King John's reign.

The main building of the castle dates from about 1263 when Prince Edward strengthened his border fortresses against the threat of Llywelyn ap Gruffydd. The main entrance was transferred from the north to the south which explains the hornwork in the moat that originally protected the first entrance into the keep. An outer ward was constructed with thick palisaded banks.

There appears to have been no siege or battle at White

Castle and unlike Grosmont and Skenfrith its buildings were purely of military nature. It was used as a rent collecting centre and as a mustering point for the war against the Scots. It belonged to the Duchy of Lancaster until the accession of Henry IV when it became Crown property. In 1825 it was sold to the Duke of Beaufort and in 1922 it passed to the Ministry of Public Building and Works, who carried out repairs in the 1920s and more recently built the gatehouse stair and platform whence fine views can be obtained.

During the last war an occasional visitor to the castle was Rudolf Hess who, after his flight to Scotland, was kept in an Abergavenny mental home.

Department of the Environment. Open normal times. Admission charge.

MONTGOMERYSHIRE

CAEREIMON
A motte and bailey castle was built here in 1156 and burnt down a few years later.

CARREGHOFA
A castle was built here in 1101 and repaired in 1212; it had a garrison and curtain walls.

DOLFORWYN
Near Newtown, Dolforwyn is a thirteenth-century ruin consisting of one tower in a rectangular ward which was one of the homes of Llywelyn ap Gruffydd.
Open at all times.

LLANDINAM
A motte and two baileys structure was built here c. 1162 of which no trace remains.

MONTGOMERY
Roger de Montgomery built the first castle here at Hendomen near the railway station. The second castle was built on the hill above the town during the reign of Henry I by Baldwin de Boller and this in turn was rebuilt by Henry III in 1223. This was the home of Lord Herbert of Cherbury, a diplomat and brother of the poet George Herbert.

During the Civil War the Herberts handed over the castle to Sir Thomas Myddelton in 1644 and the Royalists promptly besieged the castle. Reinforced by Sir William Fairfax, brother of Thomas, Myddelton beat off Byron's attack and in spite of Fairfax being mortally wounded, the Roundheads won the day. Montgomery Castle was demolished in 1649 and only a few stones now remain.

Open every day. Admission free.

POWIS

A few miles south-west of Welshpool, Powis was built at the end of the thirteenth century to command the upper Severn valley. It has been in continuous occupation since the day it was built and was altered in the seventeenth and nineteenth centuries. The first builder was Gruffydd, Baron de la Pole, who supported Edward I. His family died out in 1551 and in 1587 Sir Edward Herbert purchased the estate and was responsible for building the Long Gallery, although much work was carried out by Sir John Cherlton who married the heiress of the de la Poles. During the Civil War Powis was captured by Sir Thomas Myddelton for Parliament and during the Commonwealth it was occupied by the Welshpool Committee. Sir Edward's grandson finally returned in 1667 and repaired the damage to the interior, putting in much of the panelling. He built the west gate used by visitors today and the state bedroom. He was a Catholic and a supporter of James II. His wife was responsible for smuggling James's son, the 'Old Pretender', to France in 1688 and he joined her at the exiled Stuart court at St Germain.

William III granted Powis to his nephew, the Earl of Rochford, who was responsible for building the Dutch style terraces with their statues of shepherds and shepherdesses by Van Nost. Lanscroom was brought in to paint the great staircase.

In 1722 the son of the exiled Marquess of Powis was reinstated. His son succeeded him and in 1748 Henry Herbert, who had fought in the Culloden campaign with distinction and had been made a general, married the niece of the Marquess and became Earl of Powis. His daughter married Lord Clive, Governor of Madras, and son of the victor of Plassey. In 1804 he was created Earl of Powis and his son changed his name to Herbert. His descendant, the fifth earl, lives at Powis today.

251

National Trust. Open Tuesdays, Wednesdays, Saturdays, 2–6, June–September and Bank Holidays, 10.30–5.30. Gardens open 2–6, May–September (closed Mondays and Tuesdays). Large car park.

PEMBROKESHIRE

AMROTH
On the other side of the bay from Tenby, Amroth has a nineteenth-century castle that stands on the site of an earlier building. It is now a holiday centre.

ANGLE
The remains of the Shirburns' fortified house stand near Angle church. They are separated from it at high tide. (*See also* Thorne Island.)

BENTON
A small privately owned castle on the west bank of the Cleddau. It has one pele tower and was rebuilt from a ruin by Mr Pegge in the 1930s.

BONVILLE'S CASTLE
Nicholas de Bonville had a tower house at Saundersfoot, which is no longer visible but the field at Watlands where it stood is called Tower field.

CAREW
Just off the main A477 between Pembroke and St Clears on a creek of Milford Haven, Carew Castle is one of the most compact and interesting ruins in Wales. The earliest building was constructed by Gerald de Windsor before 1116. He obtained the property from his wife Nesta who was granted it in her dowry from her father Rhys ap Tewdr. His son William took the name Carew and another Carew, Nicholas, built the three circular towers, the chapel and the west front. He died in 1311 and the next important addition was the gatehouse and the porch and steps to the great hall which were added by Sir Rhys ap Thomas who leased the castle from Sir Edmund Carew. Sir Rhys welcomed Henry Tudor when he landed nearby in 1485 and marched with him to Bosworth Field. Sir Rhys held a great tournament here on St George's Day 1488 and 600 Welsh nobles with their attendants were present.

Queen Mary granted Carew to Sir John Perrot, the Lord Deputy of Ireland. Sir John was believed to be the natural son of Henry VIII and looked much like him. He hoped to entertain Elizabeth I at Carew and built the lavish north hall with its great windows, two of which are oriels. This building was never finished as Sir John was accused of treason and imprisoned in the Tower of London, where he died in 1592. There is a secret hiding place between the Tudor additions and the old castle which was probably used by Catholics.

The castle passed to the Carew family again and during the Civil War a ravelin was built outside the outer gatehouse, but this did not prevent the castle falling to Parliament in 1644.

There is a grisly legend associated with Carew. Sir Roland Rhys lived here during the reign of James I. When he was young, Sir Roland had fought against the Flemings, and he had hoped his son would marry into the nobility, but when his son Ewen ran off with the daughter of a Flemish merchant, Margaret Horwitz, he went insane. The girl's father called one stormy night to ask for time to pay his rent. The knight set his tame ape on Horwitz and the latter had to defend himself. The night was so wild that Sir Roland's servant gave Horwitz a room for the night. There was a fearful scream at midnight and Horwitz and the servant rushed into the great hall to find Sir Roland, dead, on the ape's lap in the centre of the blazing hearth. The ape was burnt to death and part of the castle caught on fire. Ewen returned to the castle with Margaret as his wife but henceforward the great hall was said to be haunted.

Open Wednesdays and Saturdays, Whitsun–September, weekdays 10–6, Sundays 2–4. Admission charge.

CILGERRAN

The village of Cilgerran on the Teifi is about two miles south of Cardigan and the castle is down a narrow lane at the Cardigan end of the village. It was built by the Norman Gerald of Windsor in c. 1110. In 1164 it was captured by Lord Rhys, ruler of that part of Wales known as Deheubarth, and in 1204 William Marshall recaptured it for the English. Again it changed hands when Llywelyn the Great took it in 1215 and held it for eight years. William Marshall's son rebuilt it and the two round towers date from this period.

In the fourteenth century Cilgerran belonged to the Hastings family, but in 1326 it had fallen into ruins. In

1377 Edward III ordered that Cilgerran, as well as Tenby and Pembroke castles, should be repaired in case of French invasion and certain minor repairs were made and the square north-west tower was added. In 1405 it fell to Owain Glyndwr and in 1414 it passed to the Duke of Gloucester, brother of Henry V. After Henry VII's accession it was granted to the Vaughan family who lived here until the building of their new house nearby in the seventeenth century.

Cilgerran is unusual in two respects. It has no keep and no wall. The east and west towers in the inner curtain served in place of a keep and the postern gate gave access to the river for water, but in a siege this must have been dangerous as the path is exposed to the opposite bank. Excavation has uncovered the old gatehouse to the outer ward. The castle is built on slate and has been well restored. *National Trust but maintained by the Department of the Environment. Open weekdays 9.30–dusk, Sundays 2–dusk. Admission charge.*

DALE

On the northern shore of Milford Haven, Dale has a new castle near the church which stands on the site of an older one which was once the home of the de Vales.

EASTINGTON

Originally called Jestynton, the Perrot family occupied this stronghold on Angle Bay for three hundred years. Sir John Perrot, supposed to be the natural son of Henry VIII, introduced pheasants to Pembrokeshire. A wall and a square tower remain incorporated in a farmhouse.

HAVERFORDWEST

Like Pembroke, the castle at Haverfordwest completely dominates the town. It was constructed about 1120 by Gilbert de Clare and after being virtually demolished was considerably strengthened by William de Valence in the thirteenth century. In 1405 it withstood an attack by over 2,000 men who landed at Milford Haven from France to support Owain Glyndwr. During the Civil War it surrendered to Parliament and after the Second Civil War in 1648 it was dismantled inside. The outside was left as a shell and, for many years, part of it was used as a prison. In the small museum there are two plans of the French landing in 1797 at Carreg Wastad. Haverfordwest sent its militia out to round up the French and two Welshmen, suspected of fraternising with the enemy, were thrown into the castle gaol.

In 1820 the gaol was demolished and a new one built which in 1875 was turned into the police headquarters. Today it has been converted into the museum and art gallery and houses the Pembrokeshire National Park information centre. *Museum open weekdays only* 10–6, *all the year except bank holidays. Castle ruins open during daylight. Admission free.*

LLAWHADEN

A few miles north of Narberth, near the junction of A40 and A476, Llawhaden Castle was built in the early twelfth century to protect the property of the Bishop of St Davids. The Bishop had his house surrounded by a palisade and a moat. Destroyed by Lord Rhys in 1193 it was rebuilt by Thomas Bek in 1280 in a magnificent style as a fortified mansion. The circular pattern of the earlier building was ignored and only the tower base of it on the west bank now remains. The new buildings, a large hall and kitchens with two very deep wells, were completed in the fourteenth century by Bishop Martyn. Later the gatehouse on the south-west side was improved.

The Bishop's Camera, or private rooms, are on the east side (separate from the garrison's quarters) and the constable had his quarters in the gatehouse. The chapel was once connected with the Camera and the tower next to the chapel seems to have been fitted with steps which are now blocked off. It is hoped that the Ministry will repair these so that the top part of the battlements can be explored by visitors.

During the early sixteenth century Bishop Morgan seized a Lady Tanglost and accused her of witchcraft. She was imprisoned at Llawhaden, but her friend Thomas Wyriott came to her assistance. He attacked the castle with his retainers and rescued her. She was imprisoned again and when freed she attempted to cast a spell on the Bishop. This came to nothing and Wyriott asked the Bishop to forgive them both. Shortly after this another bishop removed the lead from the castle roof in a vain attempt to enforce the removal of the see of St David's to Carmarthen. Llawhaden thus became a ruin.

Department of the Environment. Open weekdays 9.30–*dusk, Sundays* 2–*dusk. Admission charge.*

MANORBIER

Three miles from Pembroke on the south coast is the famous castle of Odo de Barri dating from the twelfth century. Its name is derived from the Welsh word *maenor* and Pyr, a sixth-century abbot of Caldy Island. Odo's famous grandson, Geraldus Cambrensis was born here about 1146. His father William de Barri sent him to Paris where he became a scholar at the university and visited Rome. He travelled in Ireland as a tutor of Prince John and wrote an account of his travels. Later he wrote his famous itinerary in which he describes in detail twelfth-century life in Wales. Manorbier is, he says, 'conspicuous by its towers and ramparts', possessing fine fishponds and 'a most excellent harbour for shipping'. Gerald's main ambition was to make the Welsh church independent by creating an Archbishopric at St Davids, and it was this unsuccessful, ecclesiastical struggle with Henry II which made him famous in his own day. The castle passed from the de Barris in the fourteenth century and then through various hands until Elizabeth I sold it to Thomas ap Owen of Treflayne. It came by marriage into the Phillips family of Picton Castle.

The structure that stands today is the inner ward with the remains of the state apartments at the south-west and a private residence, which was added in the nineteenth century and stands next to the twelfth-century round tower. The only siege it withstood was during the Civil War when it surrendered to Major-General Laugharne in 1645, but it escaped slighting. The present dilapidation dates from the eighteenth century when the castle was owned by Lord Milford Haven. The first floor chapel is well worth seeing and there are two fine undercrofts with barrel ceilings.

Lady Eaton. Open daily 11–6 (*closed* 12.30–1.30) *April–September. No dogs.*

NARBERTH

Sir Andrew Perrot built Narberth about 1246 and it belonged at one time to Lord Rhys of Carew Castle. Today its ruins are very overgrown but one undercroft remains and there is a fine view from its broken walls.

NEVERN

The first castle built in Kemes, the ancient hundred of central Pembrokeshire, Nevern belonged to the Rhys family and the double motte and bailey were built to keep out the Welsh.

NEWPORT

Built by Sir William de Martin in the eleventh century, Newport took over from Nevern as the seat of the Lord of Kemes. It passed to the Owens and for many years was a ruin until being restored by Sir Thomas Lloyd (in 1859) who converted the original entrance into a house using the stones from the eastern gatehouse.

Mrs J. Hawkesworth. Not open to the public.

PEMBROKE

Built by Arnulf of Montgomery in 1090 at the end of a creek connected to Milford Haven, the first castle at Pembroke was a small timber and turf Norman fortress with the creek on one side and the river on the other. The first custodian, Gerald de Windsor, kept off the Welsh warriors of Cadwgan ab Bleddyn by cutting up four hogs and throwing the pieces to the enemy to convince them that they had ample supplies and could hold out until Arnulf came with assistance. Gerald later married the Welsh Princess Nesta who was able to keep the Welsh and Normans at peace by her beauty, in spite of the jealousy of Henry I. In 1138 Gilbert de Clare became the first Earl of Pembroke and he built the great keep which is 19 feet thick at the base and rises to over 75 feet. It is now open to the top but once it had four storeys. Richard 'Strongbow', 2nd Earl, used Pembroke as the base for his war against Ireland. His daughter Isabel married William Marshall who became the next earl and built the Norman hall and most of the castle which stands today. William's five sons succeeded him in turn and the last of them bequeathed the castle to his daughter who married Warine de Munchensy. The northern hall was built at this time and was connected to the creek by a passage and staircase leading to the famous Wogan Cave.

Pembroke resisted the rising of Owain Glyndwr and the constable, Francis a'Court, paid a large levy to escape siege. In the fifteenth century Pembroke was held by Jasper Tudor and here the future Henry VII was born, son of the Earl of Richmond and Margaret Beaufort, Jasper's sister. He is supposed to have been born in a room in the tower now called after him and in 1471 after the Yorkist victory at Tewkesbury Jasper and Henry and his mother escaped to Brittany. Fourteen years later Henry returned to Milford Haven with a small army and successfully captured the throne of England at Bosworth. Young Henry VIII was created Earl of Pembroke by his father who looked upon the castle as his home.

The most famous period of Pembroke's long history, however, was during the second Civil War in 1648. Three Parliamentarians, Major-General Laugharne, John Poyer, the mayor, and Colonel Powell seemed to have enjoyed themselves and prospered so much during the first Civil War that they were very reluctant to disband. Poyer demanded his share of money for his services and when it was not forthcoming he shut himself up in the castle with his troops. Cromwell appointed Colonel Fleming as constable but some of Colonel Powell's men set on Fleming and drove him out of the town capturing two culverins that had been landed from a ship in the harbour. In April 1648 there was a small battle between Powell and Fleming in which Fleming was killed and at this stage Laugharne, a brilliant soldier, arrived from London where he had been held on suspicion of being involved in a Royalist plot. The Parliamentary commander Horton was at Cardiff with about 3,000 men, and Laugharne and Powell raised a force of mixed Royalists, clubmen and disbanded Parliamentary soldiers of almost 8,000. For a long time the battle that ensued at St Fagans on 8th May was in doubt but Okey's dragoons and the New Model infantry won the day and Laugharne and Powell retired to Pembroke. Cromwell arrived in person on 24th May and the siege lasted for seven weeks. The big guns opened up on 1st July but someone betrayed the water supply to Cromwell who cut it off and Laugharne was forced to surrender. Most of the rebels were set free but the three ringleaders were tried by Parliament and allowed to draw lots. The gallant mayor was taken to the Piazza in Covent Garden where he was shot. Three days before Pembroke capitulated the Scots had crossed the border. Had the defenders of the castle known this they might have held out a few days longer and the battle of Preston, which effectively finished the second Civil War, would not have taken place.

The inevitable slighting occurred and Pembroke remained a ruin until being partially restored in 1880 by J. R. Cobb of Brecon. The walk round the ramparts is rewarding and many of the towers have floors.

Pembroke Borough Council. Open Easter to September, weekdays 10.30–8.30, Sundays 11–8; rest of the year 10.30–dusk every day. Admission charge.

PICTON

About five miles south-west of Haverfordwest in a large park, Picton dates partly from the twelfth century. It has been the home of the Philipps family since it passed from the Pictons, by marriage, in 1425.
Open in the afternoon four times a year under National Gardens Scheme.

ROCH

A striking building with a tall pele tower, Roch Castle is six miles north of Haverfordwest on A487. It was built by Adam de Rupe, according to legend, on a rock because he was afraid of adders, but one was brought into the castle with some firewood and killed him. In 1601 the Walters lived here and their daughter Lucy became the mistress of Charles II in The Hague. Her son was the luckless Duke of Monmouth. In 1900 Roch was restored by Viscount St David and now belongs to an American.
Not open to the public.

ST BRIDES

On the headland overlooking Skomer Island, St Brides has a ruined thirteenth-century house, probably fortified, by the church which was the home of John St Bride, a follower of Henry III.

TENBY

The castle above the harbour was built about 1153 but the few remaining pieces are of a later date. Tenby was sacked by Maelgwyn ap Rhys in 1187 and by Llewelyn ap Gruffydd in 1260. The town was strongly fortified at the time of the Armada. During the Civil War it was captured by Colonel Laugharne for Parliament and then in 1648 it was garrisoned by the Royalists and withstood another siege. Today it harbours a small museum of local history and nearby is the monument to Prince Albert.
Museum open June–September, 10–6, October–May, 10–1 and 2–4, weekdays; 2–6 Sundays. Closed Friday afternoons and Sundays October–May. Admission charge.

THORNE ISLAND

Near Angle, at the entrance to Milford Haven, there is a fort on Thorne Island. A blockhouse was built at Angle by Henry VIII but never completed.

UPTON
On the Cosheton peninsula looking over the Carew river, Upton belonged to the Malefants and dates from the thirteenth century. It has a chapel with some remarkable effigies of an unknown date.
It is now a private house and is not open to the public.

WISTON
The very extensive, overgrown remains of a Norman keep and bailey are opposite the church. Formerly the home of the Wogans it is very close to Llawhaden.

RADNORSHIRE

ABEREDW
Llywelyn's castle stood on the heights above the village. From a cave nearby he set out on his last journey.

BLEDDFA
A motte and bailey castle was probably built by Bledewach to the south-east of the church.

CASTLE COLLEN
Near Llandrindod Wells, Castle Collen was built on a Roman site once used by the second Augustan legion. It was mentioned in 1144, 1196 and 1215.

CEFNLLYS
Near Penybont on A44 once stood Cefnllys Castle, home of Roger Mortimer, ally of Edward I.

CLYRO
A portion of the motte and bailey remains near Hay-on-Wye. There was once a Roman fort here.

CRUG ERYR
A motte and bailey castle is still visible in the village of Llanfihangel-nant-Melan between New Radnor and Builth.

KNIGHTON
There is a motte and bailey in the town and another by the river. The one may have been destroyed to build the other.

KNUCKLAS

Near Pilleth, scene of Owain Glyndwr's victory over the Mortimers, Knucklas is associated with King Arthur. By tradition he is supposed to have married Guinevere here and to have killed the giants of Bron Wrgan, the largest of whom had his head cut off and used as a stepping stone.

PAINSCASTLE

North of Clyro and Hay, Painscastle is called after Payn St John, one of Henry I's counsellors. It was rebuilt in about 1231 by William de Braose and called Castru Matildis after his wife. Henry III held his court here and in the nineteenth century it was used as the setting of Garde Doloureuse in Walter Scott's *The Betrothed*.

RADNOR

There were two castles here, Old Radnor, which was reputedly destroyed by Harold, and New Radnor, a Norman castle which belonged to the de Braose family. It later passed to the Mortimers and was destroyed by both Llywelyn and Owain Glyndwr. During the Civil War the town and remnants of the castle were held for Charles I and only submitted after being bombarded by artillery.

RHAYADER

Nothing remains of Rhys ap Gruffydd's castle which stood on the Wye. It was destroyed by his sons, rebuilt and finally destroyed in 1194 by Llywelyn ap Iowerth who killed the garrison of Hubert de Burgh's soldiers. In 1783 some skeletons, found in a line when the foundations of the new church were being dug, were believed to have been these men.

GLOSSARY

Arrow-slit: a long narrow opening for firing arrows through. To accommodate cross-bows they had small holes at the end of the slit or were cross-shaped with holes. After the fourteenth century they became gunports.

Bailey: the castle courtyard or ward. There were inner and outer baileys each with a separate gate and sometimes with a second drawbridge connecting the inner to the outer bailey.

Ballista: a large bow for shooting missiles (iron bolts). It was reasonably accurate and led to the mini-ballista or cross-bow.

Barbican: the gateway, watch-tower or outwork defending the drawbridge.

Bartizan: a small overhanging turret projecting from an angle. Usually placed on top of a tower or battlements.

Bastion: a small tower at the end of a curtain wall or in the middle of an outside wall.

Bastle: a rectangular two-storey building with an outside stair used for defence by northern small holders. The stock would be shut in on the ground floor and the occupants on the first floor (*see* Northumberland).

Batter: the sloping part of the wall, usually at the bottom of the curtain so that rocks and missiles dropped from the battlements will hit the batter and bounce on to the besiegers.

Battlement: a wall or parapet on top of a building with embrasures or indentations with raised portions between. Also called crenellations.

Belfry: a tall wooden tower with stages and covered in hides that was moved up by attackers to obtain access to the parapet. It was sometimes equipped with a base for a battering ram.

Berm: the flat space between the base of the curtain wall and the inner edge of the moat or ditch.

Bore: an iron-tipped pole used for making holes in the base of a castle wall.

Brattice: the wooden hoarding constructed on and overhanging the crenellations and fitted with a roof to protect the defenders. Missiles could be thrown from a brattice at anyone attempting to scale or undermine the walls.

Cabalus: a type of trebuchet.

Caponiere: a covered passage often used to connect one part of a fort to another or to protect an entrance as at Hurst.

Crenellation: *see* Battlement. The licence to crenellate was a permit from the Crown to fortify a house or to build a castle.

Curtain: the wall or rampart enclosing a courtyard. Bastions were sometimes placed at intervals along it.

Donjon: the strong central tower or keep to which the garrison retired when hard pressed – from the Latin *dominionem* meaning 'with the lordship.' Dungeon is the same word but now has a different meaning.

Drawbridge: a wooden bridge that can be raised towards a gateway. Usually placed over a moat.

Embrasure: a door or window with inside slanting sides. Later used as a gun port.

Enceinte: an enclosure; the area of a fortified place.

Forebuilding: an additional building next to the keep in which the chapel was often contained and a stair to the keep entrance.

Garderobe: the latrine. Often situated off the tower stair and cut into the wall.

Hoards or **Hourdes:** brattices. The holes for the supporting timbers, often clearly visible today.

Keep: the donjon or strong central tower.

Machicolation: the projecting stone parapet or gallery with openings through which the defenders could pour molten substances or missiles on the attackers. The word also applied to the openings themselves.

Malvoisin: a 'bad neighbour' or large earth or stone mound thrown up by the attackers near the wall of a castle from which they could fire into the wards or bailey.

Mangonel: a stone-throwing engine working on the torsion principle.

Merlon: part of a battlement wall between two embrasures or crenellations.

Motte: an eleventh- or twelfth-century mound of earth on the edge of the bailey.

Newel: a stair built in a spiral form with the steps keyhole-shaped to fit on top of each other and descending clockwise.

Petraria: stone-throwing engine. Could be a mangonel, ballista or a trebuchet.

Portcullis: an iron or wooden grille gate with spikes that was raised and lowered in vertical grooves in front of the main gate. There were sometimes two or three to pass under (as well as machicolations) before one reached the keep.

Postern: a back door or a covered passage between the main ditch and outworks of a fort, guarded by a postern gate.

Rampart: the surrounding wall or raised earthwork. (Hence a ram was used to batter down a rampart or rampart gate.)

Ravelin: a detached earthwork with two embankments.

Sap: the undermining of a wall.

Slight: to destroy a castle in such a way as to render it useless for fortification.

Solar: the parlour or lord's private apartment. Usually on the first floor with access by a private stair.

Springall: *see* Ballista.

Trebuchet: more powerful than the mangonel, it was a stone-throwing engine worked on the counter-weight principle.

Turning-bridge: a wooden bridge pivoted on an axle fitted with a counterweight on the end nearest the gateway.

Vice: a spiral turret stair commonly found in a keep. The handrail was carved out of the outside wall so the defender, when descending, had his right hand free for his weapon.

Ward: *see* Bailey.

Yett: An iron grille on hinges. A common form of gate in a Scottish castle.

BIBLIOGRAPHY

Castles of England Vols. I and II; Sir James D. Mackenzie; Heinemann (1897).

History and Legends of Old Castles and Abbeys; John Dicks (1880).

Early Norman Castles of the British Isles; E. S. Armitage; John Murray (1912).

Military Architecture in England during the Middle Ages; A. Hamilton Thompson; OUP (1912).

Castles of Great Britain; Sidney Toy; Heinemann (1953).

Castles; B. H. St J. O'Neil; HMSO (1954).

Norman Castles in Britain; Derek Renn; John Baker (1968).

Ministry and private guidebooks.

Abbeys, Castles and Ancient Halls of England and Wales North, Midland and South; J. Timbs and A. Gunn; Warne (1930).

Antiquaries Journal; Vols. XLIX and L (1969–1970).

Edward I's Castle-Building in Wales; J. Goronwy Edwards; British Academy Reprint (1944).

British Castles, Follies and Monuments; E. M. Hatt and Paul Sharp; Reprint Society for National Benzole (1960).

The English Castle; Hugh Braun; Batsford (2nd Ed. 1942).

Castles; Charles Oman; Great Western Railway (1926).

Castles in England and Wales; W. Douglas Simpson; Batsford (1969).

William I (1066–1087)
1066 Battle of Hastings. William crowned, 25th December.
1068 Subjugation of the West.
1069 Subjugation of the North.
1070 Harrowing of the North. Subjugation of the Welsh Marches. Hereward the Wake defeated.
1072 Malcolm III of Scotland subdued.
1075 Rising of the Earls: Roger of Hereford, Ralph of Norfolk.
1085 Domesday survey.
1086 Great Meeting at Salisbury.
1087 William dies besieging Mantes.

William II (Rufus) (1087–1100). *Third son of the Conqueror*
1088 Rebellion of the barons. Bishop Odo banished. Ranulf Flambard king's favourite.
1093 Malcolm III killed at Alnwick.
1095 Rebellion of Robert Mowbray.
1099 Godfrey of Bouillon takes Jerusalem.
1100 Rufus killed in New Forest.

Henry I (Beauclerc) (1100–1135). *Youngest son of the Conqueror*
1101 Invasion of Robert of Normandy.
1102 Rebellion of Robert Belleme crushed.
1106 Robert of Normandy captured at battle of Tenchebrai.
1120 Prince William drowned in White Ship.
1126 Roger, Bishop of Salisbury, supports Matilda.
1134 Death of Robert of Normandy (eldest son of the Conqueror).
1135 Death of Henry, caused by lampreys.

Stephen (1135–1154). *Nephew of Henry I*
1135 Stephen seizes the throne. CIVIL WAR.
1138 Defeat of David I at the Battle of the Standard.
1139 Invasion of Matilda supported by Robert, Earl of Gloucester.

Matilda (1141). *Daughter of Henry I*
1141 Stephen a prisoner after the Battle of Lincoln. Robert of Gloucester exchanged for Stephen.

Stephen
1147 Death of Robert of Gloucester. Matilda to Normandy.
1153 END OF CIVIL WAR. Treaty of Wallingford.
1154 Death of Stephen.

Henry II (Plantagenet) (1154–1189). *Son of Matilda*
1162 Thomas à Becket Archbishop of Canterbury.
1164 Constitutions of Clarendon.
1170 Murder of Becket at Canterbury.
1171 Richard Strongbow, Earl of Pembroke, to Ireland.
1174 Henry's scourging at Becket's tomb. Ranulf de Glanville captures William the Lion, the king of Scotland, at Alnwick.
1183 Rebellion of Henry's troublesome sons Richard and John.
1189 Death of Henry.

Richard I (Lionheart) (1189–1199). *Son of Henry II*
1190   Richard sails to Crusade. Persecution of the Jews (York).
1199   Death of Richard while besieging Chalus.
John (Lackland) (1199–1216). *Son of Henry II*
1200   William Marshall, Earl of Pembroke, takes office.
1203   Murder of Prince Arthur, John's heir and nephew.
1204   Normandy lost.
1206   Stephen Langton elected Archbishop of Canterbury.
1208   England laid under the Pope's Interdict.
1209   John excommunicated.
1214   Battle of Bouvines.
1215   Magna Carta signed at Runnymede. JOHN'S CIVIL WAR.
1216   Invasion of Louis, Dauphin of France. Hubert de Burgh holds Dover. Death of John.
Henry III (1216–1272). *Son of John*
1216   William Marshall, Earl of Pembroke, regent. Henry aged nine.
1217   Louis defeated at Lincoln.
1219   Death of Earl of Pembroke. Hubert de Burgh in power.
1224   Revolt of Falk de Brent.
1227   Henry, 19, declares himself of age. Peter des Roches, Bishop of Winchester, Henry's guardian (1216–27).
1232   Fall of Hubert de Burgh.
1234   Fall of Peter des Roches.
1236   Henry marries Eleanor of Provence; Simon de Montfort one of many unpopular invaders at court.
1240   Death of Llywelyn ab Iowerth, 'The Great', Prince of North Wales, (1173-1240).
1257   Richard, Earl of Cornwall, son of John, crowned 'King of the Romans'.
1258   Provisions of Oxford, drawn up by earls of Gloucester, Hereford, Leicester, and William Valence, Earl of Pembroke.
1263   CIVIL WAR. Rebellion of De Montfort.
1264   Battle of Lewes.
1265   De Montfort's parliament. De Montfort defeated at Evesham.
1272   Death of Henry.
Edward I (Longshanks) (1272–1307). *Son of Henry III*
1272   Llywelyn ab Gruffydd, grandson of Llywelyn the Great, refused homage to Edward.
1277   Edward's first Welsh campaign. Llywelyn surrenders.
1282   Second Welsh campaign: Llywelyn killed.
1283   David, Llywelyn's brother executed. Edward's great Welsh castles begun. Statute of Rhuddlan.
1284   Birth of Edward, Prince of Wales, at Caernarvon to Eleanor of Castile.
1290   Death of the Maid of Norway, betrothed to Edward, Prince of Wales.
1291   John Balliol elected king of Scotland.
1295   'The Model Parliament'.
1296   Death of William Valence, Earl of Pembroke. Balliol dethroned after the Battle of Dunbar.

1297   Wallace defeats the Earl of Warenne at Stirling Bridge.
1298   Edward defeats Wallace at Falkirk.
1301   Roger Bigod (1245–1306), Earl of Norfolk, reigns as Marshal.
1305   Wallace captured, and executed at Tyburn.
1306   Rising of Robert Bruce.
1307   Death of Edward, while marching on Scotland.

Edward II (1307–1327). *Son of Edward I*
1307   Piers Gaveston, favourite, Earl of Cornwall.
1308   Gaveston exiled.
1310   Power to the 'Lords Ordainers', under Thomas, Earl of Lancaster.
1311   Gaveston surrenders at Scarborough to Earl of Lancaster.
1312   Gaveston executed by Guy de Beauchamp, Earl of Warwick, and the Earl of Lancaster. Hugh de Despencer, favourite.
1314   Battle of Bannockburn.
1321   Despencer exiled.
1322   Lancaster captured at Boroughbridge, and executed. Edward triumphant. Despencer restored.
1326   Invasion of Isabel and Mortimer; Despencer captured and executed. Edward forced to abdicate.
1327   Edward murdered at Berkeley Castle. Accession of Edward III aged 14 years.

Edward III (1327–1377). *Son of Edward II*
1327   Roger Mortimer, 1st Earl of March, and Isabel rule together.
1328   Edward marries Philippa of Hainault.
1330   Edward asserts himself. Mortimer seized at Nottingham and executed at Tyburn. Birth of Edward, the Black Prince.
1333   Edward defeats the Scots at Halidon Hill.
1337   HUNDRED YEARS WAR.
1340   Birth of John of Gaunt (Ghent). Sea-battle of Sluys.
1346   Battle of Crecy. Defeat of the Scots at Neville's Cross.
1347   Fall of Calais.
1348   Black Death.
1356   Battle of Poitiers.
1376   Death of Black Prince.
1377   Death of Edward III.

Richard II (1377–1399). *Son of Black Prince, grandson of Edward III*
1381   The Peasants' Revolt. Wat Tyler leads the march on London.
1383   Michael de la Pole, Lord Chancellor (1383–6).
1386   Chief ministers: Thomas, Duke of Gloucester; Michael de la Pole, Earl of Suffok; Robert de Vere, Earl of Oxford.
1387   Gloucester and party defeat the king's forces at Radcot Bridge; de Vere and de la Pole flee.
1389   Richard seizes power for the Crown.
1394   Death of Anne of Bohemia, Richard's queen and creator of fashions.
1396   Richard marries Isabella, 8-year-old daughter of the king of France.
1397   Quarrel of Henry of Hereford and Thomas Mowbray, Duke of Norfolk.

1399   Death of John of Gaunt, Earl of Richmond, Duke of Lancaster by marriage (1362), third son of Edward III and uncle to Richard II. Richard confiscates the Lancaster estates. Henry Hereford, son of John of Gaunt, lands at Ravenspur.

Henry IV (1400–1413). *Son of John of Gaunt; grandson of Edward III. Earl of Hereford by marriage to Mary Bohun*

1400   Richard's supporters defeated at the Battle of Cirencester. Richard murdered at Pomfret (Pontefract). Uprising of Owain Glyndwr.

1402   Henry Percy defeats Scots at Homildan Hill.

1403   Revolt of the Percys. King Henry prevents union of Northumberland and Glyndwr at Battle of Shrewsbury. 'Hotspur' slain in the battle.

1404   Death of William of Wykeham, Bishop of Winchester (1367–1404); Chancellor, 1368–71, 1389–91.

1405   Henry Percy rebels again. Warkworth, Berwick and Alnwick assaulted by King Henry.

1408   Henry Percy, Earl of Northumberland, (1342–1408) killed at Bramham Moor.

Henry V (1413–1422). *Son of Henry IV*

1414   John of Lancaster, Duke of Bedford, third son of Henry IV, governor in Henry's absence. Lollards meeting in St Giles's Fields. Sir John Oldcastle, Lord Cobham, denounced by Thomas Arundel, Archbishop of Canterbury.

1415   Battle of Agincourt.

1416   Henry Percy, son of 'Hotspur', restored to his estates.

1419   Richard Whittington, Lord Mayor of London for the third time.

1422   Death of Henry.

Henry VI (1422–1461). *Son of Henry V and Catherine of France*

1422   Henry aged 9 months. Henry V's brothers the Duke of Bedford, and Humphrey, Duke of Gloucester, responsible for government of England and France. Henry Beaufort, Bishop of Winchester, the young king's tutor.

1428   Fifth Earl of Warwick, Richard de Beauchamp, the king's tutor.

1431   Joan of Arc burnt at the stake.

1435   Death of Duke of Bedford. Richard, Duke of York, regent in Normandy.

1441   Eleanor Cobham, wife of Duke of Gloucester, prosecuted for witchcraft, imprisoned at Chester, then Kenilworth.

1445   Marriage of Henry and Margaret of Anjou, by arrangement of William de la Pole, Earl of Suffolk.

1447   Humphrey, Duke of Gloucester, arrested.

1447   Death of Henry Beaufort.

1448   William de la Pole supreme.

1450   Jack Cade's rebellion in Kent. Death of William de la Pole. Duke of Somerset chief adviser.

1452   York demands removal of Somerset.

1453   END OF HUNDRED YEARS WAR. Richard, Duke of York, Earls of Salisbury and Warwick, and the Duke of Norfolk oppose the king, the Duke of Somerset, the Earl of Northumberland, and Lord Clifford.

1454   York appointed Protector during Henry's illness. Somerset sent to the Tower. Henry regains his sanity and dismisses York, and releases Somerset.

1455   WARS OF THE ROSES. Battle of St Albans: York kills Somerset.

1459   Battle of Bloreheath: Queen Margaret's army routed by Yorkists. Battle of Ludlow: Yorkists defeated, York flees.

1460   Battle of Northampton: Warwick defeats queen's army. York claims the throne for his heirs. Battle of Wakefield: Richard of York killed. Earl of Salisbury beheaded. Second Battle of St Albans: Queen Margaret defeats Warwick and southern Yorkists.

1461   Battle of Mortimer's Cross: Edward, Earl of March, eldest son of Duke of York, defeated Lancastrians. Edward takes London with support of Warwick and is proclaimed king.

Edward IV (1461–1483). *Eldest son of Richard Duke of York*

1461   Battle of Towton. Warwick defeats the queen's army. Deaths of Earl of Northumberland and Lord Clifford.

1464   Battles of Hedgeley Moor and Hexham. Warwick crushes opposition to Edward. Henry VI captured and imprisoned. Richard Neville, Earl of Warwick, 'the Kingmaker' supreme. Edward marries Elizabeth Woodville. Quarrels between Woodvilles and Nevilles result.

1468   Warwick plots with George, Duke of Clarence, brother of King Edward.

1470   Revolt of the Earl of Warwick. Alliance of Warwick and Queen Margaret. Warwick and Clarence land at Dartmouth. Warwick releases Henry VI.

1471   Earl of Warwick killed at Battle of Barnet. Queen Margaret defeated at Battle of Tewkesbury. Prince Edward murdered. King Henry VI dies.

1478   George, Duke of Clarence dies in the Tower.

1483   Death of Edward IV.

Edward V (1483). *Son of Edward IV and Elizabeth Woodville*

1483   Edward aged 13 years. Edward taken into the care of his uncle Richard, Duke of Gloucester, in the Tower. Joined there by his brother, Prince Richard. Richard of Gloucester declared Protector.

Richard III (1483–1485). *Son of Richard, Duke of York. Married Anne, daughter of Warwick, the Kingmaker*

1483   Richard assumes the Crown. Duke of Buckingham prepares Richard's overthrow. Duke of Buckingham captured and executed at Salisbury.

1485   Henry Tudor lands at Milford Haven. Battle of Bosworth. Richard killed. END OF WARS OF THE ROSES.

Henry VII (1485–1509). *Son of Edmund Tudor and Margaret Beaufort*

1486   Henry marries Elizabeth of York.

1487   Battle of Stoke.

1499   Execution of Perkin Warbeck.

1509   Death of Henry VII.
Henry VIII (1509-1547). *Second son of Henry VII*
1513   Battle of Flodden.
1536   Pilgrimage of Grace.
1539   Dissolution of larger monasteries.
1547   Death of Henry VIII.
Edward VI (1547–1553). *Only child of Henry VIII and Jane Seymour*
1547   Battle of Pinkie.
1549   Kett's Rebellion.
1553   Death of Edward.
Mary I (1553–1558). *Daughter of Henry VIII and Catherine of Aragon*
1553   Lady Jane Grey proclaimed queen.
1554   Wyatt's Rebellion.
1558   Loss of Calais. Death of Mary.

THE CIVIL WAR

Charles I (1625–1649). *Son of James I*
1637   Trial of John Hampden.
1642   Arrest of the Five Members. Royal standard raised in Nottingham. Battle of Edgehill.
1643   Battle of Chalgrove Field. Battle of Lansdown. Battle of Roundway Down. First Battle of Newbury.
1644   Battle of Marston Moor. Parliament victorious. Siege of Gloucester. Second Battle of Newbury.
1645   Battle of Naseby. Parliament victorious.
1646   Charles surrenders to Scots.
1648   Renewal of war. Battle of Preston. Parliament victorious.
1649   Execution of Charles I.

Burneside Hall 183
Burradon 121
Burton in Lonsdale 193
Burwell 16
Bury 96
Buttercambe 193
Bytham 104
Bywell 122

Cadwallon 233
Caereimon 250
Caergwrle 229
Caerleon 243
Caernarvon 213–214, pl. 42
Caerphilly 233–234, pl. 46
Caerwedros 219
Caerwent 243
Caister 111
Caldicot 243–244
Caledon 177
Callaly 122
Calshot 61–62
Cambridge 16
Camps Castle 16
Candleston 234
Canterbury 81
Cardiff 234–235
Cardigan 219
Cardinham 20
Carew 252–253, pl. 50
Carisbrooke 67–68
Carlisle 26–27
Carlton 104
Carmarthen 220–221
Carreg Cennen 221
Carreghofa 250
Cartington 122
Castell Cawr 225
Castell Coch 235
Castell Crwm 210
Castell Garndochan 241
Castell Gwalter 220
Castell Howell 220
Castell Lleiniog 210
Castell Meurig 220
Castell Y Bere 241
Castell Y Gaer 241
Castle Acre 112
Castle Ashby 115
Castle Bromwich 177
Castle Cary 154
Castle Collen 260
Castle Combe 186
Castle Donnington 101
Castle Dore 20
Castle Eaton 186
Castle Frome 70
Castle Hedingham 49–50, pl. 8
Castle Neroche 154–155
Castle Rising 112–113, pl. 21
Castlethorpe 15
Castleton 193
Catterlen Hall 27
Caus 147
Caverswall 158
Cawood 193
Cefnllys 260

Chalgrave 9
Charlton 147
Chartley 158
Chatham 82
Chepstow 244–245, pl. 49
Chester 18
Chichester 171
Chideock 41
Chilham 82–83
Chillingham 122
Chipchase 123
Chirk 225–226
Christchurch 62
Cilgerran 253–254
Cirencester 56
Clare 161–162
Clifford 70
Clifton (Westmorland) 183
Clifton (Yorkshire) 193
Clitheroe 96
Clophill 9
Clun 147
Clyro 260
Cockermouth 27
Cocklaw Tower 123
Cockle Park Tower 123
Codnor 34
Coity 236
Colbridge 83
Colchester 50–52, pl. 9
Colcombe 37
Coleshill 177
Compton 37
Conisbrough 193–194
Connington 79
Conway 7, 214–215, pl. 44
Cooling 83
Corbridge 123
Corby 28
Corfe 41–42, pl. 7
Cotherstone 194
Cottingham 194
Coupland 123
Coventry 177
Cowdray 171–172
Cowes 68
Craster Tower 123
Crayke 194
Cresswell 123
Criccieth 215–216
Crickhowell 211
Croft 70–71
Crogen 241
Cromwell's Castle 25
Crowhurst 172
Crug Eryr 260
Cuckney 136
Cusop 71

Dacre 28
Dale 254
Dalley 123
Dalston 28
Dalton-in-Furness 96
Danby 194
Dartmouth 37–38
Deal 83–84, pl. 15

273